THE POLITICS OF INCLUSION
AND EXCLUSION

THE POLITICS OF INCLUSION AND EXCLUSION

Jews and nationalism in Hungary

Vera Ranki

HOLMES & MEIER

NEW YORK / LONDON

To my mother, Kató Ránki,
to the memory of my father, Jenő Ránki,
and to my daughter, Natalie Ungar-Ranki

Published in the United States of America 1999 by
Holmes & Meier Publishers, Inc.
160 Broadway • New York, NY 10038

United Kingdom:
Holmes & Meier Publishers, Ltd.
c/o B.R.A.D.
Hadleigh Hall, London Road • Hadleigh, Essex SS7 2DE
Telephone: (44) 01702 552912

Library of Congress Cataloging-in-Publication Data

Ranki, Vera.
    The politics of inclusion and exclusion : Jews and nationalism in
Hungary / Vera Ranki.
    p. cm.
    Includes bibliographical references and index.
    ISBN 0-8419-1401-X (cloth)
    ISBN 0-8419-1402-8 (paper)
    1. Jews—Hungary—History—20th century. 2. Antisemitism—Hungary.
3. Nationalism—Hungary. 4. Holocaust, Jewish (1939–1945)—Hungary. 5.
Hungary—Ethnic relations. I. Title.
    DS135.H9 R36 1999
    943.9′004924—ddc21   98-45937
                                                                   CIP

Set in 10/12 pt Galliard BT by DOCUPRO, Sydney
Printed by South Wind Productions, Singapore

10 9 8 7 6 5 4 3 2 1

Contents

* *Modernity, liberalism, antisemitism and nationalism*
* *Nationalism—East and West* • *Antisemitism—modern antisemitism* • *Assimilation*

* *The age of founding: economy in the Monarchy* • *Hungarian society* • *The historical development of Hungarian nationalism* • *The making of a modern nation–state: the role of language and culture* • *The gentrification of culture* • *Nationalism and modernisation*

* *Hungarian society and the Jews: emancipation, assimilation and antisemitism* • *The emancipation of Jews and the 'Jewish question' in Hungary* • *The evolution of modern antisemitism in Hungary* • *The 'Jewish question'—a public opinion poll* • *Assimilation versus tradition* • *The split of the community*

* *Defining historical events* • *Post-Trianon Hungary* • *The rise*

Foreword

The destruction of the Jews of Hungary constitutes one of the most perplexing chapters in the history of the Holocaust. It is a chapter that ought not to have been written: by 1944, the leaders of the world, including the national and Jewish leaders of Hungary, were already fully aware of the realities of the Nazis' 'Final Solution' program.

It is one of the great tragedies of World War II that the Jews of Hungary—the last relatively intact Jewish community of over 800 000 (including the approximately 100 000 converts identified as Jews under the racial laws)—were destroyed on the eve of Allied victory. Although subjected to many discriminatory measures that claimed close to 64 000 lives and violated their basic civil rights and liberties, the bulk of Hungarian Jewry survived the first four-and-a-half years of the war. The Jews enjoyed the physical protection of the conservative–aristocratic government of Miklós Kállay and were convinced that they would survive the war relatively intact. Patriotic and committed to the Magyar cause, they were confident that what happened to the Jews of Poland and other countries in Nazi-dominated Europe could not possibly happen to them in civilised Hungary. Secretly rooting for the victory of the Allies, they could not envision the possibility that Hungary might one day be occupied by its erstwhile ally, Nazi Germany.

The chain of events that led to the German occupation of 19 March 1944 began shortly after the crushing defeat of the Hungarian and German armies at Voronezh and Stalingrad early in 1943. Realising that the Axis had lost the war, the Kállay government became increasingly eager to emulate the example of Italy, which managed to extricate itself from the German alliance during the summer of that year. However, the Hungarians' attempt at finding an honourable way out of the war was neither realistically conceived nor adequately planned. Hitler was fully aware of their 'secret' negotiations with representatives of the Western Allies and resolved to frustrate their plans in order to protect the military and strategic interests of the Third Reich in the Balkans—a military decision that sealed the fate of Hungarian Jewry.

The occupation enabled the Nazis and their Hungarian accomplices to implement the 'Final Solution' program at lightning speed. Time was clearly of the essence. The Red Army was fast approaching Romania; the Western Allies, already in control of much of Italy, were finalising their plans for D-Day. By this time in 1944, the Nazis' machinery of destruction was already well-tested. With experience gained through the mass murder of Jews all over German-dominated Europe, the Nazis were well able to handle a speedy operation in Hungary. Anticipating the imminent 'solution' of the Jewish question in Hungary, they updated the death factories in Auschwitz and extended the rail lines leading to the immediate vicinity of the gas chambers in Birkenau. Within Hungary, the Eichmann–*Sonderkommando*, consisting of a relatively small number of SS 'advisers', enjoyed the wholehearted support of the newly appointed government of Döme Sztójay.

Without the unequivocal and often enthusiastic support by the Hungarian government, the Nazis would have been helpless. The leaders of the SS commandos themselves were amazed at the enthusiasm with which their Hungarian counterparts were ready and eager to implement the 'Final Solution' program. The Sztójay government, constitutionally appointed with the blessing of Miklós Horthy, Hungary's head of state, placed the instruments of state power at the disposal of the *Sonderkommando*. With Horthy remaining at the helm, providing the facade of national sovereignty, the Hungarian police, Gendarmerie and civil service collaborated with the SS in the 'solution' of the Jewish question with a routine and brutal efficiency that often surpassed that used by the Nazis themselves. Within less than two months—from late March to mid-May, 1944—they and their Nazi 'advisers' completed the first phase of the anti-Jewish drive: the Jews were isolated, marked, expropriated and placed into ghettos. During the next two months, the Jews were subjected to the most barbaric and speedy deportation and extermination program. It was so massive and so speedy in fact that the crematoria in Auschwitz-Birkenau, updated as they were, could not cope. Special ditches had to be dug to burn the thousands of victims the crematoria could not handle. The Nazis' last major campaign in the war against European Jewry involved the deportation of close to 440 000 Hungarian Jews. By the time the deportations were halted on 9 July—the very day Raoul Wallenberg arrived on his mission of rescue—all of Hungary, with the notable exception of Budapest, was already '*judenrein*' ('Jew-free').

The magnitude of the catastrophe that befell Hungarian Jewry is dramatically illustrated by the following comparative statistical data. For example, on 6 June 1944 (D-Day)—one of the most magnificent days in the annals of military history, when the greatest multinational armada ever assembled under one command stormed the beaches of Normandy—three transports arrived in Auschwitz-Birkenau with close to 12 000 Jews from Northern Transylvania. By the end of that day, the casualties incurred by all the Allies were about half of that suffered by the Hungarian Jews. And while the casualties of the Allies declined dramatically after safeguarding the beaches of Normandy, the Hungarian Jews continued to be murdered at the same high rate, day after day, until 9 July, continuing the awesome daily massacre that began on 16 May. Another statistical reference point: the wartime losses of Hungarian Jewry exceeded those incurred by the military forces of the United States in all theatres of war by almost a third. And finally, the combined military and civilian casualties of Britain—a country that bore much of the German military onslaught—represented but half of the losses of Hungarian Jewry. These comparative figures are cited not to minimise the sacrifices or diminish the heroism of the Western Allies, but simply to underscore the magnitude of the Holocaust in Hungary.

This phase of the Holocaust represents not only the greatest tragedy in the history of Hungarian Jewry, but also the darkest chapter in the history of Hungary. Never before in the 1100-year history of the Hungarian nation were so many people killed in so short a time as in 1944. The catastrophe that befell Hungarian Jewry during the Nazi era engenders a number of provocative questions. What were the political–ideological and socio-economic factors that enabled the Jews of Hungary to experience a 'Golden Era' during the lifespan of the Austro–Hungarian Empire (1867–1918)? In what sense did these factors change after the collapse of the Empire in 1918? What were the major domestic and foreign political considerations behind the anti-Jewish measures taken after

World War I? Finally, how can one explain the linkage between the anti-Jewish measures enacted in Hungary after 1938 and the Holocaust?

Dr Vera Ranki, a respected scholar associated with the University of New South Wales, Australia, provides many of the answers. Her study on the impact of nationalism, assimilation and antisemitism on the politics of inclusion (1867–1918) and exclusion (1918–1944) pursued by the various Hungarian governments since 1867 is both cogent and well-documented. Dr Ranki argues convincingly that nationalism had been exploited during both periods for the advancement of national interests as determined by the needs of the particular rulers. During the 'liberal' era of the Austro–Hungarian Empire, the various governments of the Hungarian monarchy exploited nationalism for the advancement of modernisation. In the absence of an indigenous middle class in the multinational society in which the Magyars constituted a minority, the Jews were needed for both economic and political reasons: thus the politics of inclusion.

After considerable debate, the Jews were emancipated in 1867 in the expectation of their gradual assimilation and acculturation, if not outright conversion. The Jews took full advantage of the opportunities offered by their emancipation, playing a pivotal role in the commercial and industrial development of a Hungary that retained many of its feudalistic political and social institutions. In accord with the politics of inclusion, many of the Jews Magyarised their names, adopted and developed the Hungarian language and culture, and, to the great chagrin of the Empire's other national minorities, played an important role in the process of Magyarisation. Devoted to the Magyar cause, the Jews, who generally identified themselves as Magyars of the Jewish faith, provided the slim political majority the Hungarians needed to rule the country.

The *Interessengemeinschaft* between Jews and Magyars came to an end with the collapse of the Austro–Hungarian Empire in 1918. In the new, truncated Hungary the Magyars constituted a dominant majority, and the Jews were no longer needed for political ends. Vulnerable and defenceless, they were once again exploited as scapegoats. During the inter-war period, they were blamed for all the ills associated with the collapse of the monarchy, including the disastrous policies of the shortlived dictatorship of the proletariat. The Jews' economic and professional achievements of the Golden Era were now looked upon with envy by the impoverished gentry and the multitude of unemployed civil servants displaced from the territories lost to Czechoslovakia, Romania and Yugoslavia: thus, the politics of exclusion.

The authoritarian counter-revolutionary regime that came to power under the leadership of Admiral Miklós Horthy in 1920 was resolved to settle accounts with Hungary's 'internal enemies', including the Bolsheviks—a term often used as a euphemism for Jews. Nationalism, denuded of its former 'liberal' content and wrapped in the Szeged idea (the ideological concept of the counter-revolutionaries), took on a highly chauvinistic, national–Christian, antisemitic colouration. In the absence of any tradition of tolerance and pluralism, nationalism became a formidable weapon in the hands of the counter-revolutionaries bent on solving the two basic issues that agitated Hungarian society during the inter-war period: revisionism and the 'Jewish question'. It was primarily the desire to undo the territorial changes imposed in the aftermath of World War I under the 'punitive' Trianon Treaty that drove Hungary into an alliance with the Third Reich, the newly emerging military power that was also pursuing a revisionist policy bent on overcoming the consequences of Versailles. While the alliance yielded considerable dividends, enabling Hungary to fulfil parts of its revisionist ambitions at the expense of the Succession States (1938–41), it was in the long run disastrous for the country and especially for Hungarian Jewry. While opposed to Nazism, the successive Hungarian conservative–aristocratic governments—consisting of 'civilised' antisemites—felt compelled to yield to the Third Reich as well as to the increasingly influential domestic Right-radical forces by adopting, with the blessing of the Christian churches, ever harsher anti-Jewish measures. Antisemitism was part and parcel of the national ethos.

Eager to preserve their privileged status, the ruling conservative–aristocratic elites tended to identify the national interests of Hungary with their own class interests. During the euphoric phase of the war, when the Axis forces appeared successsful on the battlefield, these elites rationalised their domestic and foreign policy decisions in tune with these interests. At home, they operated on the quixotic assumption that by focusing attention on 'solving the Jewish question', they could divert the attention of the Right-radicals, who while rabidly antisemitic were also dedicated to the socio-economic transformation of the basically feudal system into a National Socialist one. In foreign affairs, they lived under the illusion that Hungary could satisfy its revisionist ambitions by embracing the Third Reich without having to jeopardise its own freedom of action.

It was a similar illusion that characterised the conservative–aristocratic elites' position after the military debacle at Voronezh and Stalingrad when, recognising that the Axis had lost the war, they attempted to extricate themselves from the Axis Alliance by surrendering to the Western Allies rather than the Soviets. Overlooking the fundamental geographic–military realities of Hungary's position and the political–strategic underpinnings of the Grand Alliance, these elites naively pursued unattainable objectives. They were striving to: safeguard the independence and territorial integrity of Hungary, including the retention of the areas re-acquired between 1938 and 1941; if possible, preserve the antiquated socio-economic structure of the gentry-dominated society; and, above all, avoid at all cost a Soviet occupation. They kept on postponing the inevitable by engaging in basically fruitless 'secret' negotiations with representatives of the Western Allies.

As a result of these elites' irresolute and basically unrealistic policies, the country was occupied first by the Germans and then by the Soviets, with devastating consequences for both Hungary and themselves. But the *real* losers of these policies were the Jews. There is clearly a linkage between the Kállay government's 'secret' negotiations, the German occupation, and the consequent destruction of Hungarian Jewry. It is in this light that this author advanced the speculative conclusion quoted by Dr Ranki on p. 147: 'Ironically, it appears in retrospect that had Hungary continued to remain a militarily passive but vocally loyal ally of the Third Reich instead of provocatively engaging in essentially fruitless, if not merely alibi-establishing, diplomatic maneuvers, the Jews of Hungary might have survived the war relatively unscathed.'

While the antisemitic policies and exclusionary legislative actions of the pre-1944 Hungarian governments made the draconic Holocaust-related measures more acceptable, the historical evidence indicates that it was the German occupation that sealed the fate of Hungarian Jewry.

History is a formidable weapon. It is particularly corruptive and dangerous in the hands of chauvinistic nationalists bent on shaping history. It is the responsibility of persons of good will everywhere to counteract them. For unless the falsifiers of history are unmasked and the drive of the history cleansers is stopped or counteracted, the historical record of the Holocaust will be tarnished. Dr Ranki has fulfilled her responsibilities in this regard. She has made a laudable scholarly contribution not only to the preservation of the integrity of the historical record of the Holocaust but also to the understanding of the rise and fall of the Jewish community of Hungary.

Randolph L. Braham
New York, August 1998

Brief chronology of Hungarian history since the nineteenth century

1848	March: revolution.
1848–49	War of independence against the Austrians.
1867	*Ausgleich*, the 'Compromise'—the Austro–Hungarian Empire is born.
	Emancipation Act XVII of 1867 declares Judaism a religion (as opposed to a nationality) and Hungarian Jewry acquire equal rights.
1882–83	Tiszaeszlár blood libel case.
1883	Istóczy establishes the Antisemites' party.
1895	Judaism becomes 'received' religion under Law XLII of 1895
1918	October 31: following the *őszirózsás* (Michaelmas daisy) revolution, new Hungarian government is formed under Count Mihály Károlyi.
1919	March 21 to August 1: the so-called 'Dictatorship of the Proletariat', communist rule under Béla Kún.
1920	The reign of the White Terror and the establishment of the counter-revolutionary regime under Admiral Miklós Horthy.
	20 June: the Treaty of Trianon is signed.
1938	The first anti-Jewish legislation, Act XV of 1938: establishment of professional chambers and limiting the number of Jews to 20 per cent.

First Vienna Award: following the Nazi occupation of Czechoslovakia, Hungary acquires the Upper Province (*Felvidék*).

1939   The second major anti-Jewish law, Act IV of 1939, is enacted.

1940   Second Vienna Award: Hungary acquires Northern Transylvania from Romania.

1941   The Nuremberg-style Act XV of 1941 anti-Jewish law is enacted.

16–18 000 'alien' Jews are deported from Hungary and massacred at Kamenets-Podolsk by the *Einsatzgruppen*.

1942   Hungarian military units massacre over 3000 people, among them 1000 Jews, in *Újvidék* (part of Yugoslavia).

1944   19 March: the Nazi occupation of Hungary.

5 April: Jews must wear the yellow star.

19 April: Jews of Carpatho-Ruthenia and northeastern Hungary are driven into ghettoes, the first ones to be ghettoised.

15 May: deportations begin.

6 July: the deportation of Hungarian Jews is completed in the provinces.

7 July: Horthy suspends further deportations.

15 October: Arrowcross *putsch*.

1945   17 to 18 January: the Pest ghetto is liberated.

13 February: all of Budapest is liberated.

4 April: Hungary is liberated.

Preface

I was born in Budapest, after the Holocaust. A year or so before I was born, one spring afternoon, my father's sister, Nelly, shouted my mother's name from the ground floor, screaming that my father was there.

This was the first news of him since May 1944, when he was taken to forced labour service. My mother ran down five flights of stairs to meet him. On the stairs she ran past a skeleton-like man. That man was my father. He survived *Mauthausen*, the forced march to Günzkirchen, during which the Germans machine-gunned them at random. He was liberated at Günzkirchen. My 178-centimetre-tall father weighed 35 kilos at liberation.

My mother was first in the Yellow Star house (*csillagos haz:* buildings allocated for Jews) at Csengery utca, where, on 15 October 1944, she witnessed one of the Arrowcross raids and massacres in a neighbouring building. Later she was hidden in the outer suburb of Rakospalota, by a woman called Dr Margit Kovacs, a lawyer, who had a Down's syndrome child and whose husband was at the front.

In January 1945, my mother was liberated there by the advancing Russian soldiers. Immediately she set out to find my grandmother. Wading her way through bombed buildings, corpses of humans and of horses, she walked into the Ghetto, went past a few houses and found my grandmother on the far side of the Ghetto, in the first building she entered. She half carried my starved grandmother to Rakospalota.

Then the waiting started for news of deported family members. Most never came back.

I grew up in Communist Hungary. Although my immediate

family (my grandmother, my mother and my father) experienced all the possible horrors of the Holocaust—hiding, ghetto, labour service, forced march and concentration camp—they never talked about it. This was not unique. The silence was part of the survival pattern of Jews, who, by choice or by circumstance, lived in Hungary.

And yet, I had Holocaust nightmares, even though I did not know what they were. In my dreams I was part of a crowd rounded up into the gymnasium of my school, where through the floor we were electrocuted. I dreamt of hiding and of being hunted. I did not tell my parents about these dreams. The silence bound me too.

At the age of 26 I emigrated to Australia.

Many years later, in December 1989, I went to Jerusalem to undertake the 'Teaching Antisemitism and the Holocaust' course at Yad Vashem. When I returned to Australia, I felt compelled to continue to research. As I read and wrote, I felt a growing sense of purpose but the direction still evaded me. I ended up writing a doctorate about the Hungarian Jewish experience.

The writing of the thesis meant facing the fate of Jews in Europe, the fate of my family. It meant that my father and my mother both started to talk to me about what had happened to them. Or at least, some of what happened. They talked about why they were silent. My father felt that his memories were so awful that he had to protect us from knowing. My mother felt that because she wasn't deported, she had no 'right' to talk. She 'only' experienced the murderous Arrowcross raid, the hiding, the not being able to go to a bombshelter during bombing in case some-body denounced her. She 'only' lived through the frequent house searches, starvation, and the fear for loved ones. She finally talked of the day she had to put on the yellow star and the terror it meant. In the face of the horror that came after, deportation and camps, she felt that her experiences were not important enough.

I found out that the silence of those years concealed not only my nightmares, but my father's, my mother's, and, although she never told anyone, I am certain, my grandmother's as well.

The thesis focused me on my roots and on my identity.

I had two thesis supervisors: Maria Markus and Professor Sol Encel. They were both wonderful. They were not just supervisors but friends and mentors. Their professional excellence, intellectual guidance and warm friendship inspired me throughout the writing of this dissertation. My life has been enriched by their guidance and friendship.

I am grateful to Professors Randolph Braham, Ferenc Erős, the late Ferenc Feher, Agnes Heller, Clive Kessler, Konrad Kwiet, Colin Tatz, Richard Weisberg, and Robert Wistrich for the discussions and encouragement they afforded me.

I am grateful to the The Australian Sociological Association for selecting me as winner of the 1997 Jean Martin Award, granted biannually to the best PhD thesis in social science.

My thanks go to the Board of Advisors of the Rosenthal Institute for Holocaust Studies at the Graduate School of The City University of New York, for allocating a grant, through the 'J. and O. Winter Fund', toward the completion of my thesis.

Finally, my daughter Natalie. With her boundless sweetness and generosity, persistent and unwavering support, she was a source of strength and warmth in the most difficult times, and shared in all the heartaches and joys this book brought me.

Introduction

This is the story of Hungarians and Jews, of nationalism and modernity, of antisemitism and of assimilation. It is a story of paradoxes and extremes. Nowhere else in Europe were Jews more actively encouraged to assimilate and to participate in modernisation. And nowhere else was the move from inclusion to exclusion faster and more dramatic.

In less than a hundred years, policies went from demanding and welcoming assimilation and controlling antisemitism, to pogroms and antisemitism as state policy. The status of Jews within Hungarian society was determined by the changing—but always complex—relationship between modernisation, liberalism and nationalism. What had started as nationalism and modernisation in the beginning of the nineteenth century, had become nationalism *versus* modernisation by the end of the century.

In Hungary, where there was no third estate of any significance, the nobility took on the project of modernisation in order to create an independent nation–state. Jews were needed to fill the role of the middle class, necessary for economic modernisation. The project of modernisation was thus a shared project for Hungarians and Jews, as was Hungarian nationalism in the simultaneous construction of a modern national identity. Assimilation was not only a vehicle for social integration but a higher ideal. Hungarian Jews became ardent Hungarian nationalists. In this Liberal Era, the 'Jewish question' was put in the social context of assimilation and in the political context of the 'nationalities question'.

All this changed after World War I. In post-Trianon Hungary, nationalism was articulated through the unbridled thrust towards reclaiming the lost territories. Its ideological content was defined by the polarity of two, often contradictory, tendencies: on one hand, the development of indigenous ideologies formulated under the impact of fascism and Nazism, and on the other, the policies of the authoritarian state which sought to control radical extremism.

Hungarian nationalism had been imbued with the irrational fear of the 'death of the nation'. This was behind the concept of racially threatened culture, articulated by the populist movement and taken on eagerly by traditional conservatives and radical right-wingers alike. Hungarian politics, intellectual life, society and institutions had to be 'purified'. The 'Jewish question', which was first perceived and articulated in the context of emancipation and assimilation, was re-articulated as overt antisemitism, which questioned assimilation and aimed to annul emancipation. Jews were perceived and cast as 'the other', the alien, the enemy. The most appropriate word to describe the policies of the state and, to a large extent, the nature of attitudes within Hungarian society *vis-à-vis* Jews in this period is *exclusion*. As importantly as the previous Liberal Era had been characterised by *inclusion*, the 1920s and 1930s were characterised by the increasing marginalisation, banishment and ostracism of Jews, leading to the ultimate exclusion, the Holocaust, in the 1940s.

Yet, until the German occupation in 1944, Hungarian Jews were exempted from ghettoisation and from the 'Final Solution' (to the point that the Hungarian Government demanded the release of Hungarian Jews caught in countries occupied by the Germans). Some scholars argue that, had Hungary remained a militarily passive but vocally loyal ally of the Third Reich, instead of engaging in essentially fruitless diplomatic manoeuvres, the Jews of Hungary might have survived the war relatively unscathed. I, on the other hand, argue that Hungarian institutions participated fully in the deportation of Jews, and that Hungarian society accommodated the 'Final Solution' *because* they were immersed in decades of state-sponsored and social antisemitism, and that this, together with antisemitic and extreme right-wing government policies, inevitably led to the Holocaust in Hungary.

Modernity, liberalism, antisemitism and nationalism

Together with liberalism, nationalism was the ideology which, to a large degree, formed modern Europe. Modernity and the development of the nation–state are inseparable from nationalism, the latter being especially relevant as a main component of the formation of the modern nation–state. National self-perception, especially strong in certain countries, became inseparable from nationalism, which, in its turn, used the image of the 'other'. Concurrently, with the rise of democratic political ideals, the politicisation of the masses, the separation of church and state, and a general secularisation within society, religious anti-Judaism evolved into modern political antisemitism. While Christian anti-Judaism focused more on the 'old', superseded religion, modern antisemitism focused more on 'the Jew'.

Both nationalism and the rise of political antisemitism are connected to modernity. Nationalism, in its modern form, emerged only with the demise of feudalism. The emergence of modern antisemitism is complex, because it is part of a continuum which stretches way back into the history of Christianity. In Western culture, antisemitism is part of folkways and individual *Weltanschauung*. The hatred of Jews arches across two thousand years through the conduits of religion, culture, and modern society. Christianity taught the hatred and vilification of Jews. Inasmuch as Christianity was central to Western culture, the hatred of Jews in this culture was central.

Nationalism itself has to be seen in its dynamics of change: first as an ideology and sentiment in the creation of the modern state and modern nation, bringing emancipation and offering assimilation for Jews. This is the time of essentially cultural nationalism. In the second phase, in alliance with conservatism and authoritarianism, nationalism changes to become an agent of exclusion. In this phase the nation is often perceived as an essentialist or even biological concept, and nationalism is typically racist and xenophobic.

The link between nationalism and antisemitism has to be examined in its dynamics. In the beginning the two were basically in opposition.[1] Jew-hatred was part of religious teaching of the churches. As vital ingredients of the feudal paradigm, religious teachings and institutions were underpinning the pre-Enlightenment hierarchies and world-view. Nationalism, on the other hand, was a concept and movement of the Enlightenment, at the early stages ideologically linked with liberalism and opposing most of the ideas and beliefs that the church and the Monarchy stood for. Liberty and equality dictated emancipation, while nationalism dictated assimilation.

By the twentieth century, nationalism became associated with authoritarian conservativism. Its closest, often inseparable, political and ideological allies were anti-liberalism and, frequently, anti-modernity (the *Völkisch* and populist movements, fascism and Nazism).[2] Nationalism embraced racism through social Darwinism (ethnic, tribal nationalism). Racism and modern political anti-semitism were extraordinarily compatible. The incessant hatred of Jews all over Christendom demonstrated that when antisemitism becomes part of an ideology it becomes pervasive. In modern times this ideology is most often nationalism. Losing its alliance with liberalism, nationalism became the carrier of antisemitism and of racism.

What was the relationship between antisemitism and modernity? Jews were perceived as embodying all the ills of modern society, and all anti-modernity sentiments and ideologies easily jelled around antisemitism. This was because:

1 the emancipation of Jews, and the consequent allowing of Jews into society, was an outcome of modernity;
2 anti-modernity ideologies and movements centred around a romanticised past which most definitely did not include Jews as equals;
3 many Jews were conspicuously benefiting from modern industry and commerce;
4 the imagery of Christian Jew-hatred seamlessly blended into, and was used by, modern antisemitism; and
5 nationalism, especially the organic concept of nationalism, made use of the 'other', the 'alien', *par excellence*, and the image of the Jew as evil was already ingrained, having been formulated as 'the other' and taught by Christianity for centuries.

The Enlightenment ideals of equality and liberty dictated the emancipation of Jews. There were two ways that Jews could enter society: as Jews and as non-Jews. Indeed this latter, in the strict form of conversion, was the only way to integrate into feudal society.[3] Christianity demanded conversion. With modernity the new demand was assimilation; and nationalism was the vehicle for this. Conversion to religion was superseded by conversion to the nation. Of course, where the nation itself was predominantly Christian, this demand often carried, openly, the requirement for the shedding of Jewishness, or at least parts of Judaism and, implicitly, the conversion to Christianity.

The modern concepts of assimilation and antisemitism were also the outcome of emancipation. Antisemitism, assimilation, Jewish nationalism, thriving for a nation–state and the reform of Judaism are particular Jewish issues of modernisation.[4] Everywhere in Western civilisation, albeit to a varying extent, Jews were instrumental in the modernisation process. All issues of modernity could be (and were) symbolised by Jews. Politically and socially the essentially modern issues often appeared synonymous with Jewish issues. More often than not the ills of modernity were articulated as Jewish attributes—and vice versa. Political antisemitism claimed that Jews were responsible for complex social conditions. *Völkisch* ideology perceived the new tensions as basically Jewish versus Christian–Aryan issues. Marxists could—and did—condemn capitalism through the Jews. Racist social hierarchy placed Jews at the bottom of the heap. With the birth of political antisemitism, religious Jew-hatred was secularised.

The universalism of the Enlightenment ideals of liberty and equality notwithstanding, it was the particularism of nationalism which shaped and created the nation–state. Liberty, equality and fraternity called for emancipation of the hitherto marginalised and disenfranchised Jews. Nationalism became the vehicle of assimilation. The initial fusion of nationalism and liberalism engendered the creation of the modern state, the modern nation and modern society.

Ernst Gellner, especially in *Thought and Change*, argues that nationalism is the crucial element in the process of change leading from traditional society to modern society (Gellner 1964). Traditional society includes everything from medieval European societies to the tribesmen of Africa, Chinese peasants or Mongolian nomads. In traditional society social, economic and political relationships are determined by social structure. Gellner stresses that rigidity of structure makes communication between people comparatively unimportant. As the rigid structure breaks down, culture becomes important. Culture includes a manner of communication in which language is central. This explains the nationalist passion for culture. In modern conditions people have to be literate and, preferably, technically competent. This calls for homogeneity—and assimilation is the instrument to achieve homogeneity. So in the period of transition from feudal society to modern state, there is a vital link, indeed alliance, between nationalism, liberalism and the assimilatory drive.

On the connection between liberalism and nationalism, Ghia Nodia, in a powerful essay, asserts that nationalism is a component of liberal democracy (Nodia 1994, p. 4). According to Nodia, the interconnection is such that one cannot exist without the other. Using Eugen Weber's study, *Peasants into Frenchmen*, Nodia argues that the title could have been 'peasants into citizens' because of the process in which peasants (*paysan*, country people) became citizens (i.e. city-dwellers): 'In fact the transformation of peasants into Frenchmen and citizen was a single process. Peasants could be made Frenchmen only by becoming citizens, and vice versa: the two moments are divisible in theory, but not in practice' (Nodia 1994, pp. 8–9).

With this argument, Nodia also highlights the link between modernity and nationalism.[5] It is also important to note here that Nodia actually fuses ethnic and political nationalism, a distinction that the vast majority of nationalism scholarship does make. According to Nodia, nationalism is two-sided: one side is ethnic and the other political. When the political side is thwarted or atrophied, as it was, for example, during the long years of soviet totalitarianism, 'a rubble of atomised individuals' are left behind who, without the structures of civil society, fall back for coherence on the ethnic component of nationalism. Writing about ex-Yugoslavia, Michael Ignatieff argues similarly:

> Historically, nationalism and democracy went hand in hand . . . The tragedy for the Balkans was, that when democracy at last became possible, the only language that existed to mobilise people into a shared social project was the rhetoric of ethnic difference. Any possibility of a civic, as opposed to ethnic, democracy had been strangled at birth by the Communist regime. (Ignatieff 1993, p. 25)

Ignatieff (who also differentiates between nationalism as a political, as a cultural and as a moral doctrine) argues that the surviving Communist élites manipulated nationalist emotions in order to maintain their power. In other words, Ignatieff identifies in ex-Yugoslavia a form of 'official nationalism', so named by Hugh Seton-Watson (1977), who observed that, from the middle of the nineteenth century, conservative, reactionary policies were adopted by élites.

Just as consequential as the early link between liberalism and nationalism was the link which developed between the conservative, authoritarian right and nationalism. By the twentieth century, both were committed to antisemitism.[6] In modernity, antisemitism started to mean to nationalism what religious Jew-hatred meant to Christianity: part of self-definition. It was inseparable from and, overtly or covertly, part of the ideology. Being on the opposing side of modernity also created the alliance between Christianity and conservatism.

The development of twentieth-century nationalism is thus determined by its fusion with authoritarian conservatism. This fusion basically took two forms:

1 fusion with Christianity and/or populism (this was the case, for instance, in Hungary and Romania) and
2 fusion with racism (e.g. Nazism, the most radical outcome of racism combining with nationalism).

Both Christianity and racism are based on the idea of superiority and on the privileges carried by the superior status. Similarly, nationalism also supports a sense of superiority. The formula of superiority is:

being 'better' + entitlement to privileges + keeping down and in control those who are 'different', i.e. inferior

Where there is no threat to the privileged status from the inferior other, superiority is expressed through disdain. When the privileged status is threatened, hatred follows—e.g. Christianity was vitally threatened by Judaism, because in the beginning the former was just another Jewish sect, and much of the early theological hatred has its roots in this need to justify, separate and be 'better'. Jews, because they refused to acknowledge Jesus as the 'Messiah' and stayed Jewish, did not convert to Christianity and thus posed a threat. Racism was also formulated as an ideology of superiority. The 'father' of racism was Comte de Gobineau, who, in his *Essai sur L'Inégalité des Races Humaines*, set out to prove the superiority of the 'blue blooded' French aristocracy.

The fusion with racism is not without theoretical contradictions. As Benedict Anderson points out in *Imagined Communities*, nationalism thinks in terms of historical destinies, while racism is outside history, with its biological determinism stretching eternally and unalterably (Anderson 1993, p. 149). The contradiction is actually dissolved in another paradox of nationalism. Many theoreticians of nationalism, amongst them Anderson himself, describe the paradox of the objective modernity of nations as opposed to the subjective antiquity of nations in the eyes of nationalists (Anderson 1993, p. 5). Since nationalists view the nation as 'the people', and its origins as reaching back to the dawn of history, it is precisely at this age-old beginning where nationalism can meet racism, both asserting to exist from time immemorial, originating in obscure beginnings. Both nationalism and racism use the idea of 'forever'—a notion inherently fuzzy and false.

When the distinction between nation and state is blurred, it becomes easy to marginalise nationalities and deny them the rights of the citizen of the state. Only members of the nation can be members of the state.[7] Assimilation brings in others, such as members of other nations: assimilation and inclusion are inter-dependent. It is through the concept of race that membership in the nation becomes exclusive, a matter of biology. In racist thinking, assimilation is impossible, unachievable. Liberal nationalism, with its assimilatory drive, creates the modern nation, and anti-liberal nationalism, defined by the fiction of racial characteristics, closes the nation and casts out 'the other'. Nationalism wants to obliterate the otherness of the other, to include the other and to make them conform, to wash away the boundaries within the state. Racism wants to identify the other, place them and keep them outside the boundaries of the state, or at least exclude them from the rights and privileges of membership in the state.

Let's examine the fusion of nationalism with Christianity through nationalism's fusion with conservatism, and through what I call the paradox of liberalism and nationalism. The dawn of the age of nationalism in Western Europe was the twilight of religious doctrines. This is powerfully expressed by Anderson, who suggests that: 'Nationalism has to be understood by aligning it, not with self-consciously held political ideologies, but with the large cultural systems that preceded it, out of which—as well as against which—it came into being' (Anderson 1993, p. 12). The two relevant cultural systems Anderson refers to are the religious community and the dynastic realm. Taking these two as a point of departure, let's substitute the social hierarchy of the feudal monarchy for Anderson's cultural concept of dynasty. And indeed, the initial stirrings of nationalism against dynasties such as the Habsburgs were towards independence.

And here is the paradox of liberalism and nationalism. The paradox was that, on one hand, nationalism was the weapon of independence-seeking nobility, who had no intention of changing existing social structures. On the other hand, liberal ideals often were introduced by the monarch, in a drive towards economic modernisation. The nobility fought for national independence by resisting modernising reform. Thus, nationalism's alliance with conservatism was already created in places where national independence and the dynasty were in conflict. Since Christianity was the doctrinal foundation of feudalism, the initial anti-religiousness of modern thought can be easily explained. But once it is seen that nationalism could be, and was, the project (weapon?) of the nobility, who did want to preserve the social hierarchy and feudal power-systems, nationalism, which also embraces conservatism, is not contradictory after all.

Initially, the aim of nationalism and of the assimilatory drive is to transform ethnic and cultural groupings into a functional state, to create the homogeneous state. State and nation, and cultural and ethnic homogeneity do not always coincide. Sometimes there is a nation without a state, or a state with many nations, and sometimes ethnic and cultural groups live in more than one state. Consequently the concept, and especially the definition, of nationality is of tremendous importance. Is nationality inherited or acquired? Philosopher Jurgen Habermas stresses the difference between citizenship and national identity and postulates that hereditary nationalism gave way to an acquired nationalism, because citizenship was never conceptually tied to national identity: 'Only briefly did the democratic nation state forge a close link between '*ethnos*' and '*demos*' (Habermas 1992, p. 4).

Most scholars of nationalism, similarly, differentiate between different types of nationalism, cultural and political, or ethnic and civic nationalism. For instance, Charles Kupchan argues that ethnic nationalism defines nationhood in terms of lineage, while civic nationalism defines nationhood in terms of citizenship and political participation (Kupchan 1995, p. 4). In both Kupchan's and Habermas's approaches the concept of democracy is vital. Civic nationalism, for instance, presupposes universal suffrage, without which there is no political participation.[8]

A similar dichotomy to that between civic and ethnic nationalism is the distinction between cultural and political nationalism. These distinctions are usually accompanied by a geographical distinction: Eastern and Western nationalism.

Nationalism—East and West

Nation, nationality and nationalism are notoriously difficult concepts to define.[9] Benedict Anderson sees nationality and nationalism as cultural artefacts of a particular kind, and gives the definition of the nation as an imagined political community (Anderson 1993, p. 6). Ernst Gellner similarly wrote that nationalism invents nations where they do not exist (Gellner 1964, p. 169).

Many authors point to the difference between Western and East European nationalism. For example, Hans Kohn postulated that while Western nationalism was built on reality, with little regard to the past, Eastern nationalism was based on myths and sentimental dreams (Kohn 1961b, pp. 329–30). According to him this was because nationalism spread to Eastern Europe before the corresponding social and economic modernisation even started (Kohn 1961b, p. 457).

In the West, 'nation' means, above all, a political entity. In multinational Eastern Europe 'nation' had a more tribal meaning. The difference between nation and nationality was especially relevant. One of the first philosophers to write about nationalism, and certainly the most influential in Eastern Europe, Johann Gottfried von Herder, differentiated between *Volk* (which stood for nationality) and nation. Von Herder's distinction was imbued with his essential liberalism. Another distinction, originating with Hegel and further developed by Marx and Engels, differentiates between historic and non-historic nations and posits that nationalities which never established or maintained states were not dominant political forces and thus did not become historically relevant nations.[10] A similar distinction was used by Hungarian nationalism in the nineteenth century to denigrate the aspirations of the national groups for self-determination, and to bolster indignant Hungarian chauvinism against the Successor States created out of parts of the Monarchy after World War I. The myth-creating relevance of history had renewed importance in this second phase of nationalism, when Hungarian national identity had to be reconstructed after World War I.

The German historian, Friedrich Meinecke, also saw a dichotomy between cultural and political nationalisms. He divided nations into cultural and political nations, the first informed by jointly experienced cultural heritage and the second primarily based on the unifying force of common political history (Meinecke 1928). The political nation is a product of the Enlightenment, although cultural nationalism often combines with 'cosmopolitan' political directions, for instance, in the case of German romanticism. To Meinecke, the highest form of nationalism is exactly this combination, forming a culturally homogeneous and absolutely sovereign nation–state

(Meinecke 1928). Again, this theory does not account for the formidably antisemitic nature of French nationalism, which formed itself into a visible movement following the Dreyfus affair. Similar to Meinecke's notion is the theory of Roman Dmowski, who made a distinction between 'the idea of state-nationality' and 'the idea of linguistic and ethnographical nationality' (Fountain 1980). But, as Andrzej Walicki pointed out, Polish nationalism, for instance, was born as a political nationalism of the Western type and changed only later into the xenophobic, ethnocentric type (Walicki 1982, pp. 66–7). According to John Plamenatz, the difference between Eastern and Western nationalism is that the former is cultural and the latter political. Eastern nationalism is both imitative and hostile to the (Western) models it imitates, and is apt to be illiberal (Plamenatz 1976, pp. 34–5).

Exploring the specificities of Eastern European nationalism, another scholar of the subject, Peter Sugar, points to its essentially messianic character. It was through the special mission of the nation that Eastern European nationalism counteracted the inclusive nationalism of the nobility, that is, a nationalism that was willing to include others (such as Jews). Sugar also pointed out the difference in meaning between the Western concept of liberty and its Eastern European counterpart. The first one stood for freedom from oppression while the second stood for freedom from foreign oppression (Sugar 1971, pp. 11–13).

Sugar distinguishes between four different types of nationalism in Eastern Europe: bourgeois, aristocratic, popular and bureaucratic. According to Sugar these distinctions are especially palpable in the early stages of development.

Bourgeois nationalism bore the closest resemblance to Western nationalism. It was prevalent in the Czech provinces of the Habsburg empire, where economic development was closely following that of the Western countries, and industrialisation created a strong middle class, while the aristocracy was foreign and never assumed a leading role in the shaping of Czech nationalism. Poland and Hungary, on the other hand, both lacked a middle class but had the most numerous aristocracy in all of Europe, in control of the administration and of the agrarian economy. In both countries the aristocracy used nationalism in their struggle against foreign rulers. Hence theirs was an aristocratic nationalism. Sugar describes popular nationalism as vaguely resembling Jacksonian democracy; it was prevalent mostly in Serbia and Bulgaria, where, due to the

Muslim rules of the Ottoman empire, there was no local nobility, and the landowners were mostly foreigners. This was the nationalism of peasantry. Bureaucratic nationalism, which is the closest to the emerging African and Asian nationalisms, was characteristic of Romania, Turkey and Greece. Bureaucratic nationalism fuses nation, state and the policies of government and is essentially irredentist (Sugar 1971, pp. 46–54).

In a 1964 essay, Endre Arató also differentiates between aristocratic and bourgeois nationalism in Hungary. He describes the former as essentially a narrow, political nationalism, and presents bourgeois nationalism as being more concerned with economic modernisation. According to Arató, aristocratic nationalism gave way to the bourgeois variety in the decades following 1830 (Arató 1964, pp. 79–142). Arguing the importance of economic considerations in aristocratic nationalism, Sugar contends that nationalism remained aristocratic until the end of World War II (Sugar 1971, pp. 46–51). In fact, the difference between Sugar's and Arató's point is in their definition of aristocratic nationalism. Sugar's approach is based more on sociological factors, while Arató's is more political, in the Marxist sense. The latter perceives economic modernisation as being against the interests of the aristocracy and thus constituting an exclusively bourgeois project.

Even using the above distinctions, it is clear that the nationalism of the nineteenth century, including the Monarchy years, differed in program, policies and by whom it was articulated. Nineteenth-century nationalism in Hungary was articulated by the aristocracy and the echelons of liberal gentry. It aimed at economic modernisation and limited social modernisation, and it was essentially inclusive. Following World War I, Hungarian nationalism was re-articulated by the Christian middle class, which was largely, but by no means exclusively, made up of the ranks of impoverished gentry. One of the effects of modernisation was precisely the development of the middle class, which, although predominantly Jewish at first, by the twentieth century was articulating a distinctly anti-Jewish platform. Until after World War I, the increasingly impoverished gentry did not consider the new professions and opportunities industrialisation introduced, partly because these professions were not considered gentlemanly, i.e. respectable, and partly because they could rely on finding positions in the Monarchy's vastly inflated public administration. When, with the loss of the empire, these jobs were gone and the gentry was ready to take the less respectable jobs and professions, they found that the Jews were already there.

Charting the history of Hungarian nationalism from aristocratic to 'proletarian' nationalism, historian George Barany also comes to the conclusion that 'the more it changes the more it stays the same' (Barany 1971, p. 259). Initially, writes Barany, Hungarian feudal nationalism was political–legal, 'i.e. premodern and a-national', but sometime between the mid-eighteenth and mid-nineteenth century it changed as a result of the literary–cultural revival. This timeframe is very similar to that of Arató's, but with a different explanation. While Arató attributes the change to economy, Barany sees it in national consciousness (Barany 1971, p. 309; Arató 1964, p. 137). According to Barany, in the first half of the nineteenth century Hungarian nationalism was part of the same broad modernisation process that arose in the West.

Both Barany and Arató consider the needs and tasks of nationalism in the process of modernisation, rather than the political content and the sociological characteristics of nationalism. It is this latter point of view, unexplored by Barany and Arató, from which I argue that Hungarian nationalism changed from the liberal, modernising 'inclusive' character of aristocratic nationalism to the exclusionary, authoritarian, conservative character of bureaucratic nationalism of the 'Hungarian Christian middle class'.

The paradox of modernising aristocracy was extended by the further paradox of the Liberal Era of the Austro–Hungarian Monarchy when, in Hungary, the governing liberal party suppressed both antisemitism and the nationalities by using the strength of the state.[11] (See the discussion 'The nationalities question' in Chapter 1.) The nationalism of the Horthy era, articulated by the antisemitic middle class, also contained several contradictions. One was the contradictory requirement of containing Jewish economic preponderance without upsetting the economy. Another was the religious nature of nationalism, which was manifest not only in the articulation of Hungarian identity on religious grounds (i.e. Christian Hungarian), but also in the religious worship of Hungary.[12]

Antisemitism—modern antisemitism

Viewing the hatred of Jews in its continuity, two phases are discernible: religious anti-Judaism and modern antisemitism.[13] In the first phase the religious concept of anti-Judaism was an integral part of Western culture, of art and of *Weltanschauung*, of social boundaries and of ethos. When the concepts of Enlightenment developed in the same Western culture, modern political anti-semitism absorbed and superseded religious hatred. Murderous antisemitism is an outcome and the climax of modern political antisemitism. Genocidal antisemitism, articulated and brought to completion by Nazism, is larger and more diffuse than Nazi ideology. For the Nazis to perpetrate the Holocaust, they needed—and received—endorsement from the non-Nazi populations. This endorsement sometimes came in the form of active collaboration, but more often from the silence of the bystanders. Although there was opposition to both the German occupation and the ideology and politics of Nazism, there was no opposition of any significance to the genocide of the Jews.

There are stages of development of modern antisemitism as an ideology and as a political movement, and there are stages of the development of murderous and genocidal antisemitism. That Jew-hatred has always carried the concept of murder, we know from the history of the Crusades, of the Inquisition, of the many mass murders sparked by blood libels and accusations of poisoning wells, and of pogroms.

The word 'antisemitism' was coined by an antisemite, Wilhelm Marr, who aimed to separate religious, 'superstitious' Jew-hatred from the new form which evolved with modern social conditions. Most social scientists agree upon a separation of medieval, theologically rooted anti-Judaism from modern antisemitism.[14] The relationship between the two, however, is not simply chronological. Modern antisemitism is not simply a continuation of Christian Jew-hatred.

Helen Fein's *The Persisting Question* surveys the dynamics and sociology of antisemitism and uses historical and comparative analyses (1987b). From a theoretical perspective it explores the differences between antisemitism and other inter-group hostilities, and looks at the evolving role of Jews in different states and civilisations. Of the many definitions of antisemitism, Helen Fein's seems to be sociologically the most relevant.

Fein defines antisemitism as:

> a persisting latent structure of hostile beliefs toward Jews as a collectivity, manifested in individuals as attitudes and in culture as myth, ideology, folklore and imagery, and in actions—social or legal

discrimination, political mobilization against the Jews, and collective or state violence—which results in and/or is designed to distance, displace, or destroy Jews as Jews. (Fein 1987a, p. 68)

There are two powerful aspects of this definition. One is the view of antisemitism as both attitude and action. Any definition that views only one or the other is too narrow and does not allow for dynamism nor for historical continuity. Simpson and Yinger, for instance, define antisemitism as action: 'anti-Semitism may be defined as any activity that tends to force into or hold Jews in an inferior position and to limit their economic, political and social rights' (Simpson & Yinger 1985, p. 253). What Simpson and Yinger provide with this is a definition for only a particular kind of discrimination, one based on the desire to marginalise Jews, but it does not explain why such a desire should arise at all, or what the desire is. Ethos and culture are contingent on antisemitic action. Without that, the idea of antisemitic action simply would not arise. Culture is the conduit, it provides the transmission belt, both historically and from the individual to society (and back); from attitude to action—and back again.

The other crucial aspect of Fein's definition is the time-context. The word 'persisting' places antisemitism in time. When viewed as stationary, frozen, in the setting of a specific time and/or a specific space, antisemitism is reduced to the particular, to the circumstantial, and becomes contingent on the parameters of the specific situation. To avoid this conceptualisation, which focuses solely on the accidental and the particular qualities, antisemitism has to be viewed as rooted in history, continually evolving, continually adapting to new and diverse situations and ideologies as well as adopting new ideologies and ideas. Recognising this evolving quality of antisemitism is of extreme importance in understanding it both as a system of attitudes and in the form of diverse actions. While there is a difference between the two, as discussed earlier, modern antisemitism cannot be understood without Christian antisemitism. This is why all theories which try to locate antisemitism within racism or within prejudice alone reduce antisemitism. It cannot be explained merely by xenophobia either. Neither the theories of racism nor ethnic prejudice enable us to distinguish what has been unusual about the hostility toward Jews (Langmuir 1987, p. 126). The ingredients of modern antisemitism include racist, prejudicial and theological elements—as ethos and as culture.

Of the many different explanations of antisemitism three major approaches are relevant: the historical, the psychoanalytical and the theological. The first focuses on the interactions of Jews and non-Jews, and the Hungarian scholar Istvan Bibó would fit here.[15] Viewing the sequence of interactions in their historical development, modern antisemitism is explored through the dynamics of interactions between Jews and non-Jews. The second approach focuses on the antisemite and tries to explain, using the tools of psychoanalysis, how fear and hostility is externalised and projected onto vulnerable minorities. Sartre, for example, who does not consider the origins or the functions of antisemitism in the pre-capitalist era, only its manifestation as a belief-system, uses the tools of psychology to explain antisemitism (Sartre 1948).

The third approach, using the tools of theology, seeks to understand modern antisemitism from its Christian roots, and explores the hegemonic institutions and ideologies of Western civilisation.[16] The problem with this approach is that it does not allow for the impact of modernity; for social Darwinism, racism, nationalism. The other extreme, which explains antisemitism as wholly a modern phenomenon, is best represented by Bibó. Although Bibó does explore medieval conditions, his explanation of antisemitism as a historical phenomenon minimises the relevance of Christian doctrine and ethos. The ideal approach has to be viewing the development of interactions and changes in ethos in historical context, yet exploring the historical dimension of prejudice and xenophobia. Thus the three schools together allow for a more complete understanding of the genesis of modern antisemitism.

Both as an ideology and as political movement, antisemitism belongs to modernity. Yet both as an ideology and as a movement it can only be understood in its connection to the history of religious anti-Judaism. Modern antisemitism is a continuity of Christian Jew-hatred. Without its historical and cultural roots its pervasiveness cannot be understood.

Pre-modern hatred of Jews was primarily against the Jewish religion and against the Jews for not becoming Christians. The tenets of Christian anti-Judaism are in the Scriptures, in theological writings and, generally, the teachings of the church. Modern antisemitism is against the Jews as individuals and as people. Drawing heavily on the stereotypes and images supplied by Christianity, the accusation is of corruption and of conspiracy to rule the world.[17] Modern antisemitism condemns Jews for being capitalists, for being Communists, for being liberals, for being nationalists (Zionists), in other words, for fitting into the modern world. The target of modern, political anti-semitism is not the 'authentic' Jew, but the assimilated Jew. Assimilated Jews, the beneficiaries of modernisation and emancipation, who had previously been ostracised, excluded, and separate, were no longer recognisable. By blending into Christian society and taking economically advantageous roles, they disadvantaged Christians. The phenomenon of exposing the 'hidden' Jew is observable, for instance, in right-wing post-Versailles Hungary, during the soviet purges of 1948–53 and in Poland in 1967–68.[18]

Bibó differentiates between three streams within modern anti-semitism. One stream is characterised by its conservative, even medieval, clerical phraseology and it is a continuation of medieval anti-Jewish prejudice. Another stronger and more distinctive manifestation dispenses altogether with the religious phraseology and cites Jewish political and economic advances as reasons. The third stream links with modern nationalism and racism, and views Jews as threatening the nation or the race (Bibó 1984, p. 192).[19] Right from the beginning, all these streams used each others' imagery and terminology. Even Nazi antisemitism was a conglomerate of various streams. These streams signify not so much different trends, but different historical stages, all of which adapted hatred to a new historical–sociological context. Modern antisemitism is an amalgam of these various antisemitic traditions.

Nazi antisemitism was the synthesis of political, social and religious anti-Jewish ideologies. The embodiment of evil that Jews became in Nazi antisemitism is directly linked to Christianity through the concept of the devil. Although the Nuremberg laws were racial, in the definition of who belonged to the Jewish 'race', it was the Jewish religion that defined the Jewish 'race'. The First Regulation to the Reich Citizenship Law, 14 November 1935, includes in the definition:

a)   who was a member of the Jewish religious community at the time of the promulgation of this law, or *was admitted to it subsequently*;

b)   who was *married* to a Jew at the time of the promulgation of this Law, or subsequently *married* to a Jew (Arad et al. 1988, p. 80). [*emphasis added*]

Thus, contradictory to the essential biological determinism of racism, an 'Aryan' could become a Jew by converting to Judaism or marrying a Jew. With this concept, religion, a spiritual belief-system, is viewed as biological (i.e. racial), tangible, able to contaminate the 'race'. The importance of religion was also perceptible in other ways. While all Jews were to be victims, Nazis especially targeted religious symbols. Prayer shawls and *Torah* scrolls were defiled, synagogues burnt. Assimilated, often converted Jews were marked with the yellow star or with a yellow armband, partly for humiliation but partly as a tool of identification. In spite of the Nazi claim to the contrary, it was not possible to know who was Jewish without the aid of the local population, who could identify Jews. Even the locals did not always know and had to use non-racial identification methods, such as accent.

Premodern, religious anti-Jewishness provided the continuity and the coherence for modern antisemitism. The imagery and the tenets of Christian antisemitism became part of folkways and of Western culture. Yet, from the nineteenth century, antisemitism became a political issue, often connected ideologically to nationalism and to racism. Through antisemitism the project of modernity was attacked. Jews were blamed for being liberals, capitalists, revolutionaries and industrialists. The focus of hatred shifted from religion to the person, and the rationalisation of the hatred shifted from religious to political and to racial. The 'solution' also shifted from conversion, i.e. inclusion by obliteration, to segregation and isolation, i.e. exclusion by political means. Nazi antisemitism synthesised the two with the ultimate exclusion by obliteration.

It was emancipation and assimilation, the two social and political outcomes of modernisation, which changed the status of Jews within society. So emancipation and assimilation have to be explored to ascertain the difference and the connection between Christian and modern antisemitism.

Assimilation

What is the link between modernisation and assimilation, assimilation and emancipation? In the period of transition from feudal to modern society, liberalism and nationalism were interdependent and in alliance. Without liberalism there is no assimilation and without assimilation no homogeneous culture. This alliance was also vital in another process: the integration of Jews into society. The prerequisite of assimilation was emancipation. The word 'emancipation' is used to signify two processes: the struggle for civil equality and the modernisation/secularisation of the tradition-bound Jewish communities. The first meaning is emancipation in the strictest sense: a political/legal process in which Jews, as individuals, acquire full citizenship and thus become part of the modern state, modern society. The second meaning of emancipation was directly connected to the previous one and was mostly carried out in the Western civilisation of the nineteenth century in the form of assimilation. Assimilation is the social process through which emancipation was accomplished. In this process Jews not only secularised their religion but also their tradition, to be more compatible with another tradition, that of Western civilisation. While the emancipation of the 'fourth estate' (i.e. the working classes), both in the political–legal and the social sense, took place within the same culture, for Jews the assimilatory path to social emancipation led into another culture.

Full assimilation, that is, social and cultural, could not have taken place without emancipation, that is, without the consent and support of the dominant society. For instance in Russia, and generally in the East, assimilation was not only rare, but more significantly, one-sided. Without emancipation, the process of assimilation did not lead into Russian society, but into the abstract realm of modern society. Hence the assimilatory vehicle was not nationalism, as in the countries which granted emancipation, namely the West, including Hungary, but through the universalism of socialist ideals. However, the opposite is not true. Although in many countries there was an expressed link (e.g. France and Hungary), assimilation could be an articulated expectation but not a pre-condition to emancipation. Assimilation is a many-faceted process, with two groups of 'participants': on the one hand, those who wish to assimilate and to whom the right of assimilation is granted by emancipation, and on the other, the society into which the assimilation process leads. In this process emancipation is a visible and concrete action. The community into which the newly emancipated group or stratum is heading, forgoes, or at least constrains, its former legal, social and cultural exclusivity. Both emancipation and assimilation of the former disenfranchised community is an indispensable part of the modernisation process. In other words, the project of modernity requires both.

What about the choices and challenges facing the emancipated community, i.e. the Jews? Emancipation itself was not a matter of choice for them, it was an action taken by the dominant community. Assimilation, however, was one of the choices to the challenges presented by modernity. Here an important differentiation has to be made between Eastern and Western Europe. In Eastern Europe, because of the persisting feudal structures and absence of modernisation, emancipation, and hence assimilation, was not an option. Yet, in another sense, as has already been mentioned, modernity was a challenge that had to be answered. There is the particular modernisation which uses nationalism and assimilation within a given country, but there is also another, more abstract aspect of modernity, which is without boundaries, when modernity is just an idea.[20] In this sense, the call of modernity was felt, albeit weakly, even in thoroughly non-modern, feudalistic countries such as Russia.

Faced with the challenges of modernity, there were basically two routes for Jews.[21] One was total negation, defiance of modernity and the reinforcing of tradition. The ultra-orthodox, including the Hasidic movement, chose isolation and insulation.[22] They tried to maintain an unchanging Jewish identity. In Western Europe where Jews were emancipated, this was an impossible task—changes were all around them. To counter the changes, to stay unmoving with all the movement around them, ultra-orthodoxy was established. In fact, a new movement was needed to stay stationary, to preserve the tradition. The other route, which actively acknowledged modernity, was through emancipation and self-emancipation. This route was taken by most Jews in Western Europe. For most, the maintenance of Jewish identity was still of paramount importance. Various movements sprang up within Judaism, which sought to modernise the religion. The most important of these was *Haskala*, the internal Jewish enlightenment movement, and within that the so-called *Wissenschaft des Judentums*, the Science of Judaism.[23]

Nationalism and socialism were the two assimilatory elements, the two ideological/social media which facilitated the merging of Jews into society. Nationalism, with its particularism, still allowed religious identity. Universalist socialism, on the other hand, meant abandonment of Jewish particularism. In a way, socialism was the non-religious counterpart of conversion, in which the previous identity is totally submerged. This previous identity, of course, was not only a religious one: Jewishness has many components. This many-facetedness was expressed in the route Zionists chose. Secular or religious, Zionism was and is a particular Jewish route to modernity. Zionism is then another emancipatory/assimilatory vehicle, but one that is different from any other nationalism. It engendered auto-emancipation, a particular Jewish way into the modern world, in which Jewish identity was not endangered, or compromised.

Leon Pinsker, at the end of the nineteenth century, a decade and a half before Theodor Herzl formulated political Zionism, warned that emancipation 'granted' from the outside would not achieve a lasting solution. Jacob Katz postulated in his *Jewish Emancipation and Self-Emancipation* that both emancipation and self-emancipation are necessary: 'Jewish self-emancipation may have transmuted the scene of the struggle for Jewish rehabilitation, but it has not succeeded in obviating its necessity' (Katz 1986, p. ix).

Before World War I, and even in the Horthy era, the assimilatory drive of Jews within Hungarian society followed an analogous pattern to that of German Jews: cultural/social identification. In other words, assimilation through nationalism. After the Holocaust, the reconstruction of the largest Jewish community in Eastern Europe took on the form of assimilation through communist ideology.

This book centres around the role nationalism played in both inclusion and exclusion and in assimilation and antisemitism. Nationalism was the common agency for all these processes and for the ideology of antisemitism. In alliance with liberalism, it was a positive force, in nation-building, in the creation of modern national identity, and, in the case of Hungarians and Jews, in the simultaneous construction of modern identity. In its quest to create a homogeneous culture essential for modern society, nationalism had essentially an assimilatory character, expressed in the policy and ideology of inclusion through assimilation. In alliance with authoritarian conservatism, it became the agent of exclusion and the carrier of antisemitism. It was through nationalism that Hungarian Jews were called on to assimilate, and it was the agency of nationalism which 'dictated' the antisemitic policies of the Horthy regime.

In the nineteenth century, national identity was constructed in cultural terms and was based on the perception of the cultural superiority of Hungarians. In the twentieth century, with the loss of empire-status and the loss of two-thirds of its territory, a new national identity, or rather the reconstruction of national identity, was necessary. This reconstruction simultaneously reflected, and was determined by, the changed nature of nationalism as it merged with conservatism. While in the nineteenth century Christianity was irrelevant in the definition of the 'other', this changed as post-Trianon Hungary truly became a nation–state, and the Jews were practically the only 'other' within. Antisemitism itself also went through a change. It became racial and radical, partly as a result of indigenous developments (especially the impact of the counter-revolution) and partly as part of a European trend. As a result of the fusion of nationalism, Christianity and antisemitism, any one of these elements stood for the other two: a good Christian was a good Hungarian and a good antisemite, or any other combination. This fusion also explains in large part why Hungarian society stood by while the Jews were deported and massacred.

Nationalism was also a defining factor in the formation of modern Jewish identity in Hungary. Modernisation became a simultaneous project and opportunity for Jews and Hungarians. Both were creating a new society and new national identity. This synchronous construction of modern identity is extremely relevant in the understanding of why the fervent Hungarian nationalism of Jews persisted in spite of the development of the organic concept of Hungary and the 'Christian national principle', after World War I.

The question arises, how racial, murderous antisemitism appeared so dramatically in 1919 in Hungary, where there was no historical tradition of pogroms. In the years of the Monarchy, superiority was understood in cultural terms, and racism was not yet relevant. Although there were racist elements in the definition of Hungarian superiority, it was primarily used against the ethnic minorities. In these decades the official policy towards Jews was of inclusion, through emancipation and assimilation. There was an underlying presence, a constancy of antisemitism, changing and accommodating the times, according to what was deemed acceptable and/or desirable; but the 'genteel' antisemitism of the Monarchy years switched from the private to the public, changed from social antisemitism—as expressed by the individual—first to pogrom, during the White Terror, and then to state-ideology, with the Horthy regime's 'Christian course', leading to the acceptance of the Holocaust.

Another question that needs to be asked is: was the 1919 pogrom just the result of the cessation of state-control? Did it erupt suddenly, throwing off the lid of oppression, and exposing the underlying antisemitism? It could be further argued that although the Horthy regime was authoritarian itself, unlike the Austro–Hungarian Monarchy, it did not suppress antisemitism. This explanation, however, accounts neither for the subsequent containment of radical antisemitic violence by the Horthy regime nor, more importantly, for the different nature of antisemitism. What emerged in 1919 was a different, reconstructed antisemitism, different from the religious anti-Jewish teachings, which pre-World War I antisemitism essentially had been in Hungary.

With the collapse of the Monarchy, the policy of inclusion, having fulfilled its purpose, had become superfluous. So there were two changes: one in state-policy and one in the underlying ideology. The change of policy was a surface change. Nevertheless, it was necessary for the dissemination of the new, modern, political antisemitism that emerged. The change in ideology was the defining one. As powerfully as nationalism, in affiliation with liberalism, engendered assimilation, and in the case of Hungary was vital to the policy of inclusion, the affiliation of nationalism to anti-liberalism engendered antisemitism and exclusion, fortified and further disseminated by the nascent ideologies of fascism and of Nazism.

The case of Hungarian Jews is in many aspects like the veterinarian's horse (a picture which illustrates all the possible illnesses to be studied): with both inclusion and exclusion as clearly and strongly defined policies, with the role of political and social institutions, ethos and culture clearly observable, the case of Hungarian Jews provides a poignant illustration of the changing politics of nationalism and antisemitism.

While antisemitism had common features in many countries, the Hungarian case had special features, which cast light on the relationship between traditional Christian anti-Judaism, modern political antisemitism, and nationalism.

PART ONE

INCLUSION

Chapter one

Modernisation in Hungary

[O]nly a few who lived in it felt the inherent weakness of an obviously outmoded political structure which, despite all the prophecies of inherent doom, continued to function in spurious splendor and with inexplicable, monotonous stubbornness.

Arendt 1967, p. 50

In Hungary attempts at modernisation started in the first half of the nineteenth century. In this period, called the 'Age of Reform', Hungary entered the mainstream of European economic life and this was a development of profound significance. The issue of national independence was part of the thrust towards modernisation. The two main areas where the battle for modernisation was fought were the Diet and the renewal of the Hungarian language. The 1848 revolution was led by the same reformers, mostly politicians and intellectuals, who were the leading figures of the Age of Reform.

By 1849 the Hungarian revolution and war of liberation were defeated. From the spring of nations Hungary entered the winter of the vanquished. The Habsburgs had won. All the achievements of the revolutionary parliament were abolished: equality before the law, taxation for all social groups, the abolition of serfdom (with state compensation), freedom of the press and parliamentary government. Between 1849 and 1867 Hungarians felt the oppressive power of the Habsburg monarch. The consolidation of absolutism blocked the path to all progress. However, as Austria became isolated internationally and felt increasingly threatened by German unification, an *Ausgleich* (Compromise) with the Hungarians became more and more desirable. Hungarians also felt threatened by an imminent German empire under the leadership of Bismarck, and by the traditional enemy, Russia. Lajos Kossuth, the leader of the struggle for independence, wrote his famous 'Cassandra letter', warning about the nationalities question, but the majority of the middle class, which traditionally supported Kossuth, did not listen any more. With the extensive celebration at the coronation of Franz Joseph and his wife Elizabeth, the Austro–Hungarian Monarchy was born. (Fortuitously conveying the cacophonous quality of the empire, Robert Musil called it *Kakania*, a colourful neologism created from the abbreviation *k.u.k.—kaiserlich und königlich* (imperial and royal)—the title of Franz Joseph as the emperor of Austria and the king of Hungary.)

The Monarchy consisted of two states, with many nationalities and ethnic groups: Germans, Magyars, Czechs, Slovaks, Italians, Poles, Ukrainians, Jews, Romanians, Slovenes, Croatians, Serbs, Gypsies, and, after the 1878 occupation of Bosnia-Herzegovina, Bosnian Muslims and others. There were two governments, two parliaments and two separate public administration systems. Foreign relations, defence and finance were in the hands of common ministers, who were primarily responsible to the emperor–king. A devout Catholic, Franz Joseph governed in the 'clerical spirit'. He was mediocre and cold, a dull bureaucrat, industrious and dutiful. He was also the commander of the army and, especially through the common ministries, much of the previous absolutist power was preserved. He relied on a large and strong army, a well-disciplined force of civil servants, a strong gendarmerie and police. The parliament did not have an important role. As Hannah Arendt pithily put it, they were little more than a 'not too bright debating society' (Arendt 1967, p. 243).

Serious antagonisms were inherent in the Empire. While economic, industrial and commercial modernisation was creating wealth and enhancing social mobility, a powerful aristocracy survived with huge estates. The Catholic Church also maintained its enormous political influence, wealth and lands. In addition to the survival of a retrograde feudal structure, the nationalities issue was another source of antagonism. The Austro–Hungarian Empire was built on a system of hierarchical dependence between nationalities, in which Austria was in the best position, closely followed by Hungary, where the nationalities were subjected to rigorous Magyarisation, and denied the right of autonomy, and whose national existence was negated.

In spite of the contentious issue of the nationalities and the survival of feudalistic hierarchy, this was a period of progress, the period when modern Hungary was born. Economy and society evolved in a dialectical interdependence, mutually energising each other. Two new classes developed: the bourgeoisie and the proletariat. The aristocracy modernised their huge estates and maintained their monopoly of power, and through them strong feudalistic remnants persisted. The lesser nobility went through a dramatic process of impoverishment while still maintaining their strong hold on public administration. The developing bourgeoisie was predominantly Jewish, while the urban proletariat had large segments of German and other ethnic minorities in their swelling numbers. Social and political tensions appeared, and were presented as the 'Jewish question' and the 'nationalities question'.

The nature and content of nationalism and liberalism were also changing. Nationalism was embraced, for different reasons, by all social strata, except for some members of the intelligentsia. Of special importance for the modernisation of legal institutions and the growing role of the state was the enactment of laws concerning civil marriage and state registration for births, marriages and deaths, and freedom of religion, which included the equality of Judaism with other faiths.[1]

The characteristic of the era was a dichotomy. On the one hand, it was an age of founding, of economic growth, of modernisation, of the development of modern legal institutions and of the modern state (even the nationalities were handled within the legal boundaries of a semi-authoritarian liberal state), where political antisemitism could not take foothold—as it did in neighbouring Austria.[2] On the other hand, it was characterised by the survival of feudal institutions choking social and political spheres, by arrogant, haughty and increasingly racial nationalism, and by the weakening of liberal political thought. It was also the time when the ethnic minorities were oppressed and their national aspirations ignored, leading to the eventual demise of the Empire. In fact, all the forces which were to lead to disintegration of the Austro–Hungarian Empire were very much in evidence.

The age of founding: economy in the Monarchy

With the Compromise, Hungary entered modernity in a rather abrupt manner and quite late compared to Western Europe.[3] Hungary in the

nineteenth century was largely an agrarian society. Around the middle
of the century, agriculture accounted for 90 per cent of the national
product (Berend & Ranki 1985, p. 14). It was a very backward
agriculture, both because of social conditions and production technologies. With the removal of most obstacles, the economy of Hungary
progressed dynamically.

Between 1867 and 1918 Hungary's population rose from 15.4
million to 21 million. By regulating the two main rivers flowing
through Hungary, the Danube and the Tisza, vast areas of land
were reclaimed. Harvests trebled. By the turn of the century half
of the grain produced was exported. Seventy-five per cent of
Hungarian trade was with other districts of the Monarchy. A huge
milling industry was built, utilising the enormous grain production.
In the 1870s the milling industry of Budapest was the largest in
the world. The rise of the milling industry had a huge impact on
the development of the railway system, engineering and tool-
industry, and stimulated modernisation in agriculture. Hungarian
wheat-export and milling were protected by high agricultural tariffs.
Primarily an agricultural country, Hungary was called the pantry of
the Monarchy. Around the turn of the century when grain prices
dwindled, intensive livestock breeding was introduced. Pig-farming
in particular took off in Hungary; the stock of pigs doubled and
pig-killing became a national custom which entered Hungarian
folklore.[4] Naturally, with all these developments in agriculture, not
only the number of mills but the whole food industry prospered.
Hungary's national income trebled during this period. Hungary
became a fast-developing agrarian–industrial state. In 1913 approximately 16 per cent of the national income was derived from
manufacturing industries. Electrical and chemical industries, especially, were progressing well (Hanak 1988, pp. 142–4).

Jewish financial, industrial and commercial expertise were indispensable in this dynamically expanding economy. Jews were
dominant in the sugar industry (which became virtually a Jewish
monopoly), and textile, food, and heavy industries (Katzburg 1966,
pp. 144–6).

Budapest

The rise of Budapest as a metropolis was the result and embodiment
of interconnected historical processes and economic trends: the
emergence of the modern state, which introduced freedom of
movement for peasantry and for Jews; the ensuing large scale

immigration from all parts of the Empire; the transformation of the traditional agrarian economy into a modern industrial one with the corollary requirement of labour; the inherently urbanising trend allowing and demanding social mobility; and even technological changes which helped to overcome distance and promote migration, thereby speeding up the urbanisation process.

Urbanisation is intrinsically part of the industrial age. Economic, technological and social modernisation produced big, cosmopolitan cities. In Hungary, the spectacular rise of Budapest as the nation's capital was part of nineteenth-century developments, including nationalism. In fact, historian John Lukacs sees a direct connection between the two: 'The extraordinary rise of Budapest depended on the extraordinary force of Hungarian nationalism' (Lukacs 1988, p. 69).

By the time Buda, Pest and Obuda were united in 1873 and Budapest was formally created, it was not only already the seat of the independent Hungarian government but also where most urban-dwelling Hungarians lived. Istvan Széchenyi, the aristocrat leader and ideologue of the reform age, first presented the idea that the little town of Pest should be united with Buda, the historical capital of the Hungarian kings, and that it should become the administrative, cultural and political centre of the country. This vision of Budapest (even the name was created by Széchenyi) became one of the rallying calls of social and political reform and of national pride.

György Ranki, the Hungarian historian, emphasised the role of social and economic modernisation: 'The birth of the capital was an organic part of the requirement of bourgeois transformation and at the same time its main vehicle and source of encouragement' (Ranki, G. 1989, p. 164).

From the technological point of view, the establishment of the milling industry was the most important component in the formation of industrial Budapest. It stimulated the growth of many other industries and the modernisation of agriculture. Acceleration of economic development usually promotes urbanisation. In the 1870s the social structure of Budapest was shaped by an overwhelming number of industrial workers and a very thin layer of middle class (Szelényi 1990, p. 175). The tiny middle class was concentrated in the middle of the city. In the following decades Budapest went through explosive growth and change in every way. There were decades when the growth was over three hundred thousand people.

As Budapest was fast becoming the commercial and political centre of Hungary, its social structure was changing too, and the numbers, especially of the middle class, surged. With the changing social structure and the expanding population there was a huge building boom and the face of the inner city developed, much as it still looks today. As street after street was built up to accommodate the middle classes, workers were squeezed into new settlements which were built outside the local administration boundaries of Budapest.[5]

Hungarian society

One of the main characteristics of Hungarian society in this period was change itself. Two new classes developed, the bourgeoisie and the proletariat. To varying degrees, all social classes were affected by the huge changes of industrialisation and modernisation. The class that changed the least was the aristocracy. They entered into the new economic paradigm maintaining their privileged social and political position. The lesser nobility was affected economically, and their intellectual and cultural resistance to these changes was expressed in fierce and xenophobic self-pitying nationalism. Another characteristic of the era was that the stronghold of political power stayed in the hands of the exclusively (or totally assimilated) Hungarian nobility, while the new class, the predominantly Jewish bourgeoisie, prevailed in economy, and the liberal-minded intelligentsia in culture. Finally, and arguably the most decisive and important characteristic was the absence of a Hungarian ethnic middle class, the prerequisite of the transition from feudalism to capitalism, from an agrarian society to an industrial one. Thus the modernisation of Hungary by two minority groups, the Jews and the Germans, became a specific development impacting on not only the social but also the political landscape of Hungary. With the growth of the middle classes, Hungarian society had taken on an essentially bourgeois character. Nonetheless, remnants of feudalism survived in the aristocracy, the gentry and in the peasantry.

At the apex of the social pyramid stood the aristocracy, complete with *latifundia* (large estates).[6] Their haughty and arrogant nationalism was fuelled by their position of power. Their monopoly on power was underpinned by two important features: their relatively large number, compared to the rest of the population, and that they were almost totally ethnic Hungarians. They were overwhelmingly Roman Catholic and they were the most obvious beneficiaries of the *Ausgleich*. The landed nobility occupied the leading positions in political life, in the army and the diplomatic corps. They entered the new age as members of the boards of banks and companies, utilising their leadership capabilities, which they had developed and cultivated unhindered for centuries. Loyal to the Habsburgs, frequenting in each other's company the (male) exclusivity of the 'National Casino' (a particularly Hungarian club established by Széchenyi, who saw this as an important step towards modernisation), their grand and lavish lifestyle did not change dramatically. Some 1000 families, affluent but with smaller estates, were part of the nobility, sharing similar social prestige. Another 5000 families, with smaller estates of 250–375 acres, filling important positions in government and public administration, holding the counties firmly in their hands, constituted the lesser gentry (Hanak 1988, p. 154).[7] Many of the lesser gentry could not switch over to the new farming technologies demanded by the industrial age. As a consequence, during the years of the Dual Monarchy, substantial numbers lost their land. Nonetheless, although impoverished, they still emulated the lifestyle of the gentry. Excluded by the insufficient blueness of their blood from Széchenyi's Casino, the gentry founded a Casino of their own (Macartney 1971, p. 714).[8]

Prestige, status and pretentious lifestyles allowed the gentry to hold their traditional positions in public administration. Business and commerce activities were considered plebeian:

> There remained only one refuge for the dispossessed: the administrative network of national and local government and the army. For these, Hungary needed a tremendous staff; and if she did not she could at least pretend to. Half the country consisted of 'nationalities' to be kept in check. To pay a host of reliable, Magyar, gentlemanly country magistrates to control them, so the argument ran, was a modest price for the national interest. The problem of multi-nationalities was also godsend; it excused the proliferation of sinecures . . . The magnates held their entailed estates, the gentry held their entailed jobs. (Ignotus 1972, pp. 81–2)

Becoming the backbone of the bureaucratic apparatus of Hungary, they exercised their hold on power less in a political and more in a bureaucratic fashion. Their disdain and contempt for the new classes and the whole modernisation of state, economy and society found expression in increasing conservatism. They were also imbued with what Seton-Watson termed 'official nationalism', which appeared in the second half of the nineteenth century in Europe: essentially conservative and reactionary policies as opposed to the earlier, popular nationalisms.

The long extension of feudalism in Hungary thwarted the formation of a local middle class and infected the values of the nobility, chiefly expressed in the scorn of the gentry towards entrepreneurship. As a consequence, the larger section of the middle class (including lower middle class) was of Jewish, German and other ethnic minority origin. The wealthiest layer of the middle classes, made up of bankers, manufacturers, mostly Jews, but some Magyarised descendants of Greek, Serbian and Armenian merchants, tried to emulate the lifestyle of the aristocracy. Jews predominantly participated in establishing a modern capitalistic economy, while Germans mostly turned towards careers in the bureaucracy and the army. These middle-class Germans successfully Magyarised and were readily accepted socially.

Jews assimilated voluntarily and enthusiastically, to the point that the decisive aspect of their self-perception became their belonging to the Hungarian middle class. They bought estates and ranks, many Magyarised their names and all were fully fledged Hungarian patriots. I shall be discussing them at length in the second chapter. It needs to be said here, however, that while they contributed substantially to the modernisation of the Hungarian economy, and rose to unprecedented heights as even ministers and in the *k.u.k.* (*königlich und kaiserlich*) army, their political power remained marginal and random.

The main characteristics of the middle classes were their separation from the ethnic minorities (even if they came from their ranks) and from the working classes, ostentatious patriotism, for the richer, affluent stratum, the emulation of the aristocratic lifestyle, and a uniformity of lifestyle for the lower middle class. The status symbols of middle-class life, according to Hanak, were a good education for their children, 'a flat with three rooms, home-cooked and freshly served midday meals, a free railway pass and domestic servants' (Hanak 1988, p. 156).

As the gentry made up part of the swelling number of the intelligentsia, they made a very important impact on its character. They fully supported the forced Magyarising tendencies and policies of the official liberal nationalist and right-wing conservative political and conceptual systems. Opposition to the prevailing hollow and melodramatic nationalism came from the neo-liberal movement.

There was, based in Budapest, a radical, educated, liberal layer of the intelligentsia.

At the bottom of the social pyramid were the smallholder peasants, the rural proletariat and the urban slum-dwelling factory workers. From the time the former serfs were allowed to purchase their emancipation and a small 'kerchief-sized' piece of land, the life of the smallholder peasants improved.[9] The famous colourful regional folk embroideries and attires developed in the second half of the nineteenth century, indicating that there was enough improvement in the conditions of peasant-living to enable folk-culture not only to flourish, but even to develop new characteristics and customs. The life of the rural poor, however, was mostly characterised by poverty and vulnerability.[10] Their everyday life, which was more and more influenced by the new age, through technology and through the effects of their changing role in industrial society, was harsh and full of depravation. Hungarian peasants were consequently conservative, anchored in feudalism. Arendt observed:

> In the Eastern and Southern European regions the establishment of nation–states failed because they could not fall back upon firmly rooted peasant classes. Sociologically the nation–state was the body politic of the European emancipated peasant classes . . . (Arendt 1967, p. 229)

With modernisation, along with the bourgeoisie and industrial proletariat, yet another new class appeared: the rural proletariat. The great mass of the rural proletariat was made up of farm servants and seasonal workers (harvesters and navvies). Their number in industry was swelling, but the great bulk were the impoverished, landless peasants who tried to earn their living by hiring themselves out for seasonal work, mostly harvesting. Many were working as '*kubikos*' (navvy) but with the grand works of river-regulations finished, many were unemployed. As the great agricultural depression was hitting Europe at the end of the century, those who worked seasonally often starved in the winter. Huge numbers (some two million) were emigrating to America. And many went to the cities and started work in factories.

Numerous satirical publications, always political but varied by the public they targeted, thrived on typical figures of society. These figures were regulars, with names, speaking habits and topics making the caricature easily recognisable by anybody, and therefore enormously popular. Even today these parodies are funny and tell much about their originals, the society they represented and the society which enjoyed reading and laughing at them. Aristocrats are pompous and polyglot, with their Hungarian often ungrammatical, forced and affected. Jews are depicted not as figures to hate but as comical parvenus and social climbers. Their insistence on speaking Hungarian coupled with their inadequacy both in accent and in vocabulary make them laughable, sometimes pathetic or even annoying, but not sinister. The gentry and the intelligentsia (lawyers, doctors, journalists, teachers and even amateur archeologists are represented), artists and critics, workers and peasants, and the nationalities all appear to give a rich cross-section of social life in the Monarchy. In 1988 a collection of these characters was republished (Buzinkay 1988). What is quite unexpected and interesting is that there are representations of figures of women, roughly in two categories: they appear as the grand ladies of the aristocracy and the lesser grand mistresses of the middle classes, but also as 'emancipated women, and feminists' (Buzinkay 1988, p. 334). At times they are hilarious: 'My beloved patriotic sister, Jesus Christ saved mankind—you are going to save womankind. Your name will be Jesa Christa' (Buzinkay 1988, p. 334). Some sentences show surprising, albeit unintended astuteness: 'Our ladies are all Jewish now. Since the Israelites are already emancipated and we aren't yet, it follows that now we are the Jews of the nation' (Buzinkay 1988, p. 331).

   The status of women was ambivalent in the Monarchy. On one hand, the suffragette movement did have to fight the same issues as in Western Europe, although it was made slower and more complicated by the surviving remnants of feudal structure. On the other hand, the very fact that there was a feminist movement, ridiculed or not, was a sign of liberalism and of a relatively open society. Women could enrol at universities from 1895. In 1897, the Women Clerical Workers' Association was founded, reaching the astounding membership of 1800 by 1914, and in 1904 the Hungarian Feminists' Association started to operate, with 306 members, one-fifth of whom were male. There was a General Association of Hungarian Women's Organisations, with which the feminists were affiliated, but which was more concerned with the upkeep of traditional roles and with patriotism (Zsuppan 1989, p. 60). Women who belonged to the Social Democratic party had their own organisation, the Social Democratic Women's Organisation.

The social democrats did not support the women, because as true socialists they believed that the 'woman's question' (just like the 'Jewish question') would be solved in socialist society. By 1867 there were some 81 women's organisations, among them clubs formed by Jewish women. The names of the central figures in the women's movement were often Jewish (e.g. Vilma Glűcklich, Szidónia Wilhelm). The founder of the Feminist Association in Hungary, Róza Bédy-Schwimmer, an outspoken pacifist, was later appointed by the Károlyi government in 1918 as Ambassador to Switzerland (*Magyar Zsidó Lexikon* 1929, p. 99). International figures of the feminist movement went to Hungary on lecture tours. The Seventh Congress of International Woman's Suffrage Alliance was held in Hungary, and members of Parliament attended the high-profile gathering, lending it much-needed respectability. By the time of World War I, there were 28 regional feminist organisations (Zsuppan 1989, p. 64).

The historical development of Hungarian nationalism

The historical symbiosis of capitalism, democracy and industrialisation forged the nation–state. West of the Rhine, nation–state and capitalism developed simultaneously. The interaction of liberalism and nationalism was indispensable in this process. As a consequence, there was a factual acceptance of belonging to the nation and of the basic freedoms and inalienable rights that this belonging meant to the citizens of that nation. East of the Rhine, where nation–states did not develop this way, national identity was forged through cultural, historical and ethnic definitions. This was clear in the case of Hungary, where, as in the rest of East–Central Europe, cultural and political boundaries were not identical, and where the horizontal cleavages of feudalism were still rigid in the nineteenth century. Here also nationalism and liberalism were the two main propelling forces, but nationalism had an additional role. The task of modernising in Hungary was not only to eliminate feudalism and to develop modern institutions, but to achieve independence from the Habsburg empire and to forge a modern national identity.

The creation of national identity was engendered by nationalism. Ernst Gellner's approach to nationalism is through stressing the importance of culture. Because initially Hungarian nationalism was based on the notion of cultural superiority, his analysis is of special relevance. Gellner defines nationalism as:

> A theory of political legitimacy, which requires that ethnic boundaries should not cut across political ones, and, in particular, that ethnic boundaries within a given state—a contingency already formally excluded by the principle in its general formulation—should not separate the power holders from the rest. (Gellner 1983, p. 1)[11]

Firmly linking the concept of state to the division of labour, Gellner gives a detailed description of the whole dynamism of what he calls 'the transition to an age of nationalism' (Gellner 1983, p. 5). Industrialisation produces a mobile and culturally homogeneous society, and vice versa. The modern industrial state needs a mobile, literate, culturally standardised population. In industrial societies communication and culture assume a new, unprecedented importance. Liberalism, which is vital to the forging of the polity, introduces egalitarian expectations and aspirations. Nationalism is the striving to make culture and polity congruent (Gellner 1983, pp. 39–50).

Anthony Smith, another theoretician of nationalism, especially the theory of nation, differentiates between nationalism, which is both an ideology and a movement, and nationhood, which nationalism aspires to attain. Nationhood comprises three basic ideals:

> autonomy and self-government for the group, often, but not always a sovereign state, solidarity and fraternity of the group in a recognised territory or 'home', and third, a distinctive, and preferably unique, culture and history peculiar to the group in question. (Smith 1976, p. 2)

The establishment of an independent nation–state was the common interest of those who wanted liberal reforms and a modern state, and those who only wanted national independence and few, controlled changes to enable economic prosperity. Since there was no real third estate in Hungary, supporters of both aims initially came from the nobility, which in Hungary was relatively numerous, comprising 5 per cent of the population. Although some of them did not even speak the tongue of the country, they were regarded as Hungarians. But even while struggling for national independence, the progressive nobility tried to defend its feudal privileges.

The success of creating a modern state was hindered by certain specific features, which, in dialectic interaction, strengthened each other and characterised Hungarian society and policies. These were: many nationalities; lack of independence and sovereignty; the strength of feudalistic social structures; lack of a third estate; lack of industrialisation. The survival of feudal social and power structures, including the ongoing influence of the churches, thwarted progress. Cultural homogeneity seemed impossible because Hungary was made up of many nationalities, speaking many languages.

The nationalities question

In 1867 Hungary had a population of about thirteen and a half million, of whom only six million were Hungarians (Kohn 1961a, p. 58). The economic development of the years of Dual Monarchy fostered the strengthening of the middle class among the ethnic minorities as well. The social structure of the southern minorities, Slovenians, Serbians and Croatians and the northern Slovakians was more advanced and stratified than that of the Romanians and Ruthenians, of whom only 4.5 per cent lived in towns (Hanak 1988, p. 151). With the exception of the Serbs, the ethnic minorities did not have *latifundia* and nobility. Their middle class did not emulate aristocratic lifestyles or values because the landowner class belonged to the hated Austro–German and Hungarian oppressors. Democratic national unities opposing the government were forged, and their programs included economic and social reform as well. In spite of the overall agrarian character of the country, the cultural level and national consciousness slowly strengthened.

One of the most important pieces of legislation, introduced by the Hungarian Parliament, was the Nationalities Act of 1868. Although it declared that politically, Hungary's citizens belong to the 'united Magyar nation', its approach was liberal by contemporary standards (Hanak 1988, p. 135). It guaranteed the use of mother tongue for all nationalities in public administration, education and at the lower levels of litigation. It ensured freedom of cultural and political association. The Public Education Act of 1868 not only made elementary schooling compulsory, but placed it firmly under state supervision.

Although religious equality was an ideal Hungarian liberalism pursued, the equality of nationalities was not. Since the state that had control over education was the Hungarian state, in spite of preserving the right of nationalities to their mother tongue in lower education, the Public Education Act was still advancing Hungarian nationalism. A recent study of assimilation and schooling around

1900 demonstrates that nationalist education policies were serving the assimilationist policies, which were designed to strengthen the dominant ethnic group, i.e. the Hungarians. Drawing on an earlier empirical survey, its author set out to assess (*inter alia*):

> the uses of higher education in the selection and social reproduction of the service élite in a society still rigidly stratified along inherited status lines, notably where ethnicity and denomination (together with noble versus common descent and the nature, as well as the quantity of inherited wealth) belonged to the ordinary criteria defining a person's position in society. (Karady 1989, p. 286)

Karady comes to the conclusion that more than 65 per cent of university graduates came from a non-Magyar background and that there was a palpable 'overeducation' among non-Magyars. Higher education was a vehicle for social mobility and, inseparably, 'a lever of cultural assimilation' (Karady 1989, p. 310).

Analysing the connection between culture, education, state and nationalism, Gellner shows that in the industrial age only the state can ensure the essential education of its members and this firmly links state and culture. He concludes: 'in the past their connection was thin, fortuitous, varied, loose, and often minimal. Now it is unavoidable. That is what nationalism is about' (Gellner 1983, p. 38).

The sociology of Magyarisation

In the nineteenth century, the construction of who is 'Hungarian' had been taking place against a multinational kaleidoscope of the Habsburg empire. This did not change during the Dual Monarchy, but it became more evident and acute with huge migration as the borders opened within the Empire in the wake of industrialisation and general modernisation. Religion did not form the basis of national identity. The ethnic minorities were predominantly Christian—some Roman Catholic, like the Slovakians and Croatians, some Orthodox like the Serbs, and large numbers of Protestants (Lutherans and Calvinists). Hungarians themselves were largely Christians, so religious identity was not a distinguishing factor. Later, with Trianon-borders, when mono-ethnic Hungary had only one 'other', the Jews, self-definition changed to accommodate that. But in the days of the Austro–Hungarian Empire, the important and relevant 'other' that Hungarians had to distinguish themselves against were the numerous other nationalities. Against the backdrop of the increasingly vocal demands of the nationalities for self-determination, the self-definition of the Hungarian national identity became primarily cultural.

Hungarian nationalism had to justify not only the lower position of the ethnic minorities and the denial of their right to self-determination, but also the policy of forced assimilation. What had to be shown was the difference. Since religion in this respect was meaningless, difference was found in culture. So Hungarian nationalism constructed the cultural superiority of Hungarians.

The predominance of the cultural aspect is one of the reasons for the relatively low racial content of Hungarian nationalism in the days of the Monarchy. National identity based on culture rather than on ethnicity can be acquired by absorbing, learning the culture. Stressing the importance of culture, Gellner wrote that with the transition into industrial society, culture is not only the confirmation and legitimation of the social order, but the essential shared medium. Hence it must be the same culture (Gellner 1983, pp. 37–8).

Another reason for the low racial content of Hungarian nationalism of this era, also connected to the status of the Magyars as a minority in the lands over which they ruled, was that while the Hungarian nobility was overwhelmingly Hungarian, the urban middle classes were predominantly Jewish and German and much of the peasantry was Slavic and Romanian. Herder, the extremely influential German theorist of nationalism, once wrote that Magyars might eventually disappear, swallowed up by the Slavic and Germanic peoples (Lindemann 1991, p. 44). Magyar nationalism reverberated with and amplified this perceived threat. After World War I, when the Empire was lost, and with it the ethnic minorities, suspicion was turned against Jews. This fear for national survival was present even within the liberal thought of Széchenyi, 'the greatest of Magyars', one of the most revered liberal leaders of the 1830s.[12]

The obsessive fear of Hungarian nationalists used the 'remedy' of Magyarisation. Since Jews willingly and enthusiastically Magyarised, they were viewed at this stage as valuable allies. Provided they totally assimilated (and preferably converted), Hungarian Jews found acceptance. There were several reasons for this, connected to certain specificities of Hungarian society. Jews did not only Magyarise themselves, they were keen agents of Magyarisation. Because of that, in pre-1914 Hungary antisemitism was stronger among Germans, Romanians and Slovak villagers who resented the Jews both as agents of Magyarisation and of capitalist modernisation. In the multinational Hungarian empire the Jews were the balancing power, particularly useful against the nationalities. Modern anti-semitism, although it found social acceptance in devoutly Christian Hungarian society, clashed with the strong state and did not develop the racist ingredient until much later, with the advent of anti-liberalism and its merging with nationalism.

The paradox of liberalism and nationalism

In nineteenth-century Hungary nationalism and liberalism together were a force for liberation, emancipation and independence. As the nineteenth century progressed, liberalism in Hungary atrophied. By the end of the century nationalism became first and foremost a movement against democracy. The organic concept of ethnic–national Hungary developed.

From the beginning there was the paradox of liberalism and nationalism. Nationalism was taken up by liberal-thinking nobility, but also by conservatives who had no intention of changing feudal power-structures. On the other hand, liberal ideals were used by the hated Habsburg monarch during the enlightened absolutism of Joseph II, whose liberal modernisations were running parallel to his retrograde anti-independence attitude towards Hungary.[13] As a result, the assertion of feudal privileges against reform appeared as a fight for independence and took the form of nationalism. The struggle of the nobility for power, and their opposition to the Habsburgs, appeared as national interest. The nobility and liberal thinkers had a common goal: to achieve independence from the Habsburgs. As a result, conservatives and liberals appeared to be on the same political platform united in the cause of independence, both using nationalism as a context, as a tool and as a weapon. Once political independence and 'empire-status' within the Monarchy was achieved, liberal and nationalist causes became disconnected, in fact contradictory. The concept of liberalism lost the support of the nobility who had every reason to strive to maintain the status quo, especially since embourgeoisement and the modernisation of the economy was mainly performed by a traditionally powerless group, that is the Jews, who put up with this status in return for economic and cultural prosperity.

The feudal origins and social basis of early liberal thought in Hungary fed the aggressivity of Hungarian nationalism. Oszkár Jászi, the most significant political thinker of the Monarchy years, saw it clearly and all through his numerous writings he underlined that in the process of justifying their position in the hierarchy of power, the patriotism of the nobility turned into nationalism. He wrote:

> The problem was the same for enlightened absolutism and for the revolutionary nobility: to open the way for the people and for the bourgeoisie in legal, economic and cultural life, and to replace the feudal state with *Rechtsstaat* [the rule of law].[14] Absolutism wanted to solve this problem from above, by creating a moderately liberal state which would blend into the monarchy as one of its crown-lands. Revolutionary Hungarian nobility wanted to solve from below: by liberating the masses, but securing the dominant role of the nobility in constitutional law. (Jászi 1986, p. 110)

Running parallel to the movement to forge a modern and independent Hungarian nation was the emergence of the Croatian, Serbian, Slovakian and Romanian national movements. This explosive issue exerted a continual influence on Hungarian political life, affecting strongly the development of the nationalist and liberal ideas, influencing Hungarian policies concerning Jews and, eventually, leading to the decline of the Monarchy.

The formation of a national identity went hand in hand with the wish to impose this identity on others. The most important objective seemed to be cultural homogeneity and this found expression in the policy of Magyarisation. All other social and political tensions became secondary and were mostly ignored. Questions of assimilation, the nationalities and the Jewish questions, along with definitions of who was Hungarian, ran parallel to the ascendent concept of Hungarian superiority. With the age of modernisation Hungary entered a new phase. It needed a strong state for the new demands of industrial age. Emptied of the now useless 'nation-creation' content, emphasis was increasingly placed on the fuzzy idea of the 'state-creative' and 'state-founding' (*államépitő, államalapitó*) character of the Hungarian nation. This was a deliberate slight to the national minorities and served to flaunt self-perceived Hungarian superiority *vis-à-vis* the ethnic minorities, who did not have their own state—ostensibly because not only were they not endowed with this 'nation-creating' ability, but they were not even deserving of it. The 'enemy' was not Habsburg Austria any more. The nationalities became the foe against whom nationalists rallied. With the forced Magyarisation programs, the nationalists teamed up with anti-modernisation forces and anti-liberalism strengthened. Increasingly liberalism came to be associated with revolution. As in the rest of the Western world, initially allies, nationalism and liberalism became competing forces in Hungary during the course of the nineteenth century, and, by the dawn of the twentieth century, liberalism atrophied and nationalism was strong.

The making of a modern nation–state: the role of language and culture

With the Compromise, the development of Hungarian capitalism entered full swing. The whole country was now defined by the industrial age. The transition into industrial society, according to Gellner, includes, as one of the factors of modernisation, a change from folk-transmitted culture to school-transmitted culture: 'Culture is no longer merely the adornment, confirmation and legitimation of social order, culture is now the necessary shared medium'; he adds that it must be the same culture for a given society (Gellner 1983, pp. 37–8).

In the case of Hungary, a huge blow (and one of the first) to the horizontal cultural cleavages of the agro-literate feudalistic society came from the Habsburg monarch, Maria Theresa. The first of successive decrees of education, the 1777 *Ratio Educationis* legislation, introduced elementary education for the peasants. In 1806 school attendance became compulsory. As literacy was spreading, the early nineteenth century saw the birth of Hungarian-language press and theatre. Travelling theatre groups roamed the countryside and produced legendary names and romantic figures. Great literary and theatrical works expanded the language. The building of a National Theatre for Hungarian-language plays was one of the strongest rallying causes and loudest demands voiced.

The creation of the nation required the creation of a new language to reflect the increasingly complex relations, ideals and conditions.[15] This happened on many levels. Writers and poets, statesmen and others participated enthusiastically and vigorously in dynamic language renewal. Words were created and discarded and changed meaning in vernacular usage. New concepts found poetic expression in a grand literary project which involved the whole nation. Authors set out to prove that the Hungarian language was suitable for the highest literary expression. When the 1843–44 Diet made Hungarian the official language, it was delivering the first blow to many centuries' tradition of Latin as the language of the law.[16] The language of administration was also Latin. One of the first clashes between the modernising monarch, Joseph II, and the Hungarian nobility was when the emperor replaced Latin with German as the prime language of administration (Seton-Watson 1977, pp. 158–61). Anderson observed the process of nationalising language in *Imagined Communities*: 'In a word, the fall of Latin exemplified a larger process in which the sacred communities integrated by old sacred languages were gradually fragmented, pluralised and territorialised' (Anderson 1993, p. 19).

Nationalism needed and created a '*dolce lingua nuova*' (sweet new language), which, in the dialectics of chicken and egg, was simultaneously a pre-condition and a product of nationalism. The Hungarian language, as it is spoken now, was invented, moulded, chiselled at the same time as the important epoch-changing social innovations, and by the same people. Many poets and writers were both language innovators and active participants in the 'Age of Reform' and in the 1848–49 revolution and war of independence:

> Most frequently, it is true nations have arisen on a linguistic basis; but in some cases, at least, the language was created for them by nationalist intellectuals. There was no Slovak nation before the nineteenth century, when a standardised Slovak literary language was created from the various Slav dialects spoken by peasants in the mountain valleys of Northern Hungary. Ukrainian nationalism has depended heavily on the virtual creation of a Ukrainian literary language by the nineteenth-century poet Taras Shevchenko. (Kamenka 1973a, p. 13)[17]

A close interconnection between culture, politics and history developed and was used deliberately. In the fomenting years of the 'Age of Reform', the preconditions for modern commerce and industry were created. From the middle of the century a rural, small-town and partly non-noble middle-class intellectual stratum began to emerge as a result of the cultural ferment and the economic upswing. This stratum in its turn produced figures who had an enormous impact on Hungarian literature, political and social movements. Amongst the most famous was one of the figureheads of the 1848–49 revolution and war of independence, around whom legends grew, the national poet of Hungary, Sándor Petőfi. Not only did he come from a 'lowly' innkeeper family, but his mother was Slovak and his father Serb. His very name was Magyarised from 'Petrovits'. He was a passionate Hungarian patriot, burning with the cause of freedom. If Kossuth was the father-figure, Petőfi was the romantic lover-figure of the Hungarian revolution. His life was synonymous with revolution and independence. His death became a symbol of the defeated cause.[18]

Most writers, poets and playwrights came from the lesser nobility. Their readership, however, cut across all strata. Waves of immigration and social mobility were reflected in the changing folk-music which incorporated new motifs and tunes (Hanak 1988, pp. 108–9). Hungarian operas were depicting great historical struggles against foreign oppression. Hungarian musical culture was reaching all strata. A product of romanticism, historical novels were enjoying enormous popularity throughout the world, and Hungary was no exception.

Its way largely paved by the *nepies* (folk) character of Hungarian romanticism and other ongoing literary traditions dating back to well before the pre-revolution age, a pseudo-folk-culture was developing, which idolised, by gross falsifications, pre-modernity peasants and peasant life. The putative folk-culture of the Monarchy days harked back to an image of highly romanticised, simple, noble peasant. It had its German counterpart in the *Völkisch* movement and in the Russian *narodnik* movement. The parallel developments of anti-modernity ideologies and of modern antisemitism had an uneven impact on Hungarian social and political thought.

The myth-creative aspect of nationalism continued to build a suitable Hungarian history complete with historical figures and cults. As with other nationalisms, Hungarian nationalism used history and culture deliberately, accentuating certain things and ignoring others. It invented Hungarian culture and history, with arbitrarily chosen historical facts, and by building myths. However, it contained controversies from the beginning. As Jászi wrote:

> The very fact that the democratisation process was led by the revolutionary minority of the nobility, which was executing the interests of another, alien class—the third estate—led to the result that the movement borrowed numerous concepts from the ideological and tactical arsenal of the kuruc freedom of the nobility. (Jászi 1986, p. 107)

Kuruc was the name of the Hungarian fighters of the war of independence against the Habsburgs at the beginning of the eighteenth century, led by Rákóczi, a Hungarian prince. A cult developed around the *kuruc*.[19] At the end of the nineteenth century a whole national romantic school of historiography engaged in the cult of this tradition. The cult became an intrinsic part of the particular *Weltanschauung* of Hungarian nationalism. It stood for a false, pathos-filled make-believe which stressed not the fight against political oppression, but the Magyar struggle against foreigners. Instead of being anti-Habsburg, it represented anti-Austrian sentiments; instead of the political, it stressed the ethnic conflict.

The importance given to history and to historical mythology continued into the early decades of the twentieth century. Historians took over the role of the literati of the nineteenth century in influencing—often forming—political thought, with two opposing lines of thought, agenda and context: conservative nationalism and radical liberalism.

The greatest figure of conservative nationalist historiography, Gyula Szekfü, did not publish his seminal work, *Három Nemzedék* (Three Generations), until 1920, but he had already written his controversial 'Rákóczi in exile', creating public outrage and resulting in his ostracism. Szekfü's evaluation of Rákóczi went against the romanticising public perception of nationalistic history. He presented the hallowed *kuruc* prince as powerless and embittered. Such was the strength of demand for *kuruc* mythology that Szekfü was denounced as a traitor by the press and by politicians.

The other direction in political culture came from the left, primarily from Jewish intellectual circles. It coalesced around Oszkár Jászi's sociology-centred publication, *Huszadik Század*. Introducing Western sociology, Jászi and his circle focused on social and ethnic problems. Initially they were more concerned with fighting against feudalism and the power of the clergy. By 1917 they had founded the National Bourgeois Radical Party. The nationalities question and their, especially Jászi's, methodological and philosophical approach to it went against the tide of Hungarian nationalism.

The impact of Jászi's tiny circle of radical liberals was to be felt during the revolutions following World War I. But conservative nationalism was by far the more popular ideology, its influence palpable in all facets of cultural life.

The gentrification of culture

At the end of the century Hungary celebrated the *Millennium*, the thousand year anniversary of the arrival of the Hungarian tribes into the Carpathian basin. The *fin de siècle* was full of ceremonies and celebrations. The *Millennium* was celebrated for a full year. The aristocracy fully participated, attired in stylised Hungarian folk-dress. It became fashionable to dress in a 'Hungarian way'. Of course this Hungarian way was a fictitious, stylised fashion-creation, worn by the upper and middle classes, not by the 'folk'.[20] Cultural life was more and more characterised by extremes. Although liberal tenets still prevailed and there was an emerging new left, as in the rest of Europe, anti-liberalism, nationalism and sentimental chauvinism were the dominant tendencies.

In spite of all the enormous social changes going on, the literature of the first decades almost never depicted the bourgeoisie. The main character was the peasant. But the thunder of revolution in the poems of Petőfi and other national popular writers was replaced by the sugary doggerel of a fictitious peasant. Similar to the German *Völkisch* movement, Hungarian romanticism glorified and idolised the myth of the Hungarian peasant, his (never her) wit, good heart and supposed nationalist sentiment. Literature was diverting attention away from the very real problems and tragedies of the peasantry. The feudal structures which choked peasantry were not only ignored, but glorified as part of the nationalist myth. Nor was the increasingly vocal national consciousness of Serbs, Croats, Slovaks and others reflected in Hungarian literature and culture. There was deafening silence on the two burning social and political issues of the two large and oppressed groups, the peasants and the nationalities.

The most typical publications of these years had no political news, only short stories and novels in instalments, poetry, critical reviews and news of literary and social life, almost exclusively of Budapest (as the name *Fővárosi Lapok* (Papers of the Capital) boldly declared):

> As in social and political life the gentry signified the paralysing survival of the vacuous formalities of nobility, similarly, in literature the spirit of the gentry-era is an anachronistic preserve of what was once lively and vital . . . Therefore novels and plays must be about counts or peasants and can talk about anything, except what really exists, presses and demands attention. (Szerb 1972, p. 393)

Theatres staged plays whose characters or plots were not rooted in any reality. The artificially created idyll of an illusory happy age abounded with jovial Viennese-flavoured pseudo-peasants and beautiful countesses, all dancing the *csardas*, the Hungarian national dance, happily and proudly.[21] This was also the hey-day of the so-called '*népszinmü*', the folk-musical. The plots were love triangles, with peasant characters, none of whom have any other existential problems. These plays with songs were extremely popular with all and sundry, regardless of social status—except the peasantry, of course, who did not go to the theatres of Budapest or the cities. Szerb remarked: 'There is no folk-play where the people would not have any money, where the people would not live under idyllic, simple and quiet conditions. But all the while whole villages emigrated to America' (Szerb 1972, p. 401).

Nationalism and modernisation

Nationalism, both as sentiment and as ideology, is intrinsically linked to the concept of the nation. In the development or creation of the modern nation, nationalism was at first a doctrine of popular freedom and sovereignty. Linked with the Enlightenment ideal of liberty, equality and fraternity, nationalism was instrumental in the emancipation of the people. According to Gellner, nationalism was the prerequisite to modernisation; it facilitated mass education and literacy, the 'minimal requirement for full citizenship' (Gellner 1983, p. 158). Nationalism was vital in the creation of a homogeneous culture, without which modernisation and industrialisation could not take place. Furthermore, modern national identity was also created by nationalism. Nationalism was the glue that enabled the development of a cohesive and sovereign state.

In the beginning, European nationalism was an instrument of modernisation. Being combined with the quest for political self-determination, it had the flexibility to embrace a variety of political, social and religious attitudes.

Toward the end of the nineteenth century, however, the supposed supremacy and cultural autonomy of the nation challenged this flexibility, as many people came to perceive the nation as a civic religion that determined how people saw the world and their place in it (Mosse 1993, p. 1).

While west of the Rhine political and social modernisation was well advanced, indeed established by this time, in the East (including

Germany), the project of modernisation did not dismantle feudal structures and did not establish firm democratic institutions. Nationalism, now politically allied with conservatism and its content infused with racism, thus was faced by the authoritarian state and stilted social structures. In Russia, for instance, the strong state used antisemitism, in the form of pogroms, to control social unrest while in Hungary the strong state suppressed antisemitic violence.

Observing the difference between Western and Eastern European nationalisms, Hans Kohn postulated that from the beginning the two were different types. The first, being born on the 'generous wave of enthusiasms for the cause of mankind', i.e. the Enlightenment, stood for open and pluralistic society, while the second, being born of xenophobia, strove for a closed society and an authoritarian state. This dichotomy, however, does not explain Hungarian nationalism, which in the first half of the nineteenth century was infused with Enlightenment ideals and was a tool for forming the modern nation.

Habermas sees nationalism as a form of collective consciousness, a term denoting the specifically modern phenomenon of cultural integration (this is very much Gellner's notion as well). Habermas has a chronological and dynamic concept of nationalism: 'the term "nation" thus changed from designating a prepolitical entity to something that was supposed to play a constitutive role in defining the political identity of the citizen within a democratic polity' (Habermas 1992, p. 3).

The development of this democratic polity (and, I would like to add, the resulting political ethos) was arrested, thwarted by the incomplete modernisation in Eastern and Central European countries, including Italy. The key issue is exactly the interplay of Enlightenment ideals, self-determination and the resulting national identity which comprises all these elements. Where modernisation was as yet incomplete at the time when nationalism changed its course from alliance with liberalism to alliance with conservatism, radical nationalism had an open political field.

In Hungary, in spite of the explosive economic and industrial modernisation, many of the feudal structures stayed intact. This, together with the waning of liberalism, thwarted the progress of democracy. Hungarian nationalism, influenced by the *Völkisch* movement in Germany, was more and more concerned with the characteristics and attributes of Hungarianness. Similar to France, where 'integral nationalism'—and in Germany where *Völkisch* nationalism—was gaining politically, nationalism in Hungary accelerated its quest for power. Like its German counterpart, Hungarian nationalism perceived modernisation as alien to the Hungarian nature. In essence, the project of modernisation was incomplete in Hungary.

Chapter two

The 'Golden Age' of security

> *When I attempt to find a simple formula for the period in which I grew up, prior to the First World War, I hope that I convey its fullness by calling it the Golden Age of Security.*
>
> Zweig 1947, p. 13

> *The birth and growth of modern antisemitism has been accompanied and interconnected with Jewish assimilation, the secularisation and withering away of the old religious and spiritual values of Judaism.*
>
> Arendt 1967, p. 7[1]

In Hungary, as in other European countries (particularly in France), the ideas of Jewish emancipation and assimilation were interrelated. This was already formulated in the legislation of the enlightened Habsburg monarch, Joseph II.[2] As the nineteenth century progressed and Hungarian nationalism took on a different, organic meaning, Hungarian nationalists further linked the two ideas. For both the Hungarians and the Jews, emancipation, assimilation and nationalism were the most important political, social and individual issues.

Chronologically and conceptually the 'Jewish question' in Hungary evolved in the context of Hungarian nationalism *vis-à-vis* the nationalities question, i.e. the numerical weakness of Hungarians, and the role Jews played in the project of modernisation. The interaction of Hungarian nationalism and Jewish emancipation in the nineteenth century fused as both Hungarians and Jews formed a new, modern identity informed by the civic religion, nationalism. Indeed the first act of emancipation came in the form of a (belated) gesture: in the last days of the war of independence, as a recognition of Jewish loyalty in the fight for independence against the Habsburgs, the revolutionary parliament decided in favour of emancipation (Gonda 1992, p. 317).[3]

What was peculiar about the legislation and made it unique was that the same law which granted equality demanded religious reform of Judaism.[4] In a declaration, the government urged the Jews to convene a rabbinical assembly to lay down the principles of reform. However, in 1867, following the Compromise, the Jews of Hungary were raised to equal footing with Christians in civil liberties and political rights and all previous laws, regulations and customs contrary to this were annulled. The reason that religious reform was not a pre-condition any more was to be found in the changed situation of Hungary: Jews were vital to the modernisation, in particular the economic modernisation, of Hungary.

The 1867 act emancipated the individual, but did not make Jewish religion itself equal to the Christian denominations. Although Act LIII of 1868 allowed conversion within the Christian denominations, this right was not extended to Judaism. In 1895, however, Law XLII was passed, making Judaism a legally received faith—equal to the Christian denominations.[5]

Although modernisation meant the development of political antisemitism (a modernisation of medieval, religious Jew-hatred), the specific social and economic conditions in Hungary were not conducive to an antisemitic political movement. The European surge of political antisemitism found its expressions in Hungary through the establishment of an antisemitic party and through the revival of the medieval blood libel.

Győző Istóczy, a deputy of the Liberal party, introduced modern antisemitism to Hungary. In 1875, starting earlier than either Stöcker or Schönerer, he set the tone of antisemitic rhetoric with his bombastic and hysterical style. In his many vigorous speeches he basically concentrated on two major issues. One concerned Jewish emigration and the other centred on opposing civil marriages between Jews and Christians.

The antisemitic movement made the most of the Tiszaeszlár blood libel. In the spring of 1882, in a small village in eastern Hungary called Tiszaeszlár, a fourteen-year-old girl disappeared. This was just before the Jewish Passover, with which the traditional medieval blood libels were connected. Within a short period of time the Jews were accused of murder. A Gentile lawyer, Károly Eötvös, took on the defence of the case. He and his colleagues proved that the whole accusation was unfounded, based on superstition, and that the evidence rested on the confession of a minor, obtained through threats.

Istóczy and his followers brought the blood libel into the parliament and used every means to capitalise on the trial. The parliament was told:

> Witnesses, live people verified that they saw her [Solymosi] pass by the Israelite synagogue, where she vanished without a trace. When people confronted the Jews, they did not answer and tried to avoid the questions. Fortuitously, the horrible truth was revealed. Now the case is in front of the Nyiregyháza criminal court. [The accusation is that] the Tiszaeszlár slaughterer lured her into the temple, tied back her hands, gagged her—and what happened after? It is claimed that she was killed to take her blood and to distribute her blood all over the place to orthodox believers, who need it for the baking of their Passover offering. (Karsai 1992, pp. 5–6)

He met political disinterest in the parliament. Although he was unable to generate a modern antisemitic movement, Istóczy managed to reactivate the dormant forces of traditional antisemitism. University students were especially susceptible. In February 1881, a group of Christian students at the university of Pest went on a rampage and attacked Jewish students. The rector admonished them and the minister of interior banned their planned public meeting. The students issued a manifesto, demanding the reduction of the number of Jewish students. Istóczy fully supported the students.

Following public meetings in the provinces, a series of petitions demanded the repeal of the emancipatory laws, reflecting the influence of a growing network of antisemitic movements in the rural areas. One of the petitions was initiated by priests. It opposed the legalisation of civil marriages and called for the repeal of Law LXII of 1867. In response, the parliamentary petitions committee presented a report, in which they called the act one of the major achievements of post-*Ausgleich* legislation and an integral element of Hungarian legal structure (Handler 1980, pp. 33–4).

There were anti-Jewish occurrences all over the country, more or less in the same form: demonstrating mobs attacking Jewish property.[6] The perpetrators were largely tradesmen, civil servants and shopkeepers, but the instigators came from the middle-class gentry. The government introduced martial law to contain the anti-Jewish violence. The liberal gentry fully kept to the 'assimilationist contract': the state protected Jews from the mob. The reason for this lay in the dynamics of Hungarian modernisation: 'As long as the Hungarian economy was expanding and the state bureaucracy was able to absorb the "historic" Magyar intelligentsia, the issue of middle-class antisemitism did not become acute' (Barany 1974, p. 80).

As a direct outcome of the blood libel, Istóczy established the Antisemitic party in 1883. Members of the new party came from both the Independence and the Liberal parties, both of which, not wishing to be associated with rabble-rousers, expelled the antisemites. The only platform of the Antisemitic party was anti-Jewishness. By the 1892 elections the party had disbanded.

However, because of the specificities of Hungarian society and economic developments, at this stage, modern political antisemitism did not gain a foothold the way it did in other parts of Europe, especially in Austria, Germany and France.

From its inception the Antisemitic party did not have government or parliamentary support and could not penetrate mainstream politics. Their political fellowship eroded soon. However, the words and sentiments, the articulated political antisemitism of Istóczy, stayed more than subliminally in Hungarian consciousness. All the more so because in neighbouring Vienna antisemitism was a legitimate political agenda.

Hungarian society and the Jews: emancipation, assimilation and antisemitism

Throughout the nineteenth century, the direction and the objective of assimilation was towards political emancipation and towards the desired—potential—integration into society. It was to serve as a path, away from the communal and individual pariah-status, away from powerlessness. In this context assimilation was a valid and authentic course. It was supported by the 'friends' of Jews within Hungarian society, that is, by the liberals and the progressives, those who wanted to make Jews part of the modern world. From the liberal Hungarian perspective, assimilation was the 'price' Jews were 'reasonably' expected to pay. Conversely, those conservatives who did not see emancipation as a right of Jews, but as a threat to national homogeneity, to whom nation mattered more than state, opposed it.

Neither the 'pro-emancipators' nor the 'anti-emancipators' viewed emancipation as an inalienable right—but as something that is *granted* by the non-Jews. This notion contained the assumption and the recognition that 'granting' was within non-Jews' power: on the fact that the power was theirs and on a sense of that power (the same dynamics of the inherent power as in 'granting suffrage' to women). Of course it was within their power—and certainly not in the power of Jews. The Jewish choice was limited to accepting the conditions. Those who, sometimes grudgingly, and in spite of antisemitic convictions, recognised that equality dictated equality for all, and that modern society must include Jews, used their inherent power in favour of emancipation; while those who denied this right used their inherent power to justify why Jews should not be 'made' equal. Thus the Jewish question in the nineteenth century was formulated as the 'right to assimilate'. The emphasis was on whether the Jews should be 'allowed' to assimilate or not. The progressives supported it, the conservatives opposed it. And this is how assimilation became synonymous with a progressive, liberal and positive route for Jews, attacked by antisemites and supported by liberals.[7]

The assimilation process of Hungarian Jews followed the general patterns of European Jewry in major ways. Emancipation created a new type: the German, French or Hungarian Jew. 'Assimilation-happy' Jews found some kind of idealistic rationalisation for assimilating. Nationalism in every country became an assimilatory element. Socialism also served for many as an ideological and social medium for assimilation.

Assimilation was understood by both Hungarians and Jews as modernisation and secularisation of Jewish religion, and as cultural assimilation, in which Hungarian speech played a vital role. Cultural assimilation was required partly because of the ethnic minorities, but also because the Hungarian language was so important to the cause of Hungarian nationalism. For the Jewish community, the task of modernisation involved the remodelling of the internal structure and organisation of the community. This was necessary not only for the institutional integration of the Jewish community into society, but also because in the process of secularisation, the normative and communal centrality and structure of Judaism changed.

The process of assimilation does not happen in a social vacuum and neither is it homogeneous. A very important feature of assimilation is the effect on the receiving community. Sociologist Victor Karady separates three aspects of the assimilation process. One is the obvious angle of assimilation, the actions of those who assimilate. While Hungarian Jews learnt Hungarian, absorbed Hungarian culture and customs, became Hungarian nationalists—in other words took on a Hungarian identity complete with a sense of shared future—Hungarian society received the assimilating Jews, and this process took place within the dynamics of modernisation. This reception is the second strand of assimilation; it means that the receiving society forgoes its cultural exclusivity.

The third strand of the assimilation process is the reaction, or reciprocal assimilation, which in Hungary meant the establishment of modern economic conditions and behaviour patterns, modern trends in cultural life and in facets of social life. Karady rates the importance of mutuality very high:

> I am convinced that without regarding the conditions of mutuality the whole Hungarian-type assimilation becomes incomprehensible and inexplicable. Mutuality on both sides constituted an integral part of the legitimation of the assimilation process, in an explicit way, that is, in the form of ideological reasoning constructed for the handling of the national minority status. This constituted the essence of the 'assimilationist social contract'. (Karady 1993a, p. 37)

I would like to add certain qualifying remarks to Karady's reasoning and the word 'mutuality' (*kölcsönösség*). Naturally, Hungarian society had to be affected. First of all, Jews, dwelling all over the country, constituted 5 per cent of the total population. By the very volume of their number, Jews had to have an impact on Hungarian society, assimilation process notwithstanding.[8] Secondly, Hungarian society itself was in flux, caught up in the process of modernisation at the very time the assimilation process was taking place. Although clearly Jews were instrumental in this, the modernisation process was determined and dictated by nineteenth-century conditions and social movements taking place all over Europe, concurrent with, but independent of, the movement of assimilation. In other words, all the economic, cultural and social modernisation was taking place following its own dynamics rather than being determined by assimilation. Thirdly, the word 'mutuality' presupposes at least some kind of balance, some kind of equivalence. Jews engaged in the assimilation process gave up religious and social traditions, habits and guidelines, to the point of significantly altering their identity. Even orthodox Jews were Magyarising to a point where their identity was affected.[9] As far as the Hungarian Jews were concerned, they became Hungarians, and until the Holocaust they held onto that belief.

Hungarian society, on the other hand, other than allowing the Jews into society, was accommodating not so much Jewish assimilation, as modernisation. Moreover, Hungarian society did not revise or reconstruct its perception of Jews to allow integration. As Karady himself points out, the 'assimilationist contract' did not mean the removal of social and cultural obstacles built by millennia-long religious hatred, discrimination, 'the left-overs of historical pariah-status, and the collective phantasms of the "other"'. These constituted a 'rigid primordial stigma-structure', which lent itself easily to vilifying Jews as collective scapegoats at any given political occasion. This paradoxical aspect of Jewish assimilation resulted in what Karady calls the first contradiction of Hungarian Jewish assimilation, namely, that although Hungarian Jewry assimilated with outstanding speed and thoroughness, it did not really integrate into Hungarian society, and the concept of the 'other' persisted on both sides. The second contradiction is that the more successful the social ascent, the stronger is the demand for assimilation, but the opposition to assimilation is also stronger (Karady 1993a, pp. 37–8).

Finally, emancipation was always connected to assimilation. The price of emancipation was assimilation, or, depending on the policy of the time (and whether it was formulated by liberals or conservatives, or antisemites), the prize for assimilation was emancipation. And this is the essence of the paradox of emancipation and assimilation. This connection proved to be the problem post-Trianon.[10]

The emancipation of Jews and the 'Jewish question' in Hungary

In the nineteenth century, the 'Jewish question' in Europe developed in the context of liberalism and nationalism, and was formulated within the dichotomy of assimilation and emancipation.

In Hungary there were two additional contexts. Due to the backward, feudalistic structure of Hungarian society and its economy, in particular the lack of a middle class and a modern economy, Jews were instrumental in both the industrialisation of the economy and in building and becoming a Hungarian middle class. Equally important is the context of the nationalities question and here, again, the vital role Jews played in this.

Emancipation is intrinsically a liberal notion. Karady lists three features of Hungarian liberalism which made it unique in East–Central Europe. Firstly, the liberal definition of Hungary was that of a political nation in the Western sense. The reason for this was that Hungary, a country of many nationalities, could not 'afford' a restrictive definition of nationality. As a result, xenophobia was not an important element of Hungarian liberal nationalism, unlike Romania, Poland, Bohemia and elsewhere. Secondly, the multi-denominational nature of Hungary put the secularisation of modern institutions on the agenda rather early. Thirdly, the social basis of Hungarian liberalism (groups of the landed gentry, together with educated professionals) was weak and not unified enough. Further-more, most of them were unwilling to perform the task of a badly needed, entrepreneurial bourgeoisie. Another important factor was that Hungarians constituted the largest ethnic minority, but not the majority. So the Hungarian ethnic middle class relied on Jews who eagerly Magyarised, unlike the Croatian, Serbian and Romanian gentry, who were committed to their own awakening national consciousness. As Karady points out, it was the 'assimilationist contract' that was of crucial importance. Since the only legal definition of ethnicity was the individual's first spoken language, a critical role was played by linguistic assimilation as a tool of political legitimation. The socio–political symbiosis was based on 'state-promoted official philosemitism' which is comparable to that of the French Third Republic (Karady 1993a, pp. 75–6). The word 'philosemitism' is very apt in this instance, especially in the sense of the witty definition, according to which a philosemite is an antisemite who loves Jews.

The projects of modernisation and the creation of a nation and of a national identity allowed those who were willing to identify to join the Hungarian nation. The conservatives' view was that Jews were not capable of assimilation. Conservatives, reinforced by the nascent ideology of racism, soon declared that Jews are 'unassimilable'. The antisemitic approach was exclusion (possibly even expulsion) of Jews from Hungarian society. The gravest accusation was at the same time a damning verdict: Jews are unassimilable. The assimilability of Jews was a 'question' not only during the decades when emancipation was increasingly perceived as unavoidable (since modernisation demanded equal treatment of citizens), but an ongoing one.

The opponents of assimilation in Hungary were not just mouthing traditional theological prejudice and popular bigotry, they objected to the Jews because of their religiousness and because of their 'foreign' culture. The liberal offer linked the emancipation of the Jews to assimilation. The condition of becoming fully Hungarian was to change Jewishness.[11] Human rights were extended to the individual and not to the group. Assimilation was not only offered, it was demanded: 'One could say that the fusion of liberal values and national interests resulted in these anti-liberal conditions' (Gerő 1992, p. 11).

As a result, emancipation and the right to assimilate were linked in such a way that, from the Jewish point of view, assimilation had to be fought for, defended, and justified.

The evolution of modern antisemitism in Hungary

Whether homogeneity is the objective need of the modern state or a demand of nationalism, Jews, traditionally powerless and unprivileged, with deeply ingrained religious–cultural habits, stood out once again—not as in the middle ages, because of the religious uniformity of Christianity, but in a much more complex way. In feudal society, culture and ethnicity served to distinguish privileged groups and underscored their distinctiveness, and there was no ambiguity of status. The same social marker-device of culture or ethnicity was used to identify and separate off underprivileged pariah groups (Gellner 1983, p. 102). On the one hand, post-*Ausgleich* Hungary, a semi-feudal society, maintained those markers. At the same time, because of the urban style of life, high rates of literacy and commercial deftness, Jews had a marked advantage in a mobile, anonymous, centralised, mass society. In the process of modernisation, with emancipation, Jews were released from the bind of many of the previous restrictions, but were not able to shed traditional political powerlessness. Their economic superiority and cultural identifiability assumed an added importance, compounding religious Jew-hatred. In spite of emancipation, Jews stayed stigmatised.

Although capitalism, owing to the feudal traditions which despised industry and commerce, was almost exclusively in Jewish hands (with the willing participation of the aristocracy and the gentry), until World War I, antisemitism played a far smaller role in Hungary than in Austria. According to Jászi, there were several reasons for this. Firstly, the 'sober and benevolent character' of the Hungarian peasants, 'devoid of any religious or race fanaticism' did not react to modern antisemitism.[12] Secondly, he cited the backward political differentiation of the country, where the large masses were unorganised. The budding social democratic movement (of which Jászi himself was a prominent member), whose ranks were filled with poor Jews, did not entertain antisemitic tendencies. Thirdly, the power of the government, which suppressed antisemitism because it needed the cooperation of the Jews 'not only for financial reasons, but also as an instrument of assimilation against the non-Magyar nationalities of the country', kept antisemitism at bay (Jászi 1961, p. 173).

Viewing it from a historical context, historian Andrew Handler argues with Jászi's observation that antisemitism played a lesser role in Hungary than in Austria (Handler 1980, p. 23). Admitting that the persecution of witches and Jews had not been pursued with the same 'passionate fanaticism' as elsewhere in Europe, he still cites three hundred witch-trials between the sixteenth and eighteenth centuries, stressing the interchangeability of the victims.[13]

Jászi notwithstanding, I argue that the reason that Hungarian peasantry did not react to modern antisemitism was that the peasantry remained in feudal conditions and, therefore, the feudal markers were operational in socio–cultural attitudes. The Hungarian peasant was living a harsh, backward life, oblivious both socially and culturally to the dynamic changes of the nineteenth century. The antisemitism of Hungarian peasants was the Judeophobia taught by Christianity. In the villages the peasants viewed the strangely dressed and behaved orthodox Jews with suspicion. Yet *tzaddikim* (the saintly Hasidic rabbis) were revered, and Christians often asked their advice. Their deeds were often incorporated into Hungarian folklore (Dobos 1990, p. 31). This, however, was due to the wonder-seeking nature of Hungarian folk-myth rather than a reflection of social contact. Hungarian folk-proverbs candidly reflected these attitudes. Most proverbs reveal the threefold nature of hostility—social, economic and religious: 'Out of the way, Jew, when the peasant comes'; 'Bargains like a Gypsy over a horse, like a Jew over cotton'; 'Three Greeks, three Turks, three Jews—nine pagans'; 'They keep together like the Jews or the Lutherans'; 'The

Jew does not have Christ to get him to heaven, only a green slipper to slide him to hell' (Handler 1980, p. 23).

The social structure of nineteenth-century Hungary was a very substantial—possibly the most significant—reason for Austrian- and German-style political antisemitism not finding a mass base. Political antisemitism traditionally drew its highest number of followers from the middle and lower middle classes. In Hungary these strata were just developing in the second half of the nineteenth century and, as pointed out earlier, the overwhelming numbers of the middle class were Jewish. The different social bases of political antisemitism in Hungary determined its scope and its viciousness. Modern antisemitism in Hungary followed neither the brutal course of Russia, with its programs and the institution of the Pale, nor the structured version of Austria and Germany:

> [I]t was an unforeseen yet not unpredictable extension of the latent anti-Semitism of the political and social reformers of the pre-Ausgleich era who feared that the future of Magyardom would be threatened by the seemingly unending and unstoppable influx of foreign Jews. (Handler 1980, p. 26)

Déclassé lower middle classes provided the strongest and widest, but numerically still weak, support to modern antisemitism. The leaders of political antisemitism came from the ranks of impoverished gentry and civil servants (Kubinszky 1976, pp. 40–53). As a result of the political and economical crisis of the 1870s, growing numbers of the landed gentry lost their land. At the centre of the political crisis was the intensifying and open commitment of the gentry to the preservation of feudalism, in the process of which liberalism essentially became synonymous with the futile fight against the *Ausgleich* on constitutional grounds (the so-called *közjogi vita*). The nobility accepted and defended the *Ausgleich* and coalesced in the Liberal party, while those who wanted to separate Hungary from Austria were in the Independence party.[14]

There were two, not easily discernible, currents in the Hungarian antisemitic movement. The less radical wing accepted assimilation as a possibility and mostly aimed towards holding Jews back from economic and social participation. They wanted to ban Jews from acquiring land, and to contain the number of Jews in industry and commerce. The rationalisation was a mixture of accusations, ranging from usury and fraud to cosmopolitanism, betrayal of Hungary, and even conspiracy to rule the world. The radical wing, under the leadership of Istóczy, deemed Jews unassimilable and wanted to get rid of Jews altogether by expulsion (Gonda 1992, p. 153). Jacob Katz, referring to the first half of the nineteenth century, makes the point that there was a visible reason for anti-Jewish prejudice:

> [T]he presence of the traditional Jews within Hungarian Jewry has to be taken into account in order to understand the nature of the debate on the possible integration of Jews into the Hungarian nation . . . The cultural gulf that separated the traditional Jew from society at large appeared insurmountable, and the negative image of the Jew tended to be reinforced rather than diminished through actual contact. The Jew appeared to be ethnically foreign, morally suspect, culturally unassimilable. (Katz 1980, pp. 231–2)

Istóczy's attempts to create an antisemitic movement in Hungary

Istóczy's initial assertions, that Jews were 'caste-like, racially pure', serving the interests of the Paris-based *Alliance Israélite Universelle*, that their aim was to subjugate the Magyar nation and his call for the foundation of a self-protecting movement against Jews, were not taken seriously. His speeches in Parliament were continually interrupted by derisive comments and outbursts of cynical laughter. He was publicly rebuked by the prime minister. Istóczy, however, was not discouraged. In the following years his speeches became more belligerent and frequent, but monotonously the same in essence. He kept issuing warnings on the destructive influence of Jews and made scathing attacks on religious and cultural characteristics he deemed as proof of the 'unassimilable' nature of Jews. He accused Jews of social exclusivism and dishonest business practices. He targeted not only merchants, industrialists and professionals in the cities (thus fostering the growing hostility of the nascent proletariat), but also the rural Jews, portraying the latter as parasitic moneylenders, innkeepers and land leasers, who exercised usury, corruption and deceit. Jews presented a threat to Christian morality and to Hungarian nationalism, he asserted (Handler 1980, pp. 28–30). He also called for termination of social contact with those non-Jews who maintained relations with Jews.

Istóczy was by no means a mere imitator. He suggested the linking of the 'Eastern and the Jewish question', as each the solution for the other, by way of the restoration of the Jewish state in Palestine. In his reasoning, Jews 'retarded the progress of European nations and threatened Christian civilisation', whereas in the East, 'among kindred Semitic tribes', they would become a 'vigorous, powerful new element, an effective component of civilisation'. The restoration of the Jewish state, with a national government and institutions, would serve the interests of Jews and Hungarians. Istóczy reasoned:

> The Jews could effect the regeneration of the Turkish Empire that suffers from a chronic shortage of money by the use of their excellent mental ability, great political, legal, commercial and financial skills, and above all, their enormous money power. As loyal, devoted subjects of His Majesty the Sultan, or as his undoubtedly reliable allies, they will become powerful pillars of the Osmanli empire, hard-pressed in so many directions and surrounded by enemies. (Handler 1980, p. 30)

Wilhelm Marr, who originally coined the phrase 'antisemite', was very impressed by Istóczy's ideas and supported him strongly. There was a constant exchange of ideas between Hungarian, German, Austrian and French antisemites (Katzburg 1985, pp. 8–9). Istóczy translated German and French antisemitic pamphlets, published excerpts from Fichte, Wagner and Schopenhauer. The 'threat to Aryans' in Istóczy's rhetoric was clearly inspired by modern political antisemitism:

> This country is threatened to be inundated by abominable teeming hordes of this religion which is based on the Talmud. They pose acute danger by demanding the very principles laid down in the teachings of the Talmud . . . they praise themselves for striving to rule the world. This seven or eight million handful of Semite race *challenged three million Aryans*, not openly, but clandestinely with the tangled teachings of the Talmud . . . it is written in this [Talmud] that the Semite race will rule over the world, that is an ambition that is destroying every maxim of humanism, which seeks its might and power in conquest, and desires to satisfy lust by extermination of nations. (Karsai 1992, pp. 8–9) [*emphasis added*]

Istóczy's antisemitic rhetoric turned the Jews' strong identification with Hungary against them. The self-description, 'Hungarians of the Israelite faith', was only a trick:

> Jews in European states are an internal Carthage, a state within the state, a separate race constituting a political and social power, not simply a religion, as Jews would like to present it . . . The Jewish race, under the shield of the widespread religious tolerance of our age, *wants to view itself purely and exclusively as a religion* and through

this to vindicate absolute immunity and limitless freedom . . . Among the countless Jewish perfidy this is the most monumental, with which the Jewish nation deceived other nations. Because quintessentially the Jews are a distinct nation, race, which has a specific national religion. (Karsai 1992, pp. 9–10) [*emphasis added*]

He said this in a speech at the Parliament during the Tiszaeszlár blood libel, after making the extraordinary statement that 'the task of the final solution (*végleges megoldás*) of the Jewish question is for our time' (Karsai 1992, p. 9).

Of the different threads that made up antisemitism as a radical ideology, nationalism and racism were apparent, together with antisemitism's reliance on its historical antecedent, the tradition of religious Jew-hatred. Both nationalism and racism were evident in Istóczy's reasoning and the Tiszaeszlár blood libel was a particularly good example of medieval religious superstition being used, indeed built into the 'modern' notion of radical political antisemitism.[15]

The Tiszaeszlár blood libel

Blood libels are one of the accusations and superstitions that modern antisemitism salvaged from Christian Jew-hatred. They were a recurring theme during Christianity, but in modernity, joining other accusations, they became part of a different pattern: that of antisemitic affairs, a phrase coined by Albert Lindemann, in his book, *The Jew Accused* (Lindemann 1991). The very possibility of the medieval superstition of the blood libel resurfacing in 1882 was rooted in the close relationship between religious and modern Jew-hatred. Continuity is not just linear; religious Jew-hatred is not only an antecedent. Christian antisemitism cultivated the interplay between fear and fantasy. By viewing and condemning Jews as biologically, historically, socially or culturally alien, racism rationalises antisemitism according to the science-centred demands of modernity. Political, racist and cultural antisemitism builds on and exploits the earlier, religious form. The charge of conspiracy, for instance, was underpinned by the old accusation of 'Christ-killers'. This repetitiousness and the very history of the old charges lend themselves to being rational proof of validity. Religious–superstitious Jew-hatred paved the way for the social acceptance, indeed 'respectability' of racial and political antisemitism. This is how the blood libel still could easily maintain a foothold, even though antisemites in the late nineteenth century distanced themselves from religious hatred of Jews.

The Tiszaeszlár blood libel was an early warning, a precursor of the Dreyfus affair. Like its French counterpart, it also brought into the open 'all other elements of nineteenth-century antisemitism in its more ideological and political aspects; it is the culmination of the antisemitism which grew out of the special conditions of the nation–state' (Arendt 1967, p. 45).

In a historical context, the blood libel at Tiszaeszlár was a combination of principally medieval superstitious Jew-hatred and trace-elements of modern antisemitism. In its dynamics, on the local administrative level, it carried all the hallmarks of the feudal state imbued with xenophobic vindictiveness and self-righteous hatred. On the higher, governmental and state-policy level, the ensuing events were handled with the principles, instruments and procedures of the modern state.

An 'affair', in Lindemann's definition, is 'more than a trial'; it refers to exceptionally divisive matters, where opposing sides are driven by overpowering emotions. But more importantly, in an affair, issues that transcend the trial itself come into play. For a trial to become an affair it must have ideological implications. It must, in other words, develop into something more than a strictly legal issue of innocence or guilt (Lindemann 1991, p. 5). I use the concept 'antisemitic affair' with a somewhat different meaning. In these cases the modern state with all the paraphernalia of modern legal and social institutions, especially the press, administer an accusation where the real issue is not simply the crime, but the person of the accused, in particular his Jewishness. The crime itself is of lesser importance. The trial becomes a convex lens, a convergence for malice, venomous hatred and self-justifying vindictiveness against the accused, who really stands trial with all Jews.[16] The difference between the Tiszaeszlár blood libel or the Dreyfus affair and the blood libels in medieval times is the difference between modern antisemitism and religious Jew-hatred. These affairs were not acted out in religiously defined communities, but in the modern state with modern institutions.

Jews were at the centre of the modern trial, i.e. the Dreyfus affair, which refocused the issue of antisemitism in the modern world. We remember the Dreyfus affair so well because it was paradigmatic, not only for Jews and not only for the French. It was an essentially modern trial, where issues of modernity were acted out and articulated by figures embodying issues of modernity.

Very importantly, these antisemitic affairs are as much about

Gentile–Jewish cooperation as about Gentile–Jewish conflict (Lindemann 1991, p. 15). Eötvös, the Gentile lawyer for the defence in the Tiszaeszlár case, did not just want acquittal; he set out to prove that there was no crime, and, further, that the whole idea of ritual murder was based on superstition and bigotry (Eötvös 1968, vol. 1, pp. 10–15, 374, 381).

These affairs were passionate, intense dramas, with committed observers taking sides. The issues evoked passionate beliefs that went beyond justice and truth, both in the narrower, legal and the wider, philosophical sense, and were compounded by political and ideological agendas and undercurrents. On trial were the legal system, the forces of history, modernity, assimilation and, of course, the connecting tissue in the affairs, antisemitism. In each affair there are two (or even more) charges: the one which is openly on trial—treason, ritual murder—and the other, the charges voiced in the popular press: international Jewish conspiracy; clandestine power-wielding; trying to distort or buy justice. But Jewish 'power' only existed as long as the interests of Jews coincided with the interests of those in real power. Once the internal or international, political or national situation changed, the basic underlying powerlessness of Jews became painfully clear again. Exposing the hidden charges and that lethal mixture of reality and fantasy, one can observe the dynamics of how stereotypes, created by prejudices, launch and strengthen prejudices, and how political movements and ideologies make use of these stereotypes. In the Tiszaeszlár case, the unsavoury local investigator, a modern antisemite, did not even believe the blood libel charge, but was ready to make use of it.

The Tiszaeszlár affair did not kindle modern antisemitism either. The importance of the Tiszaeszlár blood libel lies in its essence and in its outcome. The Dreyfus affair defined modern antisemitism in France for decades to come. Symbolising the failure of Jewish assimilation, it sparked the development of Jewish nationalism and was essentially modern. The Tiszaeszlár blood libel was essentially pre-modern: the very accusation was medieval. The trial itself, with its triumphant outcome, also showed a totally opposite institutional interference to that of the Dreyfus affair. In France the army, the government, the judiciary and the legal institutions were anti-Dreyfus, anti-Jewish. In Hungary not only was there a fair, lawful trial, but the state suppressed sporadic antisemitic violence fuelled by Istóczy's tiny party. Unlike Austria, Germany, or indeed France, antisemitism in Hungary only became a serious political force after World War I.

Especially in comparison to the Dreyfus affair, the Tiszaeszlár blood libel and the ensuing events were handled in an exemplary manner. The legal procedure (apart from that at the local government level), the conduct of Eötvös, the Gentile lawyer, the way the government and institutions contained—in fact clamped down on—antisemitic riots, bore the hallmarks of strong commitment to liberal values.

Why did Hungary handle its affair so much better than France? France, the country where Enlightenment was born, a country where Western democracy was firm, allowed not only a serious miscarriage of justice to take place and be repeated over an extended period of time, but allowed free rein to ensuing antisemitism. Yet Hungary, a semi-feudal country to which democracy was new and not firmly established, shines by comparison in the upholding of liberal values. I think the answer lies precisely in the strength of democratic institutions. There was a very important dimension to the protection of Jews against mob antisemitism. As the Hungarian minister of culture said: '. . . antisemitism serves only as a pretext to undermine the foundations of social order . . . [Riots] begin with Hershko and Itzig [characteristic Jewish names in Hungary] and lead to Prince Esterhazy' (Handler 1980, p. 55).

The Hungarian state was doing all it could to avoid social unrest. Istóczy's failure to gather parliamentary support was spectacular when compared to the successes of various antisemitic movements outside Hungary. While in France there was no need to fear that antisemitic movements would lead to revolution or social unrest, in semi-feudal Hungary, where the peasantry was still living in medieval conditions, there was a very real threat of initial mob antisemitism, which, after satisfying its first anger, might turn into widespread social unrest. On the other hand, Hungary was not as authoritarian as Czarist Russia, where pogroms were in fact used to channel potential social unrest into anti-Jewish violence, and an enormous police force guaranteed that a pogrom would not turn into anything else.

Essentially, political antisemitism stayed pallid in Hungary until the years of World War I. The role of Jews in modernisation, especially their role in building a modern economy, and the role Hungarian Jews played in the Magyarisation program of multinational Hungary, ensured their protection by the strong state, while the 'missing' Hungarian middle and lower middle classes meant that this protection did not have to be vigorous or constant. These reasons and considerations, however, were not permanent. With a few decades of vigorous capitalist growth, Hungarian national middle classes started to develop and make demands for more financial and economic clout. Mikszáth, the master story-teller of the *Millennium* years, put these words into the mouth of one of his gentry-figures: 'A country who gives out of its hands commerce and the press will perish, like Poland . . . The task in front of the nation now is not to wrench the flag out of the hands of the Turks, but to wrench the pen out of the hands of the Jews' (Mikszáth 1910, p. 16).

The reference is to one of the legends of Hungarian history, when a defender of a besieged Hungarian fort threw himself on a Turkish soldier who was just about to pin the Turkish flag on the tower, and, by using his own weight, he hurled the flag, the soldier and himself off the tower. The idea of being besieged this time by the Jews reflected the sentiments of the lower gentry.

Even though Istóczy's antisemitic movement met with the restrictions of the strong state, Katzburg quotes the observations of the British Consul in Budapest at the time: 'M. Istóczy only blurted out his share of the general antipathy, an antipathy which shows itself in various social phases, and which, though it is rarely expressed in public, no Hungarian gentleman is in private conversation at any pains to conceal' (Katzburg 1985, p. 3).

Hungarian nationalism was more and more articulated as Christian ethnic commitment. Catholicism itself was politicised. There were two trends visible within political Catholicism. To one wing, anti-Jewishness was not important, because its main thrust was a return to religiousness. The other wing, which rallied the Christian middle classes, was outspokenly anti-modern and, as such, had a large dose of antisemitism. The Catholic People's party, established in 1895, used much of the ideology of the defunct antisemitic parties. Its platform was politicised Catholicism and its antisemitism was largely old, pre-modern, religious antisemitism. The party's agrarian ideology juxtaposed patriotism and cosmopolitanism on obvious ethnic–social lines. It differentiated between land-owning or land-cultivating classes as opposed to the new industrial/commercial middle classes. This was clearly a distinction between Hungarians and Jews. Owing to the increasing insecurity afflicting both rural and urban lower middle classes, it was predominantly the urban lower middle classes, the peasantry and the lower clergy which supported antisemitism as in Germany, Austria and France. Robert Wistrich pointed out that while Christian antisemites maintained the traditional religious accusations and imagery, such as the blood libel, these medieval concepts were transmitted through essentially modern techniques of mass agitation. Christian social antisemitism perfectly expressed the 'vacillating radicalism' of the lower middle classes. It was anti-capitalist, anti-liberal and anti-immigrant, and, mixed with strong conservative neo-feudal elements, it attacked the 'materialist, anti-clerical ethos of modern bourgeois civilisation' (Wistrich 1990, pp. 32–3). This meant that antisemitism was primarily aligned with conservatism. But the 'left' was not free from antisemitism either. Wistrich pointed to the dangers of identifying conservatism with antisemitism and vice versa, because doing so: 'unjustifiably assumes an a priori inborn immunity to antisemitism within the socialist movement' (Wistrich 1990, p. 34).

Logically, the socialist movement, being associated with the idea of 'progress', should have been ideologically opposed to antisemitism, and sometimes it was. But the socialist movement was also part of Western culture, and antisemitism was an integral part—and even expression—of that culture. Enlightenment ideals did not necessarily provide immunity. It is one of the historical commonplaces that Voltaire exposed Christianity through attacking the Old Testament, and thus Enlightenment philosophy itself carried on the Christian tradition of the hatred of Jews.[17] All issues of modernity could be (and were) symbolised by Jews. *Völkisch* ideology perceived the new tensions as basically Jewish versus Christian–Aryan issues. Marxists could, and did, condemn capitalism through the Jews. Even Jewish Marxists were not exempt.

Jászi, the radical editor of the seminal, progressive academic journal *Huszadik Század*, (Twentieth Century), himself Jewish, wrote very critically of Jewish big business. He went as far as writing that Hungarian Jews never established 'the right contact with the original soul of the land'. He condemned the 'uncertain equilibrium of the Jewish soul in consequence of half-assimilation', and even used one of the expressions of antisemitic jargon, 'Jewish capitalist press', admonishing 'it' for serving the purposes of oppressive Magyarisation policies (Barany 1974, p. 81). Jászi, who fully believed in the success of assimilation, described Jews as the chief representatives of capitalism and of Hungarian nationalism.

The 'Jewish question'—a public opinion poll

During World War I, antisemitism became more and more palpable. Hungarian Jews tended to attribute the anti-Jewish sentiments partly to the hardships caused by the war and partly to another influx of Jewish refugees from Galicia (a region in Eastern Europe that belonged to Poland until Austria annexed it in 1772). However, the Zionist writer, Patai, wrote in his journal, *Múlt es Jövő* (Past and Future):

> Hungarian antisemitism and the so-called *'Galicianer'* refugees have nothing to do with each other. The truth is that a section of Hungarian Jews do not notice, or close their eyes and do not want to notice that when in the parliament or in the press, the antisemites write about 'the *Galicianer*', they do not mean those few hundred refugees from Galicia, but the children and grandchildren of yesterdays *Galicianers*, that is, the entirety of Hungarian Jewry, children and parents. (Patai, J. 1918, p. 283)

In 1917, the editors of the *Huszadik Század* decided to start a public debate on the 'Jewish question'. Religious, intellectual and other leaders, selected by the editors, were asked to answer three questions:

1 Is there a 'Jewish question' in Hungary and if yes, what do you consider its essence?
2 What are the causes of the 'Jewish question' in Hungary? What traits of Hungarian society; which Jewish and non-Jewish social conditions, institutions, characteristics and customs are relevant in producing the Jewish question?
3 How do you see the solution of the 'Jewish question', what kind of social or legal reforms do you deem necessary? (Hanak 1984a, p. 15)

Out of some 150 people, more than one-third answered (60). Ten did not answer the specific questions, thirteen denied that there would be a 'Jewish question', and 37 deemed it as an existent and crucial problem. The answers were grouped into 'those who think there is' and 'those who think there is not' (a 'Jewish question'), and were published in alphabetical order.

Those who denied the existence of the 'Jewish question' deemed it the creation of antisemitic propaganda, the ghost of religious hatred, leftovers of defunct theories. Some viewed it as the machination of clerics, others as poorly veiled economic contradictions. One regarded antisemitism as lack of education and culture. Many of those who considered the 'Jewish question' a significant problem of society gave very astute and penetrating analyses. Some saw its roots in capitalism, others wrote about the remnants of ghetto-mentality. The Galician emigration was also given as a cause. Some saw it as a manifestation of ideological, ethical and national problems. Some offered psychological analyses. The solutions proposed were just as varied. Quite a few saw the solution in the democratisation process, others wanted to stop any further Jewish immigration by legislation. There were invitations and recommendations to assimilate fully. József Patai suggested that deepening Jewish consciousness and self-respect would liberate Jews. Others put their trust in education, and the Zionists expressed their hope in the creation of a Jewish state and the evolving national consciousness. The editors of *Huszadik Század* remarked on the similarity of the Zionist and antisemitic approaches. Both condemned liberalism and assimilation, and both camps were pessimistic regarding a solution within Hungary. Others linked the solution of the 'Jewish question' to the peasant and nationalities problem.

The nationalist commitment of Hungarian Jews, even in the face of growing antisemitism, was not unparalleled in the Monarchy. Not even the rise of an essentially antisemitic *Völkisch* movement among ethnic Germans in Prague and in the Sudetenland shook the German loyalties of most Bohemian and Moravian Jews, whose nationalism (and language) stayed German.[18]

Assimilation versus tradition

Hanak identifies three phases of Jewish assimilation, which he sees as coinciding with cycles of economic prosperity. The first stage is settlement. In this stage the original identity and language is largely retained, although there is limited interaction with the recipient society. The second stage is characterised by linguistic, cultural and social integration. He calls this stage bicultural. Immigrant Jews of this phase already spoke Hungarian, learned Hungarian literature, history and ethos, as well as Jewish (and Yiddish) tradition. It was not uncommon for Jews to celebrate both *Chanukah* and Christmas, and even to keep *Pesach* as well as Easter, and 'eat *matzos* with smoked ham' (Hanak 1984a, p. 238). This stage, according to Hanak, is also characterised by dual commitment. The third stage is that of true assimilation. Hungarian Jewish assimilation had certain specificities when compared with Western-style assimilation patterns. Firstly, the speed with which Hungarian Jews Magyarised was unparalleled. Large masses of Jews only arrived in Hungary in the nineteenth century. Secondly, the thrust of assimilation was towards an ethnic minority, Hungarians being the largest, nevertheless still a minority within the multinational empire. Thirdly, the intensity and voluntary nature of assimilation were coupled with an institutional self-assimilation, which was manifest in the Magyarisation of the liturgy, of parish-administration (registers of births, marriages and deaths) and, in particular, of the language of education in the Jewish denominational schools. Fourthly, according to what Karady calls the 'political–cultural status of assimilation patterns', compared to Jews in other European countries, Hungarian Jews assimilated into a retrograde, provincial society. That, according to him, was a higher level of achievement than the assimilation of other European Jewish communities into modern societies (Karady 1993a, pp. 35–6).[19] The feudal nature of Hungarian society affected Hungarian Jewish assimilation and gave it a special quality, unparalleled elsewhere. Karady also points to the number of Hungarian Jews as the most visible feature of Hungarian-style assimilation: the percentage of Jews in society around the turn of the century was 6 per cent (close to a million). There was no other Western European country with comparable numbers (Karady 1993a, p. 35).

There were certain quantitative and qualitative factors which that relevant to the process of assimilation. One was the mass immigration of Jews in the nineteenth century as a result of which the overall growth of the Jewish population surpassed the growth of the non-Jewish population (Barany 1974, p. 77). Another crucially important feature was education, the major instrument in the Magyarisation process. The nationalist education policies of the Liberal Era resulted in a highly efficient, modern school system, which in its turn produced not only a sharp decline in illiteracy but, just as importantly, the interesting phenomenon of the relative aggregate 'overeducation' of the middle classes.[20] For Jews, traditionally literate, education was the means by which the desired integration into society could be achieved. As Wistrich pointed out, all over Europe Jews entered modernity through *Bildung* (self-cultivation) in its cosmopolitan sense (Wistrich 1990, p. 87). In the nineteenth century, Hungarian Jews took on Hungarian culture in much the same way as German Jews had done a century earlier.

As in Austria, schooling in Hungary was a key factor not only in cultural assimilation, but in social mobility as well.

Jewish settlement in Hungary was geographically and chronologically linked and the assimilation patterns were accordingly discernible. In the eighteenth century, the first (small) wave of Jewish settlers came from the Czech–Moravian provinces. They spoke German, were mostly urban-dwellers, and were engaged in industry and commerce. They were fairly enlightened and settled mostly in the southern parts of Hungary (Hanak 1984a, p. 239). The next wave came from Galicia. Between 1840 and 1880 the majority of Jews came from Galicia. The province of Galicia had the largest population of Jews in Europe outside of Russia. They were not only the most numerous, but the poorest, most religiously orthodox, and educationally backward. After the 1867 emancipation, these Jews migrated to Hungary in large numbers. Popularly known as *Ostjude* (eastern Jews), *Galizianer* (Galicians), or '*polisi*' (Polish), they spoke Yiddish. The Jews of Galicia were Hasidic Jews and formed their own communities, occupying the lower strata of commerce and industry (Handler 1980, p. 13).

In 1819, there were 130 000 Jews in Hungary, in 1842, 241 632 (Barany 1968, p. 157; Venetianer 1922, p. 454). At the time of the first census, in 1869, there were 553 641 Jews, by 1900, 846 254, and in 1910 the official figure was 938 458 (*Magyar Zsidó Lexikon* 1929, p. 553).[21] The cultural and social assimilation varied depending on the region and on the composition of the Jewish community: social strata, occupation, level of education, time of immigration, place of emigration were all important determining factors, along with the type and region of location—villages or cities, eastern or western Hungary.[22]

Nationalism and Hungarian identity

Nationalism and Hungarian identity were vitally important issues to Hungarian Jews. Demanding assimilation as the price of emancipation produced the same nationalist commitment as that of Jews in France and in Germany. From the Jewish point of view, the requirement of assimilation did not appear as unreasonable. Linguistic and cultural identification, secularisation and urbanisation were basic strategies of assimilation wherever Jews were institutionally emancipated.

East Central European embourgeoisement meant not only economic and social modernisation, but the construction of national identity. Jews, instrumental and central to the first process, could not be unaffected by the second. In the nineteenth century, Jewish national aspiration did not fire the imagination of Jews across Europe, and even when Zionism appeared as a movement, it was an idea and not a country. To perceive Zionism as a realisable national aspiration took a great deal of insight and visionary zeal. Even Herzl himself did not necessarily see the land of Israel as the new home of Jews. There were ideas which even included the Kimberley in Australia. Without a definite geographical location on which to focus, Jewish national identity looked more like a chimera than a viable route to modern society. In a century when nation and state were developing through modernisation, it is not at all surprising that Jews, who were also coming out of the cold of feudal ostracism into the era of Liberty, Equality and Fraternity, embraced nationalism which, alongside liberalism, was the ideological propelling force.

In examining the effect of the formation of the Hungarian national middle class, Hanak points to three important historical facts concerning the Jews of Hungary (Hanak 1984a, p. 241). Firstly, the Jewish community was neither ethnically nor culturally homogeneous. Secondly, the community was divided socially by class stratification. Thirdly, the Hungarian Jewish community was experiencing the same effects of Enlightenment and *Haskala* (Jewish Enlightenment) as the Jews of Western Europe, and as a result of rationalism and positivism there was a weakening of religiosity. Nationalism, with the irresistible force of the *Zeitgeist*, cemented modern identity which unavoidably had to develop. It was only natural that 'the Monarchy's Jewry, having already reached the stage of dual commitment at the time of the *Vormärz* [prior to the March 1848 revolution in Hungary] had no other option than to choose a national identity adequate to the age, to the place and to its interests and inclinations' (Hanak 1984a, p. 241).

Hungarians were forging a new modern national identity at the same time as the emancipation of Jews was becoming a political and legal issue. For Hungarians, the Habsburg oppression and the fight for liberty and independence had more than a superficial similarity with the social oppression of Jews. The connecting tissue was feudalism. The Hungarian fight for independence was a fight against feudalism and achieving it meant entering the modern era. The synchronicity of purpose was even more pronounced as modernisation became a simultaneous project and opportunity for Jews and Hungarians.

The fact that Hungarians needed the Jews, both for keeping the Hungarian numerical supremacy amongst the many nationalities and for industrial and commercial modernisation, produced an openness which was unparallelled anywhere else.

During the heady days of the nineteenth century, Hungarians and Jews were caught up together in the excitement of creating a new society and new national identity. Lipót Lőw, the first rabbi to deliver his sermons in Hungarian, went so far as to argue that the Diaspora had terminated the national identity of Jews (Venetianer 1922, p. 101). President of the Israelite Magyar Literary Society, Dr Samuel Kohn, rabbi and historian, declared in 1896:

> During these vicissitudinous thousand years Magyar Israelites exulted, wept and bled together with the Magyar nation and learned to love this sacred land that has sustained them and received the remains of their fathers. They have also learned to love it as their mother before it accepted them as it children.
>
> We, to whose joy this nation has acknowledged the legality of our religion, not only feel, but *know* that we are Magyars. For us the word Israelite, even in religious life that is Israelite as far as the faith is concerned is the adjective of the word Magyar. Let us proudly declare: it signifies a Jewish Magyar. (Handler 1982, p. 8)

Yet the Hungarian–Jewish 'symbiosis' was very similar to the one-sided, unrequited love affair of the Jews for German culture. As both Scholem and Wistrich pointed out, concerning German Jews, 'there never has been a meaningful encounter but only a tragic process of self-alienation, of self-surrender and Jewish national self-negation' (Wistrich 1990, p. 99).

In the Liberal Era, assimilation and social mobility went hand in hand. The same strategies and techniques that engendered assimilation also generated social mobility. The door opened for assimilated Jews to enter Hungarian society. Less well-to-do, lower middle-class Jews Hungarianised their names in droves.[23] Hungarian became the language of education in Jewish primary schools. In 1884, out of 509 Jewish primary schools, Hungarian was the exclusive language in 368 of them, 128 had bilingual (German and Hungarian) classes and in only 13 schools was German the language of teaching. Out of the 979 teachers in these schools, 96 per cent could teach in Hungarian. Nevertheless, for a long time to come,

German and Yiddish remained the primary language amongst Jews themselves (Gonda 1992, p. 164). Still, Hungarian was a cherished and cultivated language for the Jewish middle classes. There were periodicals and journals, and even an Israelite Hungarian Literary Association (Gonda 1992, pp. 165–6). From 1862, the idea of a Jewish secondary school (*gimnázium*) was gathering momentum. Although there was opposition to the idea, from those who favoured assimilation to the point of not having a separate *gimnázium*, it was steadily gaining support. Arguments were put forward for a Jewish *gimnázium*, stating that it would be beneficial so that 'Jewish students would not have to endure the derision, mockery and other minor torments of fellow students and teachers' (Felkai, 1992, pp. 10–11). This sentence is indicative of the fact that, although political antisemitism was controlled and repressed by the state, dislike of Jews was socially widespread. Another argument was put forward that it would mean jobs for Jewish teachers. Finally, in 1892 a foundation was established which led to the building and establishment of the Jewish *gimnázium*, but in another era, in 1919 (Felkai 1992, pp. 11–13).

In Hungary then, as in Central Europe, the higher rate of literacy and the successful maximisation of educational opportunities were closely related to the fact that in the pre-1914 era, 'the urbanisation of Jews took place at a faster pace than that of the Gentiles' (Wistrich 1990, p. 96).

Hungarian Jews and Zionism

Theodor Herzl, who conceived and established Zionism as a political movement, was born in Hungary, was educated and lived in Vienna, and described himself as a 'German-speaking Jew from Hungary' (Barany 1974, p. 65). Herzl was an exception, in both his tongue and his lack of Hungarian identification. By this time the overwhelming majority of Hungarian Jewish intelligentsia spoke, wrote and published in Hungarian. The notion of a Jewish homeland did not inspire Hungarian Jews. They did not need Jewish nationalism, they had Hungarian nationalism. Their Judaism was emphatically expressed as a religion. The self-description and concept of 'Hungarians of the Israelite faith' was akin to that of German Jews, with the notable difference of the official Hungarian policy of inclusion.

Zionism sounded very much like Istóczy's antisemitic proposition of establishing a Jewish state in order to get rid of the Jews in Hungary. Articles had already appeared in 1896, the same year that Herzl published his *The Jewish State*, denouncing the new movement: 'Herzl forgot about the patriotism of the Jews. No tribulation can come to us here which would not be preferable than the misery of having to change homelands' (Gonda 1992, p. 171).

Hungarian Jews felt that they did have a homeland, one that they had already fought for, toiled for, one that accepted them. They felt they already had the freedom that Zionism was seeking to achieve. The Zionist notion that Jews needed a national and political framework in which they could determine their fate as a people did not work with Hungarian Jews. The way the nationalities were treated during the days of the Monarchy made the idea of Jews as a nation, as a nationality, as an ethnicity, undesirable. This added a further reason to their insistence on describing themselves as Hungarians of the Israelite faith and to treating the idea of a Jewish nationhood with suspicion and animosity.

It was not only the assimilated Jews who did not want to have anything to do with Jewish nationalism. The orthodox rejected Zionism on religious grounds as, according to Judaism, the ingathering of the exiles can only come when the Messiah arrives. *Múlt es Jövő*, the Jewish and Zionist journal, was attacked by antisemites and anti-Zionists alike. The editor was accused, for instance, of fostering Jewish self-consciousness and seclusion by writing about Zionism and Jewishness and by publishing articles of Jewish literature making Judaism attractive (Patai, R. 1989, p. 26). Slowly, but visibly, the first Zionist organisations appeared around the turn of the century, mirroring the growth of antisemitism.[24] However, all in all, the Zionist movement remained comparatively anaemic, in the 'Golden Age' of security and inclusion.

Jewish nobles

An interesting phenomenon accompanied the assimilation of Hungarian Jews. Unlike German Jews, who copied the image of the German burgher as they entered society, or the Jews of Vienna and Prague, who looked at the Gentile middle class, wealthy Hungarian Jews emulated the nobility. The simple reason for that, of course, was that there was no Hungarian middle class into which to assimilate, no role-models to follow. Polish Jewry also emulated the nobility—to the point that even now the various *Hasidic* sects wear the attire of nineteenth-century Polish nobility, complete with fur-rimmed hats and boots. But this was a different type of imitation as its aim was certainly not assimilation.

As Jews assimilated and became the middle class, they had to invent themselves. The same dynamism applied to the Magyarising German population (Hanak 1984a, p. 242). The whole modernisation process was executed by Jews, Germans and (lower) nobility.[25] The nobility, traditionally and socially accustomed to leadership, provided ethnic and traditional authenticity to this process. For Jews, entering modern society also meant the disintegration of the traditional, close-knit community and their individual role in it. In this sense there was some similarity to the disintegrating feudal cleavages and the search for new identity in the new order in non-Jewish society. There was, however, a 'double impasse of love and hate' within Hungarian nobility regarding Jews as more and more emphasis was placed on the Christian character of the Hungarian nation and state according to Endre Ady, the decadent revolutionary poet. In 1917, Ady compared this love–hate relationship between Hungarians and Jews to a corroboree:

> [T]wo equally alien species are making love to each other under the rules of corroboree. With the musical instruments of already developed cultures here are the Jews. And we, who call ourselves Hungarian, with hate and desire sway the love-dance. Here, choking each other with love, we either produce a new nation or the deluge is after us. (Ady, cited in Hanak 1984a, p. 371)

The role that the nobility and the gentry played in the modernisation process had another, interesting aspect. According to the American historian, William McCagg, who wrote extensively on the subject of Jewish nobles, between 1863 and 1900 almost a hundred Jews were ennobled in recognition of their economic achievements. McCagg lists 346 Jewish noble families (McCagg 1972a, p. 89).[26] The ennoblement of Jews in Hungary is a significant and revealing development. It does tell about the importance of Jews in the Hungarian economy. It is also revealing that the Monarchy was willing to ennoble such a comparatively large number of Jews. It signifies acceptance and recognition. The fact that this acceptance and recognition took the form of ennoblement is a powerful indication of how deeply feudalistic this society was, where the ultimate recognition was a title. After 1848, ennoblement did not include feudal privileges since they had been abolished. The nobility nevertheless preserved its leading role in politics, legislation and state administration. There were three peak periods in which many Jews were ennobled. These periods denote times when Jewish participation was especially important.[27] Through ennoblement, some Hungarian Jews entered politics and state administration. In addition, as McCagg pointed it out, ennoblement in Hungary implied political choice: 'It implied both a degree of social conservatism or "feudalisation" and a willingness to be considered Magyar as opposed to any other nationality' (McCagg 1972a, p. 17).

The ennobled Jews, however, were also caught up in conflicts of identity, which could be summarised as emulating the values of the nobility while forging a bourgeois ethos and upholding a Jewish cultural framework in private life:

> In public life they had to accept the rules and habits of the traditional middle class, the formalities, parades, the gala dress, the rhetorical style of the nobility, its pseudo-heroical feudal value system. In public life they intransigently exercised their business minds and entrepreneurial spirits, following the bourgeois ethos; they ostentatiously upheld their fathers' German-Jewish names, Goldberger, Deutsch, Weiss, even if these were prefixed by Magyar titles such as 'Budai', 'Hatvani' or 'Csepeli'. (Hanak 1984a, p. 245)

The split of the community

The new identity, based on Hungarian nationalism, engendered other conflicts. Disunity between the orthodox and the progressive Jews was growing. At the core of the dissent was the question of which direction the Jewish community would take. For some decades the Reform movement was winning popularity within certain segments of the Hungarian Jewish community. An outcome of the Jewish Enlightenment or *Haskala*, the Reform movement originated in Germany and spread from there. It introduced innovations to liturgy and generally stood for introducing Western culture and Enlightenment ideals into Judaism. It was vehemently opposed, not only by the orthodox, but sometimes by modernising Jews as well. The reformists pushed for religious alterations to further emancipation, while the traditionalists argued that maintaining Jewish religion is not contradictory to good citizenship. The orthodox rabbis organised to stop the assimilationist Jews from establishing modern institutions for training rabbis. In 1865 the orthodox rabbis passed a resolution which threatened to place under a ban any Jew delivering a sermon in any other language than

Yiddish, or anyone entering a synagogue where the *mechitzah* (the traditional partitioning) between men and women was transparent, or where a choir sang (traditionally the cantor chanted) (Handler 1980, p. 17).

Progressive Jewish leaders persuaded the minister of Cults and Public Instruction to convene a general Jewish Congress. The aim of the Congress was to organise the structure of the Jewish community in the same manner as the Christian denominations regarding religious and educational matters—to create full autonomy for Jewish institutions and integrate them into the state's structure. Although the minister kept insisting that the law only recognised one Jewish faith and did not allow for various strands, the orthodox community would not accept the program of centralisation and demanded complete autonomy (*Magyar Zsidó Lexikon* 1929, p. 999; Handler 1980, p. 18). Finally, the Jewish Congress passed the resolutions on the administrative structure of the Jewish community without the participation of the orthodox. The orthodox community, however, managed to get the parliament to decree that forcing a minority within a religious denomination to conform to the decisions of the majority was an act irreconcilable with the principle of religious freedom. With this extraordinary demonstration of the liberal understanding of civil rights, the split of the Hungarian Jewish community was officially recognised and sanctioned.[28]

The split was into three parts: the progressive, the orthodox and the so-called *status quo ante* group, those who wished to retain the pre-Congress status. With it, in fact, parishes (*hitközség*) were established not only by territory, but by the three different groups. This was a unique occurrence in the history of European Jewry. Only in Hungary did the conflict between the reform and the orthodox factions lead to such a spectacular split. Everywhere else in Europe the *neologue* (reform) and the orthodox established their own synagogues within the same parish. The structural disunity of the Jewish community was to become chronic and paralysed the leadership in a number of ways in the following, important decades leading up to the Holocaust.

Enlightenment ideals, indeed modernisation, demanded emancipation. Cultural homogeneity is an imperative to both modernisation and to nationalism. Nationalism is thus linked to assimilation: it presumes, demands assimilation. This role of nationalism was especially relevant in multinational Hungary.

Emancipation, demanded by modernisation and assimilation, demanded by nationalism, resulted in the policy of inclusion. Emancipation made Jews equal. However, in spite of the success of cultural, linguistic assimilation, Jews were perceived as 'the other'. With the advent of racism this 'otherness' was defined as unchangeable and dangerous to the organic unity of the nation. It was due to the crucial role played by Jews in the process of modernisation and in the multinational empire, that political antisemitism did not become a political movement during the years of the Monarchy. The relevance of the strong state was thus twofold: firstly, it was capable of providing protection; secondly, it did protect Jews, for two reasons: Jews were needed economically and ethnically.

The process of embourgeoisement ran parallel to emancipation and to the forging of a new national identity, both for the Hungarians and for the Jews. Assimilation and emancipation were linked in a way that the liberal offer made emancipation dependent on assimilation, while the antisemitic approach was questioning the ability and the willingness of Jews to assimilate and sought to deny emancipation. For Hungarian Jews, the right to assimilate had to be fought for, defended, and its success continually proven. The outcome of this was an identity which saw itself Hungarian by nationality and Jewish by religion. Consequently Jewish nationalism, i.e. Zionism, did not take hold in Hungary during the Liberal Era. With the process of assimilation the Jewish middle class regarded itself first and foremost Hungarian, ethnically, politically and culturally. Jews made an investment in being committed to the Hungarian state, nation and culture.

In the Liberal Era the 'Jewish question' was put in the social context of assimilation and the political context of the nationalities question. By the twentieth century the 'right to assimilate' became superfluous. With the development of the secular modern state and of democracy, it ceased to be a legitimate political question on the one hand, and on the other, assimilation itself became a sociological reality. Jews were emancipated and many of them assimilated.

In the Monarchy, Jews were identifying with a declining power, a vanishing reality. What Zweig called the 'Golden Age of security' was disintegrating irrevocably. Yet Hungarian Jews kept on believing in the state's desire to protect them well into the twentieth century, all through the decades that led into the Holocaust.

PART TWO

EXCLUSION

Chapter three

Constitutional protofascism: the emergence of the ethos of exclusion

From the beginning of the second decade of the century, the defining policy regarding Jews was that of exclusion. The historical events which traumatised Hungarian society and brought on the changes resulting in state-condoned antisemitism and the policy of exclusion have to be seen in the context of the growing ideology of the time, fascism.

The complex, contradictory profile of Hungarian fascism developed through some characteristic specificities. Being predetermined by a different cultural, historical and socio-economic background, vital components of fascism, like nationalism and antisemitism, had national attributes. Fascism in Hungary never really found one leader who could have congealed all the parties into one, around whom fascists and sympathisers could have rallied. It existed practically by default, without an ideologist to develop an ideology acceptable to all. Another important leitmotif was an aggressive Christianity, inherent in all forms of Hungarian fascism, in contrast to the 'heathen' rituals and ritual secularism of Nazism. Hungarian protofascism in the 1930s, unlike Nazism (which still incorporated socialist ideals), was not anti-capitalist and in some ways even allowed and cultivated limited liberalism. Lacking the ideology of *Lebensraum*, instead of wanting to conquer the world, Hungarian fascism confined itself to the irredentist aims of re-establishing the *status quo ante Trianon*. Industrially well-developed Germany looked at the whole world, while provincial and semi-feudal Hungary only wanted to rule the immediate region. In Hungary, 'legality' and operating within parliamentary forms were an intrinsic part of political life. While Nazism, both as an ideology and as a form of government, was anti-parliamentary, Hungarian fascism was largely acted out within the constitutional framework. In the years after World War I, both countries experienced similar and even analogous events but the reactions were different. Much less developed capitalism, a backward economy and a corresponding social structure and culture produced attitudes, politics and ideology peculiar to Hungary. In Germany, fascism was a movement, a mass force and was in power by the 1930s. In the Hungary of the same decade, it was an ambience that pervaded social thinking, values and awareness, and set political parameters.

Nationalism and antisemitism were the dominant leitmotifs of the period. Hungarian nationalism was articulated through the unbridled thrust for the revision of the Trianon-imposed borders. Its ideological content was defined by the polarity of two often contradictory tendencies—the development of indigenous ideologies formulated under the impact of fascism and Nazism on one hand, and the policies of the authoritarian state attempting to control radical extremism on the other. The main trends of Hungarian political thought met on the common platform of antisemitism and nationalism. The irrational fear of the 'death of the nation' found further expression in the concept of a racially threatened culture, articulated eloquently by the populist movement, the traditional conservatives and the radical right-wingers. Hungarian politics, intellectual life, society and institutions had to be sacrosanct. Jews were perceived and cast as 'the other', the alien, the enemy. Describing the relationship and the nature of Hungarian society *vis-à-vis* Jews, the most appropriate word is *exclusion*. As importantly as the previous Golden Age (also known as the 'Golden Era') was characterised by *inclusion*, the 1920s and 1930s, leading up to the ultimate exclusion, the Holocaust in the 1940s, could be summed up by the increasing marginalisation, banishment and ostracism of the Jews.

As the Empire collapsed, the situation, the role and the perception of Jews changed:

- *ethnically*: after Trianon there were no more minorities, so Jews were not needed to make up the Magyar balance;
- *economically*: the increasingly impoverished gentry and the huge numbers from the state-bureaucracy who were made superfluous by the Trianon treaty found Jews obstructing their own progress;
- *politically*: the political culture had turned to anti-liberalism and anti-bolshevism and targeted Jews for both; carrying the racial

concept, fascism, as an ideology (and later as a state-ideology), advocated exclusion.

Defining historical events

The era between the two wars has many names. The Horthy era, post-Trianon, Trianon Hungary. Each describes an important characteristic of the time. Horthy's 'neo-baroque edifice' as Szekfü called it, was just as much of a determining feature as were the effects of the treaty of Trianon. Essentially, Horthy's was a right-wing authoritarian regime, in which fascism and Nazism were a pervasive ambience (Ranki, V. 1990, p. 156).[1]

The end of World War I brought the end of the Austro–Hungarian Empire. In October 1918, with the 'Michaelmas daisy revolution' (*őszirozsás forradalom*), Count Mihály Károlyi became the prime minister. Politically close to Jászi, a radical member of the nobility, Károlyi was popular and it was widely hoped that his government would be able to secure a favourable peace treaty for Hungary. While Serb, Czech and Romanian troops (the 'little Entente') occupied two-thirds of the country, in early November Hungary was declared an independent republic. In the growing confusion the promised social policies did not work fast enough.[2] By March 1919, Károlyi and his government resigned, and a soviet-style republic (*Tanácsköztársaság*) was created, under the leadership of Béla Kún, a member of the Communist party. The communist government took over not only without public resistance, but was greeted with considerable enthusiasm. This was due to Kun's defiant stand against the Entente demands. However, the Communist regime proved to be powerless in the face of unrelenting international pressure to sign the peace treaty. It also failed to meet domestic challenges. In spite of nationalisation, peasants were not given land and that meant that the largest mass support that the Commune could have rallied was not forthcoming.

The genesis of the Horthy era: the White Terror

In the upheaval caused by the lost war, the looming peace treaty and the climactic changes of government, various anti-Communist groups—mostly ex-officers of the Austro–Hungarian army and unemployed civil servants—rallied at Szeged to fight against the proletarian dictatorship. With them, the first strands and the characters of Hungarian fascism appeared. These groups could be called 'professional' right-wing conspirators because from the time of the collapse of the Monarchy this is how they spent most of their time (Erős 1970, p. 115). In Vienna, the conservative big and medium landowners were gathering under the guidance of Count Bethlen, a Transylvanian aristocrat. Later on, as consolidation was setting in, the political chasm of these months deepened, between the Szeged men, ideologically more fascist, and the Vienna group. This latter group represented the political direction that served fascism by default, more as a by-product of ambivalent foreign and internal policies and less by design, 'victims' of their own irredentism and conservatism. Both groups yielded prominent leaders. Gömbös and Imrédy, both of whom became prime ministers in the following decades, belonged to the first group, while Bethlen, twice prime minister, came from the second, more aristocratic group.[3] Admiral Horthy, being on good terms with all these groups, became their leader. (Horthy held on to his rank of 'Admiral', even though post-Trianon Hungary had no sea and no navy. The title spoke of the grand days of 'Greater Hungary', complete with sea ports and fleet.)

The Entente powers waited impatiently for Hungary to sign the peace treaty. Romanian troops occupied Budapest. Horthy's army did not combat the occupying Romanian army. They engaged in pogroms instead. The internally and externally besieged Communist government resigned in early August 1919. The White Terror gripped Hungary.

Bands of armed men roamed the country. They extracted ransoms, carried out public executions and perpetrated mass murders. For the first time in Hungarian history internment camps were set up (Braham 1981, pp. 16–20). One of the most bloodthirsty units was called 'Black Legion of Death' (*fekete halállégió*). They wore black uniforms decorated with skulls and cross-bones. Both the name and the symbols were to be reinvented by the SS *Einsatzgruppen*.

Ferenc Fejtő, the historian, wrote about the White Terror:

> The greatest surprise of the next months, or rather years was how easily a few hundred political, military and clerical agitators succeeded in the kindling and maintenance of the enormously powerful antisemitic campaign which spread all over the country. (Fejtő 1990a, p. 44)

Not only supporters of the Commune were targeted. Jews were specifically sought out. In the following decades there were tenuous attempts to justify this by the preponderance of Jews among the leaders of the Commune.[4] The relevance of pointing to their Jewishness was to mark them as the 'other', different, alien, the enemy. Christian or Jewish, Communist leaders regarded themselves Communists and nothing else. As true Communist revolutionaries, they shed their religious background. They were against the bourgeoisie, and if the bourgeois happened to be Jewish, that did not change anything. Jewish middle classes were not exempt from the economic decrees of the Commune. Furthermore, the number of Jews amongst the counter-revolutionary army-officers was also well above the percentage of Jews in society.[5] Another rationalisation used the charge which emerged in the war years, namely, that the Jews 'back-stabbed' Hungary in the war. This accusation was as unfounded as its counterpart in Germany (Mendelsohn 1983, pp. 94–8). Throughout the Horthy era the connection between Jews and Communists was stressed and became another conduit through which Nazism, too, seeped into the conservative creed. The 'Judeo-Bolshevik' description was especially absurd in Hungary, where the Jewish middle classes held a much larger part of industry and commerce than in Germany. The deliberate linking of Jews and Communists continued all through the Horthy era. Courts regularly stressed the Jewishness of the illegal Communists who were prosecuted, and, according to current research, between 1920 and 1943, the death penalty was imposed overwhelmingly on Jewish Communists (Borsányi 1992, pp. 149–51).[6] Bethlen (twice prime minister during the Horthy era) expressed the common justification of anti-Jewish policies and sentiments which was the social and official view predominant in the Horthy era: 'Hungary was largely pushed into the revolution by the bellicose Masonic lodges which were built up as fronts for Jewry engaged in politics' (Bethlen 1988, p. 126).

There was no articulated ideology during the White Terror. Revenge can hardly be called an ideology and revenge was what the special squads set out to do. The name 'counter-revolution' was the essence and the entirety of the 'ideology'. It defined and condemned itself to a reflected identity (Weber 1988, p. 441). However, it had the fuzzy, nebulous program, the 'Szeged idea' (*Szegedi gondolat*), which promoted antisemitism, chauvinistic nationalism and anti-Communism. While the antisemitism of the Szeged men was primarily nationalist and economic in character, it already had a distinctly racial ingredient, palpable in the pogroms wreaked by the special squads.

During the reign of the Communist dictatorship, a total of 587 people were killed, many of whom were actual criminals (Braham 1981, p. 35).[7] The White Terror murdered 5000–6000 victims, 3000 of them Jews (*Encyclopaedia Judaica* vol. 8, p. 1095). The squads went on murder rampages and conducted pogroms. Their vicious brutality introduced a qualitative change in Hungarian antisemitism.

The White Terror made violence, if not exactly *comme il faut*, at least socially acceptable. The traditional elements of Magyar self-definition—fierce nationalism, Christianity and provincialism— were becoming aggressive, racist.

The Treaty of Trianon

In November 1919, Admiral Horthy entered Budapest on a white horse, heading his counter-revolutionary army. As a sordid anti-climax to the revolution and the two 'chromatic' terrors, the peace treaty was finally signed at Trianon in June 1920. In the following year, under the premiership of Count Bethlen, political consolidation started.

Without doubt, Hungary suffered the biggest loss of territory, two-thirds of the land together with one-third of the population and commensurate economic losses. There was a further stipulation to pay reparations. All of Transylvania went to Romania, the northern provinces became part of Czechoslovakia. Austria gained some territory, and a large chunk in the south became part of Yugoslavia. Hungary lost Fiume, its only sea-port, to Italy. Even Poland acquired a small piece of Hungarian territory. More than three million Magyars were suddenly under foreign domination. The drawing of boundary-lines was arbitrary and unfortunate. The right of self-determination was invoked when a territory was to be severed from Hungary, but was consistently denied when it would have favoured Hungary. The actual determination of boundary questions was left to the foreign secretaries of the principal Allied Powers. They were faced with border-populations mixed by centuries of intermarriages, unreliable statistics and at times deliberate falsifications. So, a working decision was made, that when 'having the choice to make between the Allied and an enemy country, the Commission must not hesitate, however strong its desires of legitimate impartiality may be, to favour the Allied side' (Lloyd George 1938, p. 919).

The economic consequences were stupendous. Before the war,

75 per cent of Hungarian trade was with other districts of the Monarchy. The Hungarian wheat-export and milling industry was protected by high agricultural tariffs. Hungary, the pantry of the Monarchy, was primarily an agricultural country. In 1913 only about 16 per cent of the national income was produced by manufacturing. As a direct result of the peace treaty, the home-market was reduced by about 60 per cent. The losses in natural resources were also enormous.

The Peace Treaty of Trianon became the source of collective confusion and anxiety, crucial in shaping the next decades. Its effect reverberates even now. Hungarians still perceive the Trianon treaty as the most painful event in Hungarian history, possibly surpassing that of Mohacs.[8]

Hungarians, who traditionally and vigorously mistreated their numerous minorities, albeit with a jovial paternalistic attitude, were now insulted by the sombre appraisal of the Western democracies. The chauvinistic minority policies and the forced Magyarisation programs were indignantly defended. The concept of 'justice', as it was understood within these parameters, created lasting tunnel-vision. Count Apponyi, who represented Hungary at the peace talks, argued in his fluent and elegant French, English and Italian that history validated the territorial status quo. He informed the Paris Conference that the terms of peace were unacceptable to his country and his reasoning included such points as Hungary's treatment being the harshest (which undoubtedly was the case); that Hungary was not responsible for the war, not being completely independent at the outbreak of the war. He claimed, 'Hungary had all the conditions of organic unity with one exception—racial unity' (Lloyd George 1938, pp. 964–5).

He used such words and sentiments as 'race', 'inferior', 'martyrdom'. His reasoning took portentous and self-defeating turns: '[T]he consequence would be the transfer of national hegemony to races which to the present day, still stand on a lower level of civilisation.' He further elaborated on this 'transfer of hegemony to an inferior civilisation . . . to a race which . . . stands on an inferior cultural level'. This did not cut ice with the participants of the Peace Conference, since it was well known that, in the words of Lloyd George, 'the Magyar and German majority . . . were responsible for the illiteracy of the Slavonic population' (Lloyd George 1938, p. 966).

The rage against what was considered the injustice of the peace treaty altogether blinded not only Apponyi but most of the country to the extent that the existing possibility of significantly softening the terms was never explored. 'Had he devoted his criticism to these areas [the border areas where Magyars were in a majority], he had at his disposal material which would have enabled him to make a powerful and, as regards some districts, an irresistible appeal for redress on behalf of his fellow-countrymen' (Lloyd George 1938, p. 967).[9]

The tone was set for thunderous patriotic slogans for decades to come. Hungarians were always given to a kind of patriotic sorrow. It was so important a part of Hungarian *Weltanschauung*, that a special word, *'honfibú'* (the patriot's sorrow), was created for it. Now, faced with serious blows to their self-identity, they responded belligerently. The quest for a revision of Trianon became the most urgent and important issue of Hungarian politics, culture and even everyday life. For eighteen years the flags were flying half-mast. Hungary was in mourning.[10]

Post-Trianon Hungary

In a daze, the country settled down to the rule of an ultra-conservative, blinkered regime, with Horthy at the helm. The liberal–conservative Vienna group consolidated its ruling position, relying on and integrating the Szeged men, although once they felt that Hungary was 'saved', the more conservative politicians pre-ferred to return to parliamentary authoritarianism, and rule via drastic legislation, a strong police force and efficient civil servants.[11]

Hungary entered the 1930s, as did the rest of the world, in the clutches of economic recession. The collapse of agricultural prices hit Hungary severely, as agriculture had provided its main export item. Hungary, primarily an agrarian country, rested on the basis of archaic *latifundia*. Out of four and a half million people engaged in agriculture, more than two-thirds were landless agrarian proletariat (Nagy-Talavera 1970, p. 60). The semi-feudal structure made the Great Depression even harsher on the peasantry. Their lives were appalling. While Budapest was part of twentieth-century Europe in glitter and in culture, in the provinces bodily punishment was still legal, accepted and widely used, administered mostly by sticks and sometimes by slapping. Women were the prey of the landlord. Hunger and hopelessness were an integral part of everyday life. The celebrated case of the 'arsenic women' who, in their misery and dark superstition, systematically poisoned their husbands, took place in the middle Tisza region. Maybe not so coincidentally, this was also the area where a fascist movement first attracted popular support in 1931 (Nagy-Talavera 1970, p. 108).

Poverty stricken (and politically immature) peasantry and the masses of unemployed made Hungary become known as the 'nation of three million beggars'. Unemployment passed the 200 000 level, about one-third of the size of the industrial labour force (Berend 1985, pp. 130, 191). The petty bourgeoisie, the stratum most susceptible to fascism, joined the ranks of former public servants, who had already lost their jobs when the Succession States (the new states created after World War I: Czechoslovakia, Yugoslavia and Romania) swiftly dismissed and even expelled a good many of them. Traditionally, administration was the turf of the Hungarian gentry. It was thoroughly nepotistic and meant long-term employment security, guaranteed promotion through seniority, was well paid and was considered gentlemanly.[12] In the decades of the Dual Monarchy, the impoverished gentry found economic haven in the public sector, while the freshly emancipated Jews entered the intellectual fields, engaged in commerce and thus embarked on the industrialisation of the economy. After Trianon, when the suddenly unemployed public servants were eager for the liberal jobs, they found them filled overwhelmingly with Jews.[13]

The semi-feudal structure of agriculture infused the social structure and the development of capitalism with its provincialism.[14] Even anti-modernity in Hungary stemmed more from provincialism than from disenchantment. The backwardness of the semi-feudal social structure was reflected in the political system which in many ways resembled that of Great Britain in the eighteenth and early nineteenth centuries (Royal Institute 1993, p. 57). Although the workers' movement was strong in Hungary before World War I, after 1918–19 the Communists and the Social Democrats were discredited. As far as social issues were concerned, disenchanted Hungarian intellectuals were looking for a 'third' or 'Hungarian way'. What was behind this fuzzy articulation was the fear of Communism and the disdain of Western democracy. The re-establishment of the open ballot in 1922 resulted in the return of a negligible working class and peasant opposition. While the Communist party was illegal all through the Horthy era, the Social Democrats were allowed reasonable freedom—but not in the rural areas. The reason for this was that the government feared the proletariat less than the three million serfs.

The rationale for foreign and internal policies in the Horthy years was determined by the tunnel-vision already symptomatic in the 1920s. The source of all problems, economic and social, was simply put down to two causes: the Entente powers were blamed for all the outside ills and the Jews for internal problems. Accordingly, the foreign policy pursued was alliance with Germany and Italy on geo-strategical lines; and *irredenta* (border-revisionist) and antisemitic propaganda and policies were cultivated. This further opened the way to fascist influence.

Coinciding with *Nazionalsozialistische Deutsche Arbeiter Partei* (NSDAP or National Socialist German Workers' Party) electoral victories, Gömbös became prime minister in 1932. An ardent admirer of Hitler, he was the first head of government to visit Germany after Hitler became chancellor. The two countries promptly signed an economic agreement, the essence of which was Hungarian agricultural export to Germany and import of German goods needed for rearmament and modernisation. Hungary depended on Germany for technical and industrial supplies and over the years the economic tie strengthened considerably, to include— amongst other things—raw materials as well. There was also a rapid increase of German investment capital (Braham 1981, p. 54). With the support of Germany, by the late 1930s Hungary was engaged in a massive rearmament program. The economic relationship was accompanied by the penetration of many Nazi-sponsored organisations. Propaganda was disseminated to the Schwabian minority and, just as importantly, to Hungarians, who were susceptible through the Germanophile strands in Hungarian culture.[15] During the years of his premiership Gömbös substantively modified the balance of power towards Germany. By the mid-1930s the various fascist factions were exerting more and more influence. This was not solely due to the good offices of Gömbös, who utilised his premiership, although it was a major factor. It also reflected the increasing responsiveness to fascist ideas of a society in moral decline, impressed by the Nazi and fascist victories.

The radicalisation of the army towards the right was an ominous phenomenon. Officers of the national army and the Ludovika military academy were becoming intensely indoctrinated by extremist political ideology. Many were members of secret societies. The participation of military personnel in civil administration started in the days of Gömbös. The army was also becoming involved in the training of students at secondary schools and universities. As the army was becoming increasingly fanatical, it started to propagate national-socialist solutions to both internal and external politics. The main aims were military–political cooperation with Germany and rearmament; these were peppered with some racist and social reforms.[16] The government gave in to army pressure and announced a program of massive rearmament. These measures were developed further as the vociferousness of the fascist parties grew.

While ultra-right opposition to the Horthy government strengthened, irredentist foreign policy, aimed at border revision, propelled the Horthy regime further and further to the right. The conservative ruling élite was supported by the majority of the middle classes and the landed gentry. The overall movement towards the right was stalled from time to time by the short-lived success of conservative moderate groups (Berend 1985, p. 38). Moderate agrarian and electoral reforms were introduced during the 1930s along semi-liberal lines. Apart from occasionally outlawing some of the right-radical parties and sometimes arresting their more offensive leaders, constitutional safeguards were strengthened to try to curtail the preponderance of extreme right elements in parliament.[17] However, against the backdrop of strengthening Nazi-style parties and more and more racist antisemitism, the temporary fortunes of moderates and the more radical right wing notwithstanding, Hungarian foreign and internal policies were shifting to the right.

Based on the two different strands of the White Terror, the Szeged and the Vienna group, two basic right-wing factions developed. The Szeged men were—as indeed they had been from the very beginning—given to radicalism in their right-wing ideology, often incorporating the rhetoric of social change. Their ideal was the corporate, totalitarian state (Mussolini's Italy), and their idea of social revolution always included the elimination of Jews from national life and, to varying degrees, some redistribution of wealth. The mass-base of the Szeged men was organised in the many secret and semi-clandestine associations and paramilitary organisations. The Vienna group, which constituted the moderate right, was closer to pre-war conservativism. They stood for parliamentarism and the legal ideal of the *Rechtsstaat* system, the functional equivalent of the rule of law, in which state and bureaucracy traditionally play a dominant role, and law and legislation were used as symbolic means.[18] Consequently, till March 1944, the 'Jewish question' in Hungary was handled within the legal framework of the *Rechtsstaat*.

The aristocrat- and gentry-dominated anti-revolutionaries were against any kind of reform and viewed the radical right-wingers with gentlemanly distaste and distrust. It was not their ideals, only their radicalism which was deplored.[19] István Bethlen, the leader of the Vienna group and prime minister for eleven inter-war years, to whose name the consolidation era is linked, was representative of the moderates. Writing about Gömbös, the prime minister under whose guidance Hungary became firmly aligned to Nazi Germany, Bethlen wrote in his memoirs:

> Gömbös was an antisemite deep in his heart, but not any more antisemitic than any other *good Hungarian* who, as a reaction to the Mihály Károlyi and Béla Kún times, came to loathe the behaviour demonstrated by a large segment of Hungarian Jews. (Bethlen 1988, p. 128) [*emphasis added*]

The moderates and the radicals shared the same basic anti-Jewish, anti-Communist and nationalist fervour. But within each camp there were many variations. Some radicals were anti-German, others in the moderate camp were committed to the Axis, at least in the inter-war years: 'Some in the counter-revolutionary camp abhorred Hitler, admired the British, and defended the capitalist system: others called themselves followers of Hitler and mobilised workers and day labourers in vast strike movements' (Deak 1985, p. 49).

This description also fits Horthy himself at various periods. From the White Terror days he was the ideal leader for both groups. In the inter-war years his policies became more and more controversial. He was an antisemite and a fanatical anti-Communist, who, although not participating in actual murders and brutalities, nevertheless condoned them. However, he was also a product of the Monarchy, an admiral of the Monarchy's navy. He also had some grudging admiration for the British and sincerely distrusted Hitler and the Nazi mob. Teleki, prime minister between 1939 and 1941, was not only anti-German but anti-Nazi, yet espoused racism:

> You can in eight or nine cases out of ten recognise the Jew. This proves that they form what we call a race. But the biological race and the blood is not so important. What is important is much more the ideological age-old seclusion, their own code of moral and the whole ideology and behaviour in all forms and actions of life which are thoroughly different from those of all the European peoples. (Katzburg 1985, p. 7)

The government's widely popular remedy for unemployment (apart from organised charity) was the promise of containment of what was conceived as Jewish economic dominance. For the unemployed *lumpenproletariat* and the petty bourgeoisie—in other words the overwhelming majority of the middle class—anti-Jewish legislation promised easy access not only to jobs but to personal economic advancement. For the ruling class this racial panacea served as a popularly accepted subterfuge to avoid real reforms. Views which held that the Jews were responsible for all poverty, even the deterioration of the peasantry, were widespread: 'A widespread and ever-growing social opinion made the Jews in general responsible for palpable Hungarian social ills which had, in fact, been caused by Hungarian capitalism' (Feher 1980, p. 12).

The inter-war and even the war years were characterised by the fight between the radicals and moderates, during which one or the other faction gained power and formed government. The moderates' overwhelming fear of hooliganism, of the mob and of social change set the measure for how far they were prepared to go on the scale that went from economic and social marginalisation of Jews, to deportation.

The rise of the extreme right

The rise of fascism was not solely an indigenous development in Hungary. There was considerable German propaganda coming through political, economic and ideological channels. As argued earlier, the Horthy regime functioned as a pluralistic system of competing groups, which, while forming an uneasy coalition, struggled against each other. The Szeged men, the officers of the special squads, the perpetrators of the White Terror, were either part of the governing political élite, or members of the burgeoning parties and societies, or, as in the case of Gömbös, both.

While Hitler did away with the parliament altogether with the Enabling Law and the *Gleichschaltung* (the 'coordination' of the Reich), the Hungarian extreme right had to accommodate the strict authoritarian rule of the parliament. Consequently a considerable part of the radical right existed in clandestine forms. The extreme-right radical parties and societies took advantage of the ambivalence of the conservative Government party. The coexistence of numerous fascist organisations and policies, leaders and diverse theories, sometimes simply copying Nazism or fascism, fighting and competing with each other, constituted an important characteristic of the Horthy era. Corresponding to the patriotic groups in Bavaria, there were the over 10 000 secret and semi-secret associations during the early 1920s (Braham 1981, p. 21). These political organisations had structural characteristics that were sometimes simply inherited from the traditional monarchical bureaucracy, and mostly they were still a far cry from the Hitlerite forms. The operation of secret societies and the conspiratorial character of early Nazism were an integral part of both the White Terror and the constitutional protofascism of the Horthy era. The various groups of the counter-revolutionary movement shared common organisations. The secret societies and patriotic association were more or less loyal to Horthy in the years to come.

The oldest and one of the most ferocious of these organisations was the Hungarian Association for National Defense known as 'MOVE'.[20] Its president was Gömbös, who had, to some extent, united the various national socialist currents in Hungary. During the Bethlen years he wrote pamphlets on international Jewry and founded the new Party of Racial Defense. He forged the social program of the radical right from agrarianism and the *Keresztény Kurzus* (Christian Course), fused with ultra-chauvinistic nationalism and rabid antisemitism. Gömbös made good use of the proliferating paramilitary organisations. After Gömbös' death in 1936, as MOVE was disarmed and paralysed, the organisational centre of rightist dynamism shifted to Szálasi and the Arrowcross party.

Szálasi was a former army officer. He believed he had a mission to save Hungary, and by emphasising the 'proletarian' character of his movement, he won the support of the poorer classes. A devout Catholic, he showed concern about the welfare of the dispossessed lower classes although his ruthlessness and violence, even in methods of propaganda, went beyond the more irredentist aims of the other parties. Szálasi's dream was a 'Danubian Carpathian Great Fatherland' and he ranted about 'Turanian Christianity'.[21] The Arrowcross party was the only fascist movement with large mass-support. It was most widespread amongst the petty bourgeoisie, lower middle classes and the working class (Berend 1985, p. 39). It was the largest opposition party, winning 25 per cent of the votes in 1939. It infiltrated the army and also had a high proportion of convicted criminals, even if convictions for political offences are discounted.[22] The Arrowcross party, however, was not as successful amongst the peasantry, even though most of the social discontent came from their ranks.

Officially condoned antisemitism, as one of the fundamental

psychological pillars of frustrated, revenge-oriented nationalism, had a tremendous appeal to students and to clerks, to officers and to workers, to grocers and to gentry. It led them to join the proliferating ultra-right parties. The inconsistencies and fuzziness of the right-wing ideologies allowed different strata to identify with them. There were many variations on the theme to choose from. There were fascist organisations which had anti-German tendencies, like the Order of the Brave, established in 1920 by Horthy, which was loyal to him.

The various forms of hatred these societies indulged in galvanised an otherwise apathetic society—giving a feeling of energy, a sense of purpose and of importance. Anti-liberalism, another classical symptom of fascism, was fuelled in Hungary partly by the hatred of the Entente powers and partly by the fear of Communism. As in Germany, this also increased the susceptibility of the masses. The fascists succeeded more and more in making a favourable impression on the gentry. Unmitigated chauvinism blinded those who otherwise would have been troubled by signs of barbarism. The lenient, somewhat absent-minded antisemitism of Horthy and the upper classes generated an atmosphere in which it was not such a huge step to move towards active, Nazi-style Jew-hatred and open fascism.

The Christian national principle

The ideological platform of the Horthy regime was the Christian national principle. Bethlen's Christian National party, apart from the ideals stated in its name, also propagated the rejection of communism, socialism and pacifism. The Christian national principle, the Szeged idea, the Christian Course—a fuzzy socio-political program which combined ultra-chauvinistic religious nationalism with rabid antisemitism—Hungarism (Nazi-style movement) and others were variations on a theme. They used antisemitism, nationalism, irredentism and Christianity as threads to weave their own patterns, varied by policies and the level of brutality they found justifiable.

The nature of Christianity, nationalism and antisemitism all changed in the Horthy era. Although open brutality and pogroms were gone with the White Terror, the 'gentlemanly' antisemitism of the Liberal Era gave way to radical antisemitism. With the organic concept of nation, the nature of nationalism also changed. The liberal and rather tolerant nationalism which characterised the period of Jewish emancipation was all but defunct. Following the collapse of the Monarchy, two basic trends of nationalism were discernible. The authoritarian conservative trend, articulated by historian Gyula Szekfü, held the basic tenets that:

a liberalism is alien to Hungarians;
b liberalism caused the nationalities' and the Jewish 'problems'; and
c it is imperative to maintain and cultivate Catholic tradition.

The other trend, radical anti-liberalism, had as its figurehead a writer, Dezső Szabó, who preached the democracy of races and immersed the movement in nationalist pessimism and romanticism. Instead of nation–state, the organic concept of ethnic–national Hungary developed. This concept of the organic nation (as opposed to the citizen of the state) moved nationalism into the realm of mystical pseudo-biology. Great emphasis was placed on the attributes of authentic, real Hungarians. As Mosse pointed out, the belief in the existence of a 'national character' was present from the beginning of modern nationhood (Mosse 1993, p. 122). The construction of the national stereotype included the construction of the 'other', the counter-image as the opposite. The national stereotype stood for everything true, good and noble, and reflected and personalised the character of the nation. In all constructions of a national character the distinction between insider and outsider was sharply drawn. Antisemitic literature cast the Jews as the very opposite of national ideals as reflected in the stereotype of national, character (Mosse 1993, p. 122). The Jews, measured against the ideals represented by the nation, were not only 'the other' and 'the alien', but the antithesis and corruption of all that was good and noble in the nation.

This counter-image, the stereotype of the Jew, was essential to the image of nationalism. The evolution of nationalism toward a full-blown civic religion had its origins in the needs of the times, but it was sharpened and further defined as it faced real and putative enemies. All these enemies—Jews, Bolsheviks and socialists (called in Germany 'scoundrels without a fatherland')—were seen as possessing identical morals, manners and looks, directly opposed to the national stereotype (Mosse 1993, p. 123).

As nationalism bloated into a civic religion, Christianity remained an active element. It also proved to be the conduit through which Jews could be perceived as the evil 'other'. According to Mosse, the connection between nationalism and Christianity was prominent at the start of modern nationalism and then again during World War I (Mosse 1993, p. 123). In World War I, the link between nationalism and Christianity became central to both. World War I was a climax in the evolution of modern nationalism. In a quest for totality, nationalism sought to coopt Christianity (Mosse 1993, p. 124).[23]

The destructive influence of Jews was a well-established notion of Hungarian social and political culture in the last years of the Monarchy.[24] In the 1920s, the Association of Awakening Magyars explained the imperative of defending Christianity:

> Antisemitism in Hungary means the protection of Christianity against progressing Judaism and does not aim only at local circumstances, sad as they may be—but embraces the interests of all Christendom in every part of Europe and of the world where Christian civilisation is or should be established. Therefore Hungary claims the aid of every Christian people of whatever nationality, to help her in the mutually vital struggle against Judaism. (Katzburg 1985, p. 9)

As Christianity, nationalism and antisemitism fused, Jewish–Gentile relations were re-articulated as Jews versus Christian Hungarians. The effect of this articulation was threefold. Firstly, it presented Jews as the enemy. Secondly, it allowed earlier religious prejudices to combine with sentiments of nationalism; and, thirdly, it formulated the context and a visible, identifiable focus for social and economical grievances of not only the middle classes (mostly the *déclassé* gentry) but also the lower middle classes and workers.

It was through the triple conduit of Christianity, nationalism and antisemitism that the right radicalism of the Hungarian middle classes was formulated and through which the 'Jewish question' was to be solved. These were the main ideals echoing through the Horthy years, governing foreign and internal politics, economic planning, penetrating cultural life, permeating entertainment and jokes, manifest in novels, newspapers and plays. These ideals were more than respectable; they became socio-political *bona mores*.

'Populists' and 'urbanists'

Nineteenth-century poets and writers in Hungary regarded themselves as being on a patriotic mission to serve the nation and to foster patriotism. Concurrently with ascendant anti-liberalism, this mission grew to include the fight against cosmopolitanism and foreign decadence. In the Horthy era these latter aspects became prevalent as the cultural expression of the Christian–national principle.

The conflict between tradition and modernism unfolded in the 1930s as a controversy which split Hungarian literary life into two: 'populists' (*népiesek*) and 'urbanists'. Liberal intellectuals, who were inspired by the development of Western democratic political institutions, were dubbed 'urbanists'. Their ideals were political emancipation, universal and secret franchise, right of assembly, trade unions, etc. The urbanists were essentially the liberals, but as the word 'liberal' was a code-name for Jewish, along with 'cosmopolitan', 'urbanist' became one of the synonyms for Jewish.

Populism was not a specifically Hungarian movement. Populism itself as a political movement was prevalent in countries where the conflict between tradition and modernisation remained largely unresolved. Where the forces of modernity were weaker than rigid social structures and hierarchy, populism became a reaction against capitalism. Populism is essentially anti-modernity, anti-liberal and generally antisemitic. Hungarian populism was not related in any way to the so-called populist trend in French literature. Reactionary as it was, the movement can be seen as a Hungarian variety of the *Völkisch* movement.

Populism assumed special relevance in Hungary, where modernity was developing within persisting, tenaciously maintained feudal structures. In Hungary, populism became a movement, a reaction, a response to the forces and processes of modernity. It was instrumental in the creation and maintenance of an anti-modern, anti-liberal and antisemitic atmosphere. Populist anti-capitalism was directed against 'foreign' or 'alien' capitalism, that is Jewish, or Jewish-controlled capitalism, very much as it was presented by Nazi ideology. So, when they were talking about the necessity of developing a Hungarian Christian middle class (*Magyar keresztény középosztály*), which everybody understood as emphatically non-Jewish, the stress was not on social change or social justice, but on antisemitism. The populists sought social emancipation, idealised the peasantry and embraced nationalism. The leitmotif was 'back to the land'. The populists romanticised and idealised peasantry as the keepers of nationhood and culture. Populism in Hungary had an increasingly antisemitic character and gave literary impetus and respectability to the racist principle. As the writers and poets of early nineteenth-century nationalism engaged in linguistic Magyarisation, now a racial Magyarisation, in the form of some fuzzy ethnic cleansing, was propagated. Not surprisingly, assimilation stayed an issue.

The largest and loudest trend within populism was characterised by those writers whose real sympathies lay with the Nazis (Lőrinc Szabó, János Kodolányi, Géza Feja, József Erdélyi). This group represented the direction of the movement with Nazi sympathies or even commitment to Nazism. The leader of the populist *(népies)* writers was Dezső Szabó. The populist approach was favoured by the Christian middle class, who associated urbanist liberalism with the Jewish intelligentsia of Budapest.

Just as not all urbanists were Jewish or pro-Jewish, the populist writers cannot be all branded antisemites. Within the populist movement there were writers who were only on the peripheries of the movement, whose affiliation to it came from their rural allegiances, but who nevertheless saw the answer to the peasants (and society's) plight within the ideals of liberalism. Bibó, for instance, believed in the liberation of peasantry in the Western sense. It was Bibó's understanding of social justice, which in Horthy's Hungary was inextricably connected to the problem of peasantry and of land-reform, that led him to the fold of the populist writers. Bibó's affiliation with the populists was primarily through their opposition to authority, in particular the authority of the reactionary Horthy regime. He did not share the populists' romantic anti-capitalist irrationalism, which made most of these writers so susceptible to antisemitism.

There were quite a few for whom the populist movement served as a front for their Communist sympathies. They later became leading figures of the 1950s and 1960s literary life (József Darvas, Péter Veres).

The 'urbanists', as they were called by the populists, represented the influence of Western democracies and cosmopolitan liberalism, concepts easily identifiable as Jewish values. Indeed many of the urbanist writers were Jewish. The urbanist–populist fight was more than an ideological or political dispute amongst the literati. It also split the Hungarian intelligentsia into supporters of liberal cosmopolitans—i.e. Jews—and supporters of Christian Hungarians and nationalist, organic Hungarian culture—i.e. antisemites. After the war, antisemitism was kept alive, albeit in a covert and subdued form within *népies* (folkish in the sense of *Völkisch*) circles and this division resurfaced in the years of Communism.

A radical historian and a racist writer

Since the end of the eighteenth century, the question of social reform was intertwined with literature and language. Poets and writers used literature to express their political views and social theories. In the wake of the revolution two works exerted tremendous influence. One was by the historian, Gyula Szekfü, and the other was Dezső Szabó's sociological novel, *Az elsodort falu* (Swept Away Village). Although the two works differed, both argued the intellectual preponderance of Jews: Szekfü discussing their role in the press, Szabó in the Budapest theatres. Szekfü's condemnation of capitalism and of liberalism, of Jews and the 'corrupt city' had its parallel in the racial mysticism of the eccentric Dezső Szabó. His glorification of Magyar racial purity was articulated in the creation of a peasant mythology. Szabó directly applied *Völkisch* concepts when he passionately attacked the 'city' as the root of all evil, and condemned foreigners (that is Germans and Jews), as the source of corruption in the simple but noble righteousness of Hungarian agrarian society. A decade later his ideas gave rise to a large-scale movement. In the mid-1930s, the radical social promises of the Gömbös government were reverberating, particularly in agrarian circles. For the first time in Hungary, authentic peasant writers—intellectuals—emerged. Gyula Illyés, one of these populist peasant-writers, was quoted as saying to Gömbös that they were united by a common goal, the elimination of the aristocracy and the clergy (Glatz 1989, p. xviii). Dezső Szabó was seen by these writers as their master.

Szekfü had a huge impact on Hungarian thinking with his treatise *Három Nemzedék* (Three Generations).[25] He wrote and published the book in 1920, at the time when Hungarian society was in a state of national shock caused by the collapse of the empire, revolution and the Treaty of Trianon. (The 'three generations' Szekfü refers to were the three generations of liberals in nineteenth-century Hungary.) It was such a success that the book sold out three times in quick succession. *Három Nemzedék* was a poignant product of the tide, which moved from emancipating and accommodating Jews, and from the 'benign' genteel antisemitism of the gentry (in other words from antisemitism as expressed by the individual), to the thoroughly modern radical antisemitism of the White Terror and the institutionalised state-ideology of the 'Christian Course'. It shifted from the private to the public domain. It was a seminal book, instrumental in the formulation, and, equally importantly, the dissemination of anti-liberalism and antisemitism. *Három Nemzedék* was one of the books that actively shaped political culture, that made vital ingredients of fascism not only acceptable but desirable and 'justified'.[26]

Analysing and describing its development in each 'generation' in the nineteenth century, Szekfű condemned liberalism as alien to Hungarian thinking and character, a foreign, Jewish machination that in fact led to the demise of Hungarian society. Charting the decline of the Hungarian 'historical' classes, Szekfű came to the conclusion that due to the misguided liberalism of three consecutive generations, Hungary was on the path of decline from 1867 onwards. Szekfű analysed Széchenyi, the 'greatest Hungarian', at length. Széchenyi's understanding of nation and state as an organism, together with his 'mission' of 'leading his nation to real Christian life', served as a ready model for Szekfű. 'Széchenyi is the true political romantic, who construed a never before seen and perfect structure from the basic tenets of romanticism: nationality, Christian morality, individual perfection and individual work' (Szekfű 1989, p. 53).

Szekfű describes early Hungarian liberalism as irrational:

> In the 40s [i.e. 1840s], Hungarian liberalism was in fact *radicalism*, not in a European, but in a specifically Hungarian way . . . Hungarian radicalism never demanded *suffrage universal* and *plebiscite* . . . Radicalism here was not expressed in principles, but in national characteristics, constitutional programs. All in all, let's admit it—we can't deny it—it was expressed in emotions, forms and moods. With us, radicalism was simply the projection of national passions onto politics, and as such, it was despotically prevailing without rivals. (Szekfű 1989, p. 133)[27]

Presenting the principle of equality in accusatory terms, Szekfű blamed nineteenth-century liberalism, because by 'denying all religious differences, [it] wanted to make all men equal, and together with the doctrine of free trade, opened a never-hoped for perspective for Jewry, the *par excellence* merchant class' (Szekfű 1989, p. 155).

Szekfű condemned Kossuth (another radical revolutionary leader) as well: 'Even though Kossuth talked of the "Jewish scum from Maramaros" [unassimilated religious Jews living in poverty], other than that, he did not admit to any difference between the immigrant from Galicia and the Hungarian' (Szekfü 1989, p. 158). And that lack of distinction between Hungarians and Jews led liberal thinking 'astray', because 'only seeing religion in Jewry, not the race, [it] did everything for emancipation' (Szekfü 1989, p. 159).

A large segment of the book is directly about the 'Jewish question'. Szekfü questioned the sincerity of Hungarian Jewish assimilation. Szekfü viewed assimilation as a one-way movement, in the direction of the assimilant, the Jews. *Harom Nemzedek* provided a justification of antisemitism using socio-historical reasoning. Pointing out the relationship between liberalism and capitalism, Szekfü saw that there was no Hungarian middle class to fill the role of economic modernisation. In Hungary especially, Szekfü surmised, capitalism and Jewry were inseparably linked:

> The next question, which was to determine the life of the third generation [of liberals], was whether foreigners should be permitted to become rulers on the richness of Hungarian soils' economy and after gaining influence on the material side to allow them to influence Hungarian culture as well? (Szekfü 1989, p. 247)

Here Szekfü quoted Sombart's statistics, according to which: 'even where Jews are admittedly poor, they are still six times richer than Christians. Jews pay 30 per cent of the totality of taxes in Berlin' (Szekfü 1989, p. 247).

The main problem, he wrote, was that generations of liberals treated Jews not as a race, but as a religion. Thus, in the second generation Jews took over the economy and in the third generation of liberal rule they gained access to Hungarian culture (Szekfü 1989, pp. 236–49). 'In the second, capitalistic stage, the profits of industrial, commercial and financial enterprises, banks almost exclusively enriched Jewry only. Now, in the third generation . . . after the financial, the spiritual leadership also falls into the lap of Jewry' (Szekfü 1989, p. 328).

Szekfü was not softened by the Jewish contribution to Hungarian cultural life. In fact, this contribution served as added accusation. Rich Jews financed the arts and press to serve Jewish purposes. Liberalism was 'Jewish ideology', and it was to be feared (Szekfü 1989, p. 336). With this accusation he completed the drawing of the 'evil' circle of liberalism, capitalism and the Jewish threat to culture. Since this 'low culture, they inherited from their forefathers', with its 'alien morality', had invaded Hungary, Austria and Germany, postulated Szekfü, small wonder that these three countries had a Jewish problem (Szekfü 1989, pp. 329–30). The mistake had to be rectified. To protect good Hungarian Christians, Jews had to be contained and liberalism denounced. The liberal illusion provided:

> the emotional basis on which we only demanded superficial, only external but quick transformation from the immigrants. We avoided looking into their soul. We were satisfied with the externalities of clothing and speech, and thus we fell prey to the gravest mistake, from which Széchenyi in mortal fear, wringing his hands tried to save us: we mistook nationality for language, Hungarianness with Hungarian chatter, the immortal soul with the transient, deceptive exterior. (Szekfü 1989, p. 331)

The concepts of racially threatened culture, liberalism as a criminal folly, and anti-capitalism, the alien as the exposed enemy, all combined to create powerful images. All merged into one. Jews were the liberals, the capitalists, the corrupters of culture. Szekfü condemned the Jewish habit of Magyarising their names, as a result of which 'the Galician alien hardly arriving to Hungarian soil, immediately shedding their most obvious distinctive feature, forever blends into the Hungarian mass' (Szekfü 1989, p. 332).

This notion of losing distinctive features and blending in sharply contradicts the racist logic and accusation of non-assimilation. If Jews blend into the Hungarian nation, it has to be their politics and their culture that makes them alien. Jews are not Hungarians, liberalism is un-Hungarian, *ergo* Jews are liberals and non-Hungarians.

Both Szekfü's and Szabó's earlier stance was modified in the late 1930s. Szekfü wrote a segment in *Trianonóta* (Since Trianon), in which he criticised the 'neobaroque edifice' of Hungarian society. He listed five areas of tension, 'antinomes': the agrarian problem, the denominational question, capitalism and Jewry, the generational problem (in which he addressed the influence of Szabó) and the problem of ethnic Hungarians in the Succession States. In this book, written in 1934, regarding Jews he recommended partly, that it would be in the interest of Jewry to let Hungarians (that is, Christians) have a larger share in every level of 'capitalist mode of production'; and, reviving Istóczy's solution, that Jews who migrated after the war should join the Zionist movement and emigrate to Palestine. These two measures would 'ease the relationship between the sincerely Magyarised, accultured Jewry and Hungarians within the Christian state' (Szekfü 1989, pp. 434–44). In 1938, Szabó wrote the essay, 'The criticism of anti-Judaism'. In this he argued that irredentism and the Jewish problem were expressions of German influence in Hungary. Szabó, who was strongly anti-German, re-emphasised all his anti-Jewish diatribes but warned that the German threat was more 'deadly'. He was against the anti-Jewish laws, because these laws had no social significance (Juhász, F. 1985, p. 55). In spite of the ideological adjustments made by both Szekfü and Szabó, their earlier notions retained their force with the general public. Antisemitism and anti-liberalism were too entrenched and pervasive, society and state were too much in unison to significantly vary or modify existing beliefs. These beliefs were reinforced by the ascendant ideology, fascism.

Fascism

The definition of fascism and its interpretations are one of the complexities of the social sciences. The word denotes both a political movement in general and Mussolini's political regime in Italy. Zeev Sternhell's analysis of fascist ideology, first in his seminal essay in Laqueur's *Fascism: A Readers Guide* (1976) and recently, in a book (Sternhell 1994), omits Nazism, because, Sternhell argues, Nazism was not a mere variant of fascism. Biological determinism and the degree of extremism made it a radically different movement. Since fascism in power is already 'corrupted' by political exigencies, Sternhell analyses fascism in its purest form: its origins. The growth of fascism has to be understood in the prevailing intellectual, moral and cultural context at the end of the nineteenth century, in the intellectual crisis of the 1890s. World War I and its consequences brought on the birth of fascism as a political movement, but its ideological roots were already fully formed before the war. Sternhell views fascism as an independent cultural and political phenomenon, not a mere reaction. Sternhell articulates his view that fascism is first and foremost an ideology. This view has two implications: firstly, that the origins are more important than the later developments and secondly, that the thinkers are more 'authentically' fascist than the doers (Paxton 1994, p. 51). Thus Sternhell concentrates on the cultural beginnings of fascism and identifies the merging of nationalism and revolutionary syndicalism as the main intellectual 'ingredients' that created fascism: 'For inasmuch as they were opposed to liberal democracy and to bourgeois society, syndicalists and nationalists were of one mind' (Sternhell 1976, p. 330).

Francis Carsten identifies the basic elements of fascist ideology as national imperialism, étatism, populist socialism, racism, backward looking romantic nationalism and corporativism (Carsten 1988, pp. 429–30). Viewing fascism together with its cultural and ideological roots *and* as a movement in action (both as striving for power and as a regime, with the obvious differences), it is clear that the main ingredients of fascist ideology are nationalism, anti-liberalism, antisemitism and brutal, terrorist authoritarianism. Analysing the fibre of nationalist ideology beyond socialism and nationalism, Sternhell examines the importance of anti-liberalism, anti-Communism and élitism in the building of the 'new civilisation' and totalitarianism. Others do not separate fascism and Nazism in trying to ascertain the most important ingredients of fascist ideology. Fritz Stern (1961) identifies anti-liberalism as the single most important aspect of both fascism and Nazism. George Mosse (1993) stresses the importance of *Völkisch* ideology, the particular German populist romantic nationalism, as the springboard for Nazi ideology.

There is further argument concerning the social base of fascism. There are two basic interpretations. One puts the emphasis on the middle classes, the other emphasises the fact that the followers of fascism came from all sections of society (Carsten 1988, pp. 415–20). There is a consensus concerning the importance of conservative allies. Not only was fascism a phenomenon of the right, essentially reactionary in character, but none of the fascist and Nazi movements could have come to power or would have survived without the political right.[28] At the same time the essential distinction has to be made between fascism and conservatism and fascism and reaction.[29] As Carsten warns: 'To equate the terms "reactionary" and "fascist" . . . is to misunderstand the nature of fascism' (Carsten 1988, p. 431).

Fascism in Hungary

Applying the above criteria and analyses to post-Trianon Hungary, certain specificities and generalities emerge. The main ingredients of the post-Trianon political culture were nationalism, anti-liberalism, anti-Communism, Christianity and antisemitism. Any of these, especially when coupled with another, provided a conduit through which various political factions could meet and strengthen each other or, often, compete with each other. Indeed, the various fascist associations and political parties frequently fought one another. All the above ingredients were present in the Szeged idea and in the Christian Course. How did these trends constitute fascism? Excluding Christianity, the above were all hallmarks of classic fascism (although Romanian fascism, especially of the Iron Guard and of the Legion of the Archangel, and in Slovakia, the fascism of Hlinka and Tiso, all contained fervent Christianity). A distinction, then, has to be made, firstly on the level of extremism, because the degree of extremism makes for a radically different movement (Sternhell 1994, p. 316). Secondly, further distinction has to be made between the movements on the basis of their revolutionary aspect, which was only present in some of these movements. Taking all this into consideration, the Horthy era was essentially an era of protofascism: while some governments (e.g. Bethlen's, Kállay's) were reactionary but not fascist, others, especially those of Gömbös, Imrédy and Darányi, were clearly close to Nazism and fascism. Amongst the proliferating organisations, all varieties of fascism and Nazism could be found, with the underlying cultural and political paradigm that of fascism.

Of these characteristics not only nationalism but antisemitism also had a particularly Hungarian character. It was rooted in the peculiarities and specificities of Hungarian history, society and culture, yet carried the characteristics of modern antisemitism. Christianity remained an important, vital part of right-wing ideology. In fact, 'Christian' came to mean not just non-Jewish, but anti-Jewish. Consequently not only the *ideological role* of antisemitism was different to that of Nazism, but also the *nature* of antisemitism. In comparison to Nazism, antisemitism was not the ideological heart of Hungarian fascism. Nationalism was. And it was through nationalism that Hungarian superiority *vis-à-vis* Jews was perceived, unlike Nazism which posited Aryan Germans *vis-à-vis* the rest of the world. Hungarian fascism was racist only inasmuch as it was influenced by Nazism. Racism was not really indigenous. The legacy of the Monarchy years still persisted, not only within the fossilised feudal structures and value-systems, but also in the perception and articulation of social problems and ideologies. Hungarian fascists, such as Gömbös or Szálasi, used Nazi, racist terminology, but the understanding of the Hungarian middle classes filtered this through Monarchy-nurtured perceptions.

Sternhell distinguishes between fascism in power and fascism in opposition. (His argument is that fascist regimes carried national characteristics more than movements.) Until the German occupation, fascism as a movement in Hungary was clearly in opposition, even though fascist ideology was pervasive. Even after the German occupation it could be argued that while Horthy was the head of state—that is, until the actual Arrowcross takeover in October 1944—fascist and Nazi politicians were tempered by Horthy. The factional fighting between the various indigenous Nazi and fascist parties also made that period ambivalent from the point of view of power. Sternhell makes a second distinction between the fundamental principles of the ideology and the operative adaptation of it (Sternhell 1976, p. 319).

Fascism in Hungary, in contrast to the much more homogeneous German Nazism, had three interlocking forms. The first, chronologically, a harbinger in essence, was the White Terror. It was followed by twenty years of ultra-conservative government with its constitutional protofascism, during the course of which the final and complete form, the many varieties of actual fascist and Nazi parties, emerged. These three strands of fascism had, however, considerably more than a chronological relationship. They overlapped and influenced each other, carried the seeds and elements of the other, and, even though at times they opposed one another and were in many ways in conflict, they also nurtured and facilitated one another (Ranki, V. 1990).

Istvan Deak points to the dichotomy of Hungarian fascism: it was at the same time a native and a foreign-inspired movement (Deak 1985, pp. 45–53). While constitutional protofascism was 'homegrown', in the 1920s there was a discernible influence of Italian fascism, especially corporatism. But the greatest influence was that of Nazism. In the confused atmosphere sustained by the ambivalence of the conservatives all through the Horthy era, people were drawn to right-radicalism. While Nazism drew on radical–social aspects, antisemitism and extreme nationalism, the underpinnings of all varieties of Hungarian right ideologies (Szeged idea, Christian Course and the radical fascist and Nazi-influenced parties and movements) were chauvinistic Hungarian nationalism and antisemitism, serving as a substitute social problem. The problems of Hungary were perceived as the loss of territory, which nationalist irredentism addressed, while the palpable social injustices and adversities of modernity were lumped under the heading of the 'Jewish question', with the accompanying, and thus justified, hatred of Jews, and the anti-Jewish legislation was to address that.

Hungarian racism had its own problems. Hungarians were not Aryans, not even honorary Aryans, as were the Japanese or the Arabs. The most popular notion of Hungarian superiority was manifest in Turanism, which 'preached the mythical kinship and historic mission of Turkic peoples (to which the Hungarians do not belong either)' (Deak 1985, p. 44). Turanism, then, was an ideology, a nationalism, complete with superiority of one and the inferiority and expendability of another, which already perpetrated genocide.[30]

Apart from the problem of Hungarians not being part of the Aryan race, there are further ambiguities of Hungarian fascism. Many Hungarian fascists were anti-German. There were also those who were supportive of Germany and Nazism, but viewed with disdain local Schwabians, who were ethnic Germans, and as such, Aryans, but still eastern peasants. Finally, according to Deak, religion and the person of Horthy were two more paradoxes of Hungarian fascism. Most Hungarian fascists were practising Christians, and in the Horthy years Hungarian nationalism itself became inseparable from Christianity. Yet national socialism was an exclusively secular religion, complete with pagan rituals and often vocal anti-religious attitudes. The prestige of the Regent was so great that it overshadowed that of Hitler. This was contrary to the demands of the '*Führer*-principle' (Deak 1985, pp. 44–5).

Ideological, historical, political and social developments inevitably led to the Holocaust in Hungary. Sucked into the black hole of fascism, Hungarian conservative politics became the casualty of the *Zeitgeist*.

Chapter four

The end of the assimilationist 'contract'

Following the collapse of the Monarchy, the position of Jews in Hungary changed dramatically and the historical and socio-political developments demonstrated that antisemitism was no longer a fringe issue. In this period, Hungarian society and political culture became openly antisemitic. As emancipation, or rather, the equality of Jews was increasingly questioned, Hungarian Jewish assimilation was increasingly queried, attacked and rejected by Hungarian society.

Bibó, in his seminal essay on Hungarian society and Jews, examined Jewish assimilation in its historical context. According to Bibó, the process of assimilation in the Golden Age was built on perilous foundations because instead of social integration, linguistic Magyarisation was demanded. This notion was similar to that expressed by Szekfü earlier, but Bibó's analysis went much deeper. According to him, assimilation was false and dishonest and Jews were deceived concerning the criteria of assimilation. The dishonesty was due to the self-delusion of Hungarian society. Both Hungarians and Jews viewed linguistic Magyarisation as a laudable nationalist and moral action. Jews believed that they were delivering what was expected from them. In post-Trianon Hungary the fallacy of this illusory and 'inadequate' assimilation was exposed and turned against the Jews (Bibó 1984, p. 249). Bibó's analysis is scrupulous and incisive, and explains why Hungarian Jews were so unprepared for the brutal antisemitism of 1919 and 1920. The false context of the Golden Age's assimilatory processes explains the suddenness of antisemitic flare-up and the headway political antisemitism made, but it has to be stressed that neither was the consequence of assimilation.

The emancipation of Central European Jewry was gradual and connected to assimilationist demands. Sometimes this connection was that the price of emancipation was assimilation, at other times (like in Hungary in the 'Golden Age'), that the prize for assimilation was emancipation.

Following the collapse of the Empire, this connection between assimilation and emancipation facilitated the change from 'genteel' antisemitism to murderous antisemitism in three ways. Firstly, the linkage of emancipation to a condition, or a set of conditions, carried a power imbalance. One party was dictating the terms, the other was accepting it. Thus the 'contract' was not negotiated and entered into by *equal* parties. Secondly, the judgment of success was reserved by the assimilator society. Thirdly, the criteria on which this judgment was based was arbitrary and changing. In the 'Golden Age', the criteria were linguistic assimilation and modernisation of Judaism.[1] Hungarian Jews tackled both conditions sincerely, and largely achieved, in some ways even over-achieved, them.

But the criteria, set arbitrarily in the first place, were changed just as arbitrarily. The success of Hungarian Jewish assimilation was questioned—but the underlying meaning was not an expectation of a different assimilation, or assimilation by different criteria (which also would have been unjust and unfair), but that Hungarian society did not accept Jews as Hungarians, or as equal. The compromise between gentry and Jews did not secure for the Jewish middle class the political power corresponding to their economic position. In fact, it implicitly excluded Jews from political power:

> In the age of nationalism only those had a chance of political leadership who were perceived as the legitimate representative of the nation. The guarantee of the political hegemony of the gentry was that the Jewish-origin bourgeoisie, assimilation notwithstanding, was not to be accepted as Hungarian, had to stay the alien, the Jew. (Kovacs 1992, p. 268)

Assimilation patterns in the Horthy era

Following the rapid assimilation of the Monarchy years, Hungarian Jews were confident in their status as integrated members of society. This very feature, the trust and the perception, the 'symbiotic' relationship of Hungarian Jews and Hungarians, was what eventually led to the horrible conclusion of the Holocaust in Hungary. This trust was developed during the Golden Age when it was based on reality. Every time the state was needed to protect Jews (against pogroms, or against the antisemitic incitement of Istóczy), the protection was provided. During the Golden Age the 'assimilationist social contract' was working. However, this situation changed dramatically in 1919 with the White Terror. The assimilationist social contract was abandoned by Hungarian society and, more importantly by the Hungarian state—but Jews still adhered to it. Hannah Arendt wrote of German Jews that their 'relationship to Germany is one of unrequited love' (Arendt 1968b, p. 184). It was based on self-alienation, self-surrender and Jewish national self-negation. Arendt's description is true of Hungarian Jews after the decline of the Monarchy. Hungarian Jews kept on insisting on the unfounded—in fact obviously refuted—belief that the assimilationist contract was still valid. Instead of rational analysis, which would have showed the precarious situation of the Jews within Hungarian society, an almost complete delusion influenced assimilation patterns of Hungarian Jews even well after the Holocaust, during the years of communism.

Viktor Karady, the sociologist who developed the concept of the 'assimilationist social contract', stressing the essential importance of mutuality in the process of assimilation, outlines the initial contract. One party to the contract (the assimilating community, which included the nationalities, albeit without the voluntary enthusiasm of the Jews) was to perform linguistic and cultural Magyarisation and the modernisation process on the nationalist platform demanded by the liberal gentry. In return, the acceptance into society and into the body politic was offered. Over the years, the contract lost most of its initial rationale. The minorities were excluded because of their reluctance and insistence on self-determination, and the program of enforced Magyarisation took the place of the 'contract'. It is important to remember, as Karady points out, that even during the Golden Age, while the contract was functioning regarding the Jews, total social integration was still obstructed. The obstacles were the consequences, on the one hand, of the century-old religious and state-enforced pariah-status, and on the other hand, the collective phantasms of the 'other'. These images in their turn:

> created a rigid, perceptually primordial (elementary, unsurpassable, non-rationalised and not built on arguments) *stigmatising structure*, which, on one hand, from time to time—at times of social

crises—served as a conduit which allowed Hungarian Jews to be cast in the role of the scapegoat, and, on the other hand, (precisely because of the above) continually forced Hungarian Jews to perform well over their 'contractual' obligation. (Karady 1993a, p. 38)

The result of this was the paradoxical situation that in the first phase of assimilation (the Golden Age), Jews assimilated much faster and much more thoroughly than other groups (the nationalities), yet their integration into Hungarian society was markedly less. Partly as a consequence of this insufficient integration they kept their sense of the 'other' and were perceived by society as such. This is what Karady calls the first contradiction of Hungarian Jewish assimilation. When the assimilationist contract was functioning, mutuality flowed unimpeded, and all social developments which stemmed from the contract were harmonious. When, however, the mutuality disappeared (as indeed it did post-Trianon), the Hungarian side enjoyed full legitimacy and Jewishness became a hardship.

Another contradiction of assimilation was that the more successful their social mobility, the harsher the antipathy against Jews; and the harsher the resentment, the more Jews felt compelled to assimilate. Thus, social mobility and assimilation went hand in hand, and the strategies and techniques of one served for the other as well, e.g. linguistic assimilation, overeducation, urbanisation and secularisation (Karady 1993a, pp. 38–9).

The positive Jewish assessment of the success of assimilation was not unfounded. It was supported by the achievements of the rapid assimilation process. From a 'contractual' point of view Hungarian Jews did fulfil their obligations. Linguistically, assimilation was almost complete and the Magyarisation of Jewish sounding names widespread. Albeit not confined to Hungary but part of a worldwide movement, even religion was modernised, especially in Budapest, the main centre of the *neologue* movement.

The strength of the assimilationist movement was palpable in the numbers of mixed marriages. From 1895, after the reception of Judaism, the numbers were steadily growing. In 1895, 4 per cent of all Jewish marriages were with non-Jews; in 1910, 9.7 per cent; in 1918, 19.6 per cent; following the White Terror, in 1920 and 1921 the numbers dropped to 16.5 per cent and 17.6 per cent; but they regained momentum (although not the rapid increase of the Monarchy years) until 1938, when the 23.9 per cent was followed by a sharp drop following the first anti-Jewish decree, dwindling to 3.2 per cent in 1942 (Zeke 1990, p. 197).

For Jews, conversion is the most extreme form of voluntary assimilation.[3] The number of conversions from Judaism to Christianity was 10 035 between 1896 and 1917 (a 21-year period; no data are available for 1918). Between 1919 and 1938, (a 19-year period) the number was 30 774, with 1919 and 1920 showing a huge increase, to 7146 during 1919 and to 1925 in 1920, the drop showing the beginning of consolidation in 1920. In 1938, following the anti-Jewish decree, the number (8584), surpassed the 1919 pogrom-related figures. (See Table 4.1.)

It is also interesting to compare the numbers of Christian converts *to* Judaism in the relevant periods. Here the numbers show a different trend. While between 1896 and 1917 the number of conversions was 2134; in the 19-year period between 1919 and 1938, 4211 people converted to Judaism. Surprisingly, between the two wars twice as many Christians converted than during the Liberal Era. This trend of becoming Jewish, at a time when racial antisemitism was becoming increasingly hostile and sinister, was borne out by an additional set of figures, that of those who reverted back to Judaism, that is, 'returning' Jews. (In this sense at least, assimilation is a reversible process.) The number in the last 21 years of the Monarchy was 539, while (with an almost threefold increase) 1744 people had returned to Judaism by 1938. Although evidently one cannot ascertain the 'origin' of the returning Jews, that is, they may not have converted to Christianity in Hungary, or not within the relevant periods, deducting those who were actually returning to their faith, between 1896 to 1918, 'authentic' converts to Judaism numbered 1595 (with 539 returnees), while between 1919 and 1938 the number was 2467 (1744 returnees).[4] The number of returnees reflects the same trend for Christians. They signify more the failure of conversion than the desirability of being Jewish. Baptised Jews stayed exactly that, baptised Jews, with the social stigma that being a Jew carried. Regarding Christian converts to Judaism, however, this increasing trend shows something different. The desirability of becoming Jewish, and the social acceptance within society can be discerned from these figures. The year 1938 is a dividing line between these periods, because with the first anti-Jewish decree, the political climate and the status of the Jews had qualitatively changed. Accordingly, the numbers show the changes. From 1939 till 1942, 16 049 Jews converted to

Table 4.1 Changes of religion

Year	J to C	C to J	CJ to J	-CJ
1896–1917[a]	10 035	2134	539	1595
1919–1938[b]	30 774	4211	1744	2467
1939–1942	16 049	768	256	512

Notes: J to C Jews converting to Christianity
            C to J Christians converting to Judaism
            CJ to J Christians who were formerly Jews reconverting to Judaism
            -CJ Christian converts without the number of returning Jews
            a No figure is available for 1918
            b Post-Trianon borders: population one-third less

Christianity. In this period of anti-Jewish decrees, labour battalions and rabid antisemitism, there were an amazing number of converts to Judaism, including those Jews who were returning to the Jewish faith. In 1941 there was the relatively high number of 89—as opposed, for instance, to the all-time low of eight re-converts in 1936 (and 54 and 52 respectively in 1940 and 1942).

As to the relationship between the patterns of assimilation and social crisis, in particular conversion, according to a recent study, two factors were at work. On one hand, there was the 'normal' rising number of conversions following the assimilationist direction (correlated to mixed marriages). On the other hand, conversions perceptibly followed the antisemitic surges in social and political life, with a different, more short-term effect on numbers (Karady 1993a, pp. 45–6).

There was an important variation in the reasons for conversions. In the Golden Age conversion was tantamount to total assimilation. It even opened the door to entering public service, which was closed to Jews. With the advent of racial antisemitism and xenophobic nationalism, converted Jews stayed converted Jews and were not accepted as (ethnic) Hungarians. Converts were not perceived as Christians. A convert was merely a Jew who converted to Christianity and often sinister motivations would be attributed to the conversion. Between the two wars, conversion did not carry social mobility or acceptance. It was an escape strategy, but not a successful one. Conversion was connected to the rise of antisemitism. Until 1918 the annual increase in the number of converts to Christianity showed a correlation to the increase in the population (Karady 1993a, p. 47). In 1919, however, the year of the White Terror, the number of converts jumped to well over ten times more than would be expected according to population figures.[5] In 1916 there were 463 conversions, in 1917, 677; no data are available for 1918 but in 1919 the number was 7416 (Zeke 1990, p. 194).

An increased number of conversions took place during the Commune, with the highest numbers converting between April and July 1919. Karady points to the anticipatory nature of these conversions. By the time the actual pogroms of the White Terror took place, the numbers returned to the pre-revolution level. It is also important to remember that with the post-Trianon territorial losses, the number of Jews in Hungary was halved. Between the two wars the numbers of conversions follow the advances of right radicalism 'with eerie accuracy' (Karady 1993a, pp. 47–8).

A noteworthy aspect was a predominance of women amongst the converts to Judaism. Between 1923 and 1942, a staggering 1894 women converted to Judaism as opposed to only 485 men (Karady 1993a, p. 50).[6] In the Horthy era, conversion to Judaism required remarkable emotional commitment. To convert to Judaism was to accept stigmatised existence and often the disapproval, indignation or disdain of (Christian) family and friends. How can the significant difference in numbers be explained?

The answer has to be in the different status of women within society and the different power-structures which controlled it. Undoubtedly, men could exercise more control over which party would convert. A Jewish man, provided that his religion was important to him, could ask his partner to convert and have his wish fulfilled. The reason for this was that traditionally men's wishes carry more weight, thus are more readily fulfilled than women's wishes (who will often not even formulate wishes, or will be reluctant to articulate them). Women were in a weaker position in another way as well. It was socially more important for women to be married than for men. To be a spinster was to be a social outcast, whereas to be a bachelor did not carry the same social stigma. This aspect of patriarchal social order firmly placed women in a position of more need, and less power. To request the conversion of the bridegroom or refuse the request to convert into Judaism carried the risk of no marriage at all. In other words, the fear of the stigma of being unmarried overrode the stigma of conversion. Although conversion to Judaism signified a high level of personal commitment because of the stigma it carried (and, after 1938, the increasingly palpable discrimination), this commitment also reflected the inherent inequality within patriarchal society.

There is another very important aspect. According to Judaism, the religion of the children follows that of the mother. Even if a Jewish woman marries out of the faith, the Jewishness of the children born of the mixed marriage is indisputable. Consequently, the conversion of the partner to Judaism is not as important even for an identifying 'authentic' Jewish woman as for a man.

The number of conversions to Judaism showed a declining trend year by year from 1938 onward until 1941. In this year, in August, the third anti-Jewish law, the Nuremberg-type racial decree, went into effect.[7] The law banned mixed marriages from 1 November 1941. In 1942, when Act VIII of 1942 repealed XLII of 1895 and turned Judaism again into a tolerated religion, as opposed to a received religion, conversions to Judaism were banned. But between the period of 1941 to 1942, there was a huge increase of Christian women converting to Judaism. In 1940, the number of conversions was 69 (which was a significant drop compared to the previous year's 160: less than half), 31 men, all of them originally Jewish, and 38 women, 23 of them reconverting. In 1941, 259 people converted to Judaism, of whom 224 were women and 35 men (91 per cent of these men—32—were returning to Judaism, so only three were 'genuine' converts). In 1942 the number rose even further, to 280 converts, of whom 255 were women and 25 men (64 per cent of men were reconverting while only 14.1 per cent of women were reconverting) (Zeke 1990, p. 195; Karady 1993b, p. 59, Table 4).

The extraordinary jump in numbers at a time when being Jewish carried real danger and discrimination, over and above the social stigma, is rather difficult to explain. Concurrently there was a parallel increase in the number of mixed marriages. This was a unique occurrence. The Christian woman who married a Jewish man in 1941 or 1942 considerably damaged her own status and the quality of her life—without helping her spouse. The Christian who converted (or reconverted) to Judaism similarly could only expect a worsening of life. A possible explanation is offered by Karady, that these were marriages where the partners realised that this was the last period when they still could get married. However, the real question is what was the function of these relationships in society, and, more generally, how could this trend be interpreted? Karady examines the phenomenon in a historical context. During the years of World War I, more Jewish men entered into mixed marriages then ever before. The war had loosened the taboo of mixed marriages, for two major reasons: the limited availability of men (taken as soldiers) and the changing status of women (both regarding work and within the family, as male heads of family were away or had died). In the two years of the counter-revolution, between 1919 and 1920, there was a comparable increase of both conversions to Judaism and mixed marriages. Karady suggests that in the increasing antisemitic frenzy, marrying into a Jewish family was a way of showing support towards Jews and in this context it could be interpreted as a kind of resistance against fascism. I find his explanation far-fetched and unsupported. Maybe there were some individuals who were driven by decency and loyalty, but even that would not explain the numbers. His further analysis, dealing with the period between the two wars, proves to be more valuable. Three reasons are offered by Karady. Firstly, men were more inclined to marry 'down', namely to marry out of their status. 'Marrying "down" became a significant compensatory possibility of the stigma of "Jewishness"' (Karady 1993b, p. 54).

Karady also points out that the secularisation of Christians was an ongoing process. Lastly, resurfacing in Karady's argument, the paradox of fascism, which prompted identification with Jews and the Jewish cause by many (Karady 1993a, pp. 51–5). Karady reiterates the 'marrying a Jew as political resistance' argument, but just as for the period of the counter-revolution, I think it optimistic and perhaps even romanticising. However I am not able to offer any other explanation.

Politics and identity: nationalism, internationalism and Zionism

For a while the forging of a modern national identity, and the establishment of the modern state and modernisation were shared projects for Hungarians and Hungarian Jews. Hungarians and Jews built modern Hungary together, sharing in the same process, the same project. In the nineteenth century, all over Europe, nationalism was the conduit for assimilation. However, there were other, albeit initially less appealing conduits. Socialism, with its internationalism, also served as an ideological medium for assimilation. There were several persuasive reasons. Nationalism was turning anti-modernity and anti-liberal and was becoming increasingly racist. Furthermore, the appeal of social justice, in face of the palpable economic and political oppression, was also a considerable factor. Even before the turn of the century, the 'Jewish question' became 'inextricably intertwined not only with modern nationalism but with the class struggle' (Wistrich 1982, p. 213). This was also true in the antisemitic context. Herzl, the father of political Zionism, wrote that Jews were becoming socialists, because 'we stand in the most exposed position in the camps of both the socialists and capitalists' (Herzl 1988, p. 87).

Herzl's alternative was of course Zionism. Since Herzl conceived the idea during the Dreyfus trial, during which he perceived increasing antisemitism as a threat to emancipation, Zionism could be seen as a reaction to assimilation *and* the failure of assimilation. But Zionism is much more than that. It is an alternative to the conundrum of emancipation and assimilation, it is self-emancipation, the integration into the world as a distinct, Jewish people, with a distinct, Jewish nationalism. Zionism naturally also uses nationalism as an emancipatory vehicle, but it is more than that. Its messianic theme, the restoration of the Jewish people to the ancestral land, is a very important component of Zionism. From the beginning, Zionism itself was made up of many trends. Possibly the most decisive of these is social revolution. Early Zionist settlers were imbued with socialist principles of agricultural co-operation. In fact, early Zionism had a distinctly socialist, Marxist–populist vocabulary. This radical, social revolutionary aspect of Zionism was a very important factor: it ran opposite to the conservative nationalism of Hungarian middle-class Jewry.[8]

Nationalism versus internationalism

By the beginning of the twentieth century, nationalism ceased to be a liberal, emancipatory, modernising movement. All over Europe the organic concept of the nation was gaining ground, fortified by the alliance with exclusionary, racist conservatism. In his *Confronting the Nation: Jewish and Western Nationalism*, Mosse examined how the Jews confronted the changing concept of the nation (Mosse 1993). He points out that Jews were ill prepared to confront the new civic religion, as Mosse calls the changed nationalism.[9] Hungarian Jews were especially unprepared for the new organic concept of nation which excluded them.

Engaged in the process of assimilation, the Jewish middle-class regarded itself first and foremost as Hungarian. Large segments of orthodoxy, who chose the path of non-secularisation, still embraced

Hungarian nationalism. Jews were committed to the Hungarian state, nation and culture. In their committed nationalism, Jews grieved the losses of Trianon. One year before her emigration to Palestine in 1938, the committed Zionist Hannah Senesh wrote in her diary how she carved the map of Hungary and the letters '*N.N.S.*' into a bench while visiting Czechoslovakia. The letters stand for '*Nem, Nem, Soha!*' (no, no, never), which was one of the irredentist Hungarian slogans, meaning never to give up the fight for the lost territories (Senesh 1973, p. 58).[10] The assimilationist patriotism of Hungarian Jews, calling themselves 'Magyars of the Israelite faith', led them to exult with the rest of the country in the 'achievements' of the two Vienna awards, regaining territories. Yearly the presidency of the National Rabbinate institutionally remembered the 'great anguish of Hungary' in the service and prayed for the 'resurrection of the Hungarian homeland which was unjustly carved up in a cursed way' (Csorba 1990, p. 242). Simon Hevesi, chief rabbi, wrote a prayer in 1941: 'I believe that Thou has worked wonders with Hungary, our beloved nation . . . Praised be Thou O Lord for restoring to our nation the lands that had been taken from her' (Handler 1982, p. 33).

From 1933 onwards, the orthodox (and anti-Zionist) *Egyenlőseg* (Equality), regularly published news-items about what was happening to German Jews. Yet the leader of the Hungarian *neologues* confidently stated that it would never happen to Hungarian Jews (Csorba 1990, pp. 234–7). His certainty was shared. In 1934 the *Egyenlőseg* wrote (waxing *echte* (pure) '*Völkischness*'): 'Our ancestors pledged their blood [ancient Hungarian tribal contract] to Hungarian soil. In 1848 and in the world war, 10 000 dead heroes and the blood of many many thousand wounded Jews was gushing not for Palestine but for Greater Hungary' (Csorba 1990, p. 237); blood (twice), Greater Hungary, pledge to the soil, rejecting Palestine—all in one sentence, an example of the oxymoron of Jewish '*Völkischness*'.

Heartened by the relative economic prosperity, Jews tried to ignore social non-acceptance and mitigate the importance of the emanating hatred. In the increasingly antisemitic atmosphere they kept proving staunch loyalty to Hungary, and everything Hungarian. This was sadly ironic, since historical Jewish allegiance to Hungary had been more then amply demonstrated. It was, for instance, manifest in the bizarre example of the Jews in the Succession States who, neglecting not only their own interest, but the traditional Diaspora principle of support for the law of the land, remained strongly Hungarian and played a powerful role in the maintenance of Hungarian political parties, culture and press.[11] Newspaper articles in Czechoslovakia complained that the Hungarian Jews in Slovakia, in spite of being fluent in Slovakian, kept speaking in Hungarian, and would consider themselves Hungarian (Vida 1939, p. 56). As late as the Munich crisis, Slovak leaders wanted to exclude the Jews from a planned plebiscite, because they would vote for Hungary (Macartney 1961, p. 299n).

By the 1930s there were clear signs of regression. The 1931–32 figures, compiled by the National Bureau of Hungarian Israelites (*MIOI*: *Magyar Izraeliták Országos Irodája*) show that between 1920 and 1930 the number of Jews declined by 0.8 per cent (while the general population showed an increase of 8.7 per cent). State support was withdrawn from 27 schools because the number of students fell below 30. Jews made up 20.9 per cent of suicides in the year of 1926 (Csorba 1990, p. 219). The figures also show that a perception of threat was developing. According to Samu Stern, the head of the *neologue* community, the real problem was economic antisemitism (Csorba 1990, p. 220).

Unlike in most other European countries, in Hungary Jews had participated in political life before the revolution. Yet the percentage of Jews in the leadership of the 1918–19 revolution was conspicuously high. The question arises, what was the relevance of their Jewishness?

Jewish revolutionaries

The large number of Jews in the revolution was examined by McCagg, who, in his study of revolutionary Jews, points out through the case of Béla Kún and Jászi that their rebellion was still within the nationalist paradigm, i.e. it was against the old nobility. McCagg comes to two basic conclusions. Firstly, Jewish revolutionaries were symptomatic of modern urban resentments against semi-feudal agrarian structures, and thus the explanation for Jewish involvement in revolutions lies not in the ethnic background or in the 'social misfit' explanations, but rather in the high percentage of urbanised Jews. Examining the social background of the leaders of the 1918–19 revolution, McCagg points out that all came from families which earned their living through education (McCagg

1972b, p. 83).[12] Thus, McCagg comes to the conclusion that the revolutionary Jews were basically modernisers:

> These Jewish revolutionaries were not . . . a sign that Jews were particularly addicted to revolution, or merely a symptom of general class conflicts within the urban sector of society. Rather they were a function of tensions between modern city and traditional agrarianism. (McCagg 1972b, p. 86)

Secondly, McCagg stresses a generational problem, the corruption and weakness of their urban 'fathers'. In his seminal essay, Gershom Scholem described the dangerous dialectic of the struggle for emancipation, 'not for the sake of their rights as people, but for the sake of assimilating themselves to the people among whom they lived' (Scholem 1976, p. 77). Scholem pointed out that at the crucial time:

> when Jews turned from their medieval state toward the new era of Enlightenment and resolution, the overwhelming majority of them—80 per cent—lived in Germany, Austria-Hungary and Eastern Europe. Due to prevailing geographic, political and linguistic conditions, therefore, it was German culture the Jews first encountered on their road to the West. (Scholem 1976, p. 78)

In the time following the French Revolution, many Hungarian Jews, like German Jews, resolved to modernise by denying Jewishness as a matter of nationality. This meant the assumption of a German national identity. By the mid-nineteenth century, with the stirrings of modernisation within Hungary, the second generation was faced with a dilemma. 'If they followed in the Germanizing steps of their fathers, they could easily find themselves pitted against Liberalism, against Jewish emancipation' (McCagg 1972a, p. 92).

The solution was fervent Magyarisation in the synagogue and at home, and in the same way that German Jews wished to be known as Germans of the 'Mosaic persuasion', Hungarian Jews wished to be recognised as Hungarians of another faith. Two generations later, most of the revolutionaries of 1918 and 1919, according to McCagg (1972a, p. 93), relinquished not only religious Judaism but the liberal nationalism of their middle-class fathers:

> It seems legitimate to hypothesize . . . that Hungary's Jewish revolutionaries were in a restricted sense specifically Jews who were responding to the problems of assimilation through radical rejection

of their Jewish identities, both secular and religious, in favor of socialist universalism. (McCagg 1972a, pp. 94–5)

Examining the role of Jews in the labour movement, one can find another connection. Jews participated primarily as intellectuals, filling the gap left by Christian intellectuals who were deserting the liberalism and radicalism of the previous era. A recent study charts the percentage and the actual number of intellectuals and Jews in the leadership of the social democratic party, both in the Liberal Era and between the two wars, pointing to parallel trends (Borsanyi 1992). Non-Jewish intellectuals found political roles in these parties. Jews readily satisfied the labour movement needs of intellectuals, especially lawyers, journalists and speakers, and in the movement Jewish intellectuals found a political base where they could feel equal. Furthermore, Communism, especially in 1918 and 1919, appeared as a secular religion, and this feature especially appealed to thoroughly secularised Jewish intellectuals who renounced Judaism but did not embrace Christianity. The study draws attention to two important facts: first, that the high number of Jews was only true for the leadership; and second, that between the two wars, antisemitism was accelerating in the labour movement itself (Borsanyi 1992, pp. 145–51). Table 4.2 clearly shows that between 1922 and 1942, in the year after the White Terror, and from 1938 onwards, there were considerably fewer Jews in the leadership of the Social Democratic party. The drop by almost two-thirds from 1939 was due to the (forced) resignation of Jewish members of the executive in 1939.[13]

The two analyses both make sense. What needs to be added is that being a revolutionary can also be perceived as the ultimate in assimilation. The internationalism of Marxism offers assimilation not to a particular nation but to humanity itself. Following their grandfathers' and fathers' trend of reducing their identity to the extreme, these revolutionaries further dissolved their identity in the perceived internationalism of revolution.

It is not at all surprising that the opposite accusation (that Jews supported the counter-revolution) also had proponents. Two wealthy Jews gave financial support to Horthy in the early Szeged days.[14] Száraz, in his seminal 'On the trail of a prejudice', states this fact (right before he quotes his own mother's words about a Jewish acquaintance who was murdered in a pogrom). Száraz infers that Jews were financing the murder and the pogrom of their own

Table 4.2 Jews in the leadership of the Social Democratic party

Year	executive	intellectuals[a]	Jews[b]
1922	14	1	2
1924	16	1	3
1925	16	1	3
1926	17	2	4
1928	16	2	6
1929	16	2	7
1930	16	2	7
1931	20	2	7
1933	20	3	7
1935	23	5	8
1937	23	5	8
1939	23	3	3
1942	23	2	2

Notes: a Minimum matriculation
         b Born Jewish, even if later converted
Source: Borsanyi 1992, p. 150

brethren. He also suggests that those (rich) Jews who supported Horthy in the worst days of the counter-revolution cared more about their class-interests than about their religious/ethnic affiliations. On the one hand one must remember that Száraz wrote as a Marxist, and what he offers is a Marxist analysis. On the other hand, in Száraz's treatment, the difference between the victim and the perpetrator is subtly washed away and the victim becomes an accomplice. But beyond Száraz's assertion, what about the fact itself? How can the support of some Jews for Horthy and his men be explained without the above pitfalls which lead to reactivated prejudices?

During the Golden Age Jews learned to trust the strong state. The counter-revolutionaries, under the leadership of the old guard, were fighting what were perceived as 'thugs' of the Commune, the 'thugs' of revolution. The revolutionaries brought social upheaval. Supporting Horthy and the counter-revolutionary movement was the same as the traditional support for the state which in its turn protected the status quo. Furthermore, did those Jews (and many others) know of the pogroms? In the social and political upheaval, with the occupying 'little Entente' forces in the country, statements were issued by some bishops and prominent figures which helped to create the impression that the pogroms were but isolated incidents and not the mainstream program of the counter-revolutionaries (*Magyar Zsidó Lexikon*

1929, p. 221). Trying to be on the same side, to be 'in' with those who controlled the counter-revolutionary forces, could have been a misguided but legitimate hope to interfere, to influence the leaders. Finally, the anti-Bolshevism and the authoritarianism of the counter-revolutionaries were not undesirable for affluent Jews who were—or at least their status and wealth were—threatened by the revolution.

The pogroms of the White Terror, the *Numerus Clausus* law, the insistent questioning of the validity, the sincerity and even the motivation of assimilation (behind all of which the answer was already there: Jews are not Hungarians), produced only an increasingly frenzied effort to prove that they were good Hungarians. This anxiety to demonstrate sincerity powerfully motivated, for instance, the authors of the *Magyar Zsidó Lexikon* (Hungarian Jewish Lexicon). Under each heading that could be used for this purpose, the authors tried not only to give information but formulate a ready defence against the numerous accusations. In a way the *Lexikon* was a propaganda publication, with answers to the charges. For instance, the 'counter-revolution' heading, on the one hand, describes how Jews suffered during Communist rule, complete with numbers of Jews murdered during the Red Terror. On the other hand, the article stresses the number of Jews who participated on the 'good' side, that is, who helped the counter-revolution (*Magyar Zsidó Lexikon* 1929, pp. 220–1). Under the heading 'assimilation', after stating that 'we know what Jewry gave to the world', the writer is fawning:

> [I]t is due to assimilation that Jewry does not stagnate, but can absorb what is valuable, elevating and exalting in European-Christian civilisation. Here we have to mention the findings of American anthropologists, according to which the assimilation of the emigrating Russian Jewry—and not only the next generation—can be demonstrated by measuring the skull. (*Magyar Zsidó Lexikon* 1929, p. 65)

This, written in 1928, also serves as an indication of the popularity of the eugenics movement in Hungary.

Another statement, 'Assimilation is altogether unknown in Islamic countries, due to the higher culture of Jewry', is partly incorrect and partly pays a backhanded compliment by implying that assimilation happens 'upwards' into the higher culture, such as Hungarian (*Magyar Zsidó Lexikon* 1929, p. 65).[15] The *Lexikon* is part of the nationalist discourse with which Hungarian Jewry was trying maintain the mirage of their specific identity as Jewish

Hungarians. Lamenting the previous high numbers of conversions and alienation due to mixed marriages, the authors argue: 'In the last eight years exactly the harsh and humiliating measures against Jewry strained the inner life of Jewry and closed the earlier avenues of assimilation for the large majority who value Judaism' (*Magyar Zsidó Lexikon* 1929, p. 65).

The overwhelming majority of Hungarian Jews were committed to their identity as Hungarian nationals. Even the nationalism of Jászi and of Béla Kún was noticeable. Jászi, who consistently condemned the nationalities policies of the Monarchy, advocated a Greater Hungary and postulated that if the policies were changed, the nationalities would eventually Magyarise (Jászi 1986 and 1988). And under the leadership of Kún, the Commune organised the Red Army to fight the invading 'little Entente' and refused to sign the peace treaty.[16] The Jews of Hungary insisted on their Hungarianness and on Judaism as a religion. In this, Hungarian Jews can readily be compared with German Jews. Gershom Scholem describes in his seminal paper 'Germans and Jews' the emotional confusion of the Jews and the process in which the love affair of the Jews and the Germans remained one-sided and unreciprocated (Scholem 1976, pp. 71–92). As German Jews embraced everything German—language, culture and nation—so did Hungarian Jews embrace everything Hungarian.

Zionism

This fervent nationalism explains largely why the Zionist movement initially had little success in Hungary.[17] All that Zionism offered and fought for, Hungarian Jews felt they had already achieved.

Zionism was a nationalism which sought to create a new state. Hungarian Jews had fought for a nationalism and participated in the heady project of creating a new state. Zionism was an ideology which strove to bring Jews into modernity, into the brotherhood of nations. Hungarian Jews were part of this brotherhood as Hungarians. There was no need for Jewish nationalism, when there was an exhilarating Hungarian nationalism which emancipated and liberated Jews. Jews could not forget that the arch-antisemite, Istóczy, labelled them in derision as a nation, wanted to send them all to Palestine—just like the Zionists. Most Jews had already invested heavily into disproving Istóczy and the antisemites. It seemed to make sense to follow the old footsteps and continue in the delusion of a Hungarian national identity and successful assimilation rather than suddenly embrace again the old, discarded Jewish identity.

Zionism, the antithesis of assimilation, posited that Jews, like any other people, must have their land and embrace Jewish nationhood. Hungarian Jews who treated Jewishness as only a religion and nothing else could not easily discard their hard-acquired nationality. In the face of increasingly vocal accusations of shallow assimilation and of not being truly Hungarians, most Jews chose to try to prove their fervent and true Hungarianness. The whole discourse was insincere and false. Hungarians only used the accusations as a rationalisation for the real message, antisemitism.

Assimilated Jews saw Zionism as an outright threat. By insisting on a Jewish nationhood it directly contradicted and threatened the development of a purely religion-based Judaism. If Jews are a nation they cannot be a faith. And this was dangerous, as most of the civil rights Hungarian Jews achieved were based on the equality of faiths (*Magyar Zsidó Lexikon* 1929, pp. 38–9). This fear, that Zionism would endanger the hard-won emancipation rights, was the basis of the acceptance of the premise that Jews have to *deserve* emancipation—that emancipation is a 'price' for good behaviour and not an inalienable human right.

The religious community also viewed Zionism as a threat. They saw it as a secular movement, more a product of Western culture than of Jewish tradition, although the love of Zion and of Jerusalem always, and in the last two thousand years the return to the land, have been central to Judaism. But early Zionism especially was primarily led by assimilated Jews, and a radical critique of Judaism was an essential characteristic of early Zionism. The orthodox community based its rejection on the hostility of early Zionism to Jewish tradition. While religious Zionists formed the *Mizrachi* movement, the religious also had anti-Zionist trends. The *Agudat Yisrael* movement was formed precisely against the secularising nature of Zionism. Other strands of orthodoxy were against the return to Zion on religious grounds. According to them, the ingathering of exiles can only happen with the coming of the Messiah.

With the growth of racist antisemitism, and as Zionism branched into various ideological wings, ranging from left to right, from secular to ultra-religious, its followers came from both camps. Following World War I, Zionism increasingly appeared as an alternative to both assimilation and to national identity, providing a third organisational theme in Jewish political life, until then basically bipolar (orthodox—*neologue*) in the days of the Monarchy. The first group *aliyah* (emigration to Palestine) took place following the *Numerus Clausus* law in 1920.[18] But even the Zionists were patriots:

> How is it that I, fully Zionist with my heart, body and soul, feel equally Hungarian and Jewish pain . . . Where do I find an analogue explanation? Only one case, but the most appropriate: the child's love for its parents. In Palestine, in the soil of my ancestors I respect and adore my father—and my mother is our sweet homeland, Hungary.[19]

Komoly, the president of the Zionists, wrote in 1943:

> In the *galut* [diaspora] our lifestyle and position should not allow us to be seen constantly in the limelight. Let us wake up to our national community and our responsibility. Apart from dispensing all our duties to our country, with all our ability we should strive to build our homeland in Palestine, where every Jew will find a place, who cannot or does not want to assimilate in the present homeland. This Jewish homeland, by regaining the respect of other nations and by raising Jews to political equality with all other nations, will enable the assimilation of those who stay back and will terminate the situation in which the Jew is the lightning-rod and the victim of every storm. (Bányai & Kis 1990, p. 98)

The nationalism of Hungarian Jews coloured and pervaded both their internationalism, even as revolutionaries, and their Zionism.

The image of change

> There is something in the Purim story which always left me puzzled. We know that the Jews in Shushan, in Persia lived very happily then. There was a flourishing Jewish community just like the one we had in Hungary. Jews occupied positions in the highest places in government. There were bankers, teachers, professors, writers and critics everywhere. Then one man, and only one man, came along; his name was Haman, and he decided because of a whim, to kill all the Jews, men, women and children. And it almost happened. Now my question is, how is that possible? Could one man change the mentality of a whole people? What happened to the liberals? To our friends in the government? To the ministers? What happened to our neighbour with whom we lived for centuries in semipeace? How was it possible that one man could usher in a threat of such magnitude? (Wiesel 1985, p. xv)

Elie Wiesel's question talks of the immense and irrational trust and commitment of Hungarian Jews to Hungary and to Hungarian nationalism. Even with hindsight (he wrote this well after the Holocaust), Wiesel talks of an overnight change. But what Wiesel describes is valid only for the bygone days of the Monarchy. After World War I, not only the mentality of the people changed, but government policies and the whole political ethos. Antisemitism in Hungary 'caught up' with modern political developments. Social and legal institutions, indeed language and policies, loudly declared that the 'assimilationist contract' was obsolete and invalid. But the nationalism of Hungarian Jews was stronger than the changed reality. Neither socialism nor Zionism were popular ideologies for the largely middle-class urban Jewry, nor for the more religious, traditional agrarian Jews.

The assimilation patterns of the Horthy era show a continuing tendency to convert to Christianity. But while in the previous era conversion was perceived as a substantial step toward social mobility, between the two wars conversion increasingly was sought as protection and safety.

However, Jews still hung on to the obsolete image of the 'benevolent' state, which protected Jews. This image, together with the continued internal squabbling within the community, proved disastrous. To paraphrase Gershom Scholem's words about German Jews, Hungarian Jews distinguished themselves by an astounding lack of critical insight into their own situation.

The process of exclusion, from the pogroms of the White Terror to the institutionalisation of antisemitism, took decades. During these decades Hungarian Jewry maintained their trust in the state, ignoring that the state was essentially different from the one with the policy of inclusion.

PART THREE

THE HOLOCAUST IN HUNGARY

Chapter five

The process of exclusion and Hungarian society

Nazi Germany was not only a genocidal state, but a genocidal society. Not every member of a genocidal society is a perpetrator, or even a potential perpetrator. For genocide to 'succeed' it is essential that the bystander stays just that: a bystander, who approves, condones or does not object to genocide. The differentiation between genocidal state and genocidal society is extremely relevant, because the perpetrators were not only Germans and the Holocaust was not primarily perpetrated within Germany. The countries whose Jews were deported, or murdered *in situ*, did not have to be genocidal states—'only' genocidal societies. These societies had a political and social ethos which accommodated the genocide of 'the other'. All occupied countries—with the exception of Denmark—allowed the Jews to be deported. Some governments like that of France and of Hungary passed anti-Jewish laws of their own accord, institutionalising the pariah-status of 'the other'. The authorities in these countries participated in the deportations. In other countries, for instance the Baltic states and Ukraine, the population massacred Jews. With the exception of Denmark, the Nazis did not meet with any significant resistance regarding the murder of the Jews.

The stages of exclusion

In the process of exclusion, the first, preliminary stage was the development of the antisemitic social ambience following the revolutions. I identify that period as the first stage, with two qualifications. The first one is connected to one of the debates in Holocaust scholarship. The so-called intentionalist–functionalist debate is about whether the Nazi regime aimed at the destruction of the Jews from the very beginning, and that every step taken was in order to achieve that, or whether the 'Final Solution' evolved step by step, in the context of the murderous ideology and of various historical events and developments.[1] The functionalist approach, especially that of Christopher Browning's moderate functionalist position, asserts that it was the crisis brought on by opening the eastern front that acted as a catalyst.

Hungary was neither a genocidal state nor was Nazism the dominant ideology. Yet when the Germans occupied Hungary, there was no resistance to the deportation of the Jews; in fact, Hungarian institutions cooperated willingly. This could have happened only as a result of the antisemitic ethos of the preceding decades. The relevance of the antisemitic ethos as a necessary preliminary phase becomes obvious in the light of the events as they unfolded. Hungarian politics and ethos carried more than the potentiality of the Holocaust. In the case of Hungary, the crisis of the German occupation was the catalyst. The logic of events did lead to the Holocaust. Hence, the decades before World War II, when the course was set, should be viewed as constituting the first phase of the process.

The second, equally important qualification, concerns the process of exclusion itself. Holocaust scholarship largely accepts Raul Hilberg's stages, which are (from the point of view of the perpetrator): expropriation, concentration and extermination. In the first phase, during which legislation was enacted that aimed at expropriation and marginalisation, the pogrom of *Kristallnacht* took place. Jews were not only marginalised, but terrorised. The second phase was ghettoisation and the third phase, the actual 'Final Solution', was really two sub-phases: first, what Hilberg calls the mobile killing units, in which the murderers (the *Einsatzgruppen*, the police and even the *Wehrmacht*) went to the victims, i.e. to the ghettoes, followed by the last sub-phase, from December 1941, when the killing centres started to operate (Hilberg 1967).

Hilberg, of course, wrote about the process of destruction as it was perpetrated by the Nazis and their helpers. Hungary was allied to Germany but was not a Nazi state. Anti-Jewish legislation did not start until 1938. However, in spite of not being Nazis, the public was ready to accept not only the economic marginalisation and the racial branding of the Jews, but the later, destruction phase as well.

The second phase of exclusion in Hungary was that of the exclusionary legislation, and the third phase started with the

German occupation of Hungary in March 1944. This third phase itself contained two stages: the period under the leadership of Horthy, and the Arrowcross period. When Hungary was invaded, Horthy and the establishment stayed on until October 1944 when, supported by the Germans, the Arrowcross party took over with a *putsch*. In the first period a semblance of law and order was maintained, which disappeared after the Arrowcross *putsch*.

The successive governments' policies, the anti-Jewish legislation and the moral breakdown of Hungarian society and leadership in the first and second phase made the third inevitable. In other words, the antisemitic ethos and the exclusionary legislation—although not its expressed aim—sealed the fate of Hungarian Jews once the Germans occupied Hungary.

Historical overview

In the 1930s, Hungary's alliance with Nazi Germany and fascist Italy was strengthened not only in the area of foreign policy but with economic ties as well. In early 1938 the government announced its readiness to tackle the 'Jewish question'. Two months later the first anti-Jewish law was adopted. (The anti-Jewish laws are discussed in detail in Chapter 6.) The 'solution' of the 'Jewish question' became synonymous with the elimination of Jewish economic power. The 1938 anti-Jewish law was conceived in the same vein as its predecessor in 1920: economic containment. It was, however, never implemented, because by the end of the year the second exclusionary bill had been submitted to parliament, and was passed as Act IV of 1939. The 1939 Act's definition of a Jew was given on racial grounds yet through religious criteria.[2] After the second anti-Jewish law, the racial definition was to be applied in every decree and enactment affecting Jews.

The main thrust of the 1939 Act was also economic containment, but it was not fully implemented until 1944. The most important reason for that was a drastic change in the economy. In 1938, the government approved a five-year plan for rearmament and economic development which revived economic activity and bolstered growth. Unemployment, along with over-production and capital-shortage, vanished in the course of 1939.[3] Instead, Hungary experienced labour shortage, insufficient productive capacity and inflation. Under these circumstances Jewish enterprises became vital assets to the national economy's rearmament efforts. In the following years an increasing number of exclusionary laws were passed, depriving Jews of rights acquired in the Liberal Era and, apart from their increasing impoverishment, singling them out for humiliation.

The anti-Jewish legislation has to be seen in the context of the perceived successes of Nazi Germany and their impact on Hungary. In 1938, following the German occupation of Czechoslovakia, a large chunk of pre-Trianon territory was 'returned' to Hungary with the First Vienna Award. In 1940 Hungary acquired another chunk of 'lost' territory: Northern Transylvania from Romania. The Nazi largesse was repaid by the adoption of the third anti-Jewish law. Hungary joined Nazi Germany in the war in 1941 by attacking Yugoslavia and got back the Délvidék. In the same year 16 000 'alien' Jews who were deported from Hungary were slaughtered by *Einsatzgruppen* at Kamenets-Podolsk.

Rocked by the enormous losses of Hungarian soldiers on the eastern front, by Italy's unsuccessful attempt to get out of the war, and by the Allied victories, pro-Western politicians attempted to establish contact with the Allies. As a result, the Nazis occupied Hungary in March 1944. Horthy appointed a new, pro-German government. The Germans arrived with contingency plans concerning the Jews. Finding, however, not only a compliant, but enthusiastic bureaucracy, ghettoisation and deportations started within days. Under the government sanctioned by Horthy, some 400 000 provincial Jews were deported—not by the Gestapo but by the Hungarian Gendarmerie.

By July all Jews from the provinces had been deported. International pressure was mounting against the cooperation of the Hungarians. When it would have been the turn of the Jews of Budapest, Horthy ordered the deportations to be stopped. After the botched attempt to leave the Axis, Horthy was replaced in October 1944 by the Nazi-supported Arrowcross *coup*, under the leadership of Szálasi. The deportations immediately resumed. The Arrowcross thugs slaughtered and terrorised the Jews, until early 1945 when the Soviet army reached Budapest and liberated the ghetto.

Institutionalising antisemitism—the anti-Jewish legislation

The direction which led to the destruction of Hungarian Jewry evolved on three crucial levels: the political and cultural antisemitism of the regime, foreign policies and exclusionary legislation. Constant, pervasive antisemitism, condoned and exploited by the regime, together with irredentist foreign policies determined the essence of the regime to the point that, even when the end was obvious and efforts were made to extricate Hungary from the war, the aims stayed confused and the efforts were half-hearted. The antisemitic and fascist content and tone of the Horthy decades pervaded Hungarian society and, ultimately, this is what proved to be stronger. In all this the exclusionary legislation played a significant role.

Anti-Jewish legislation[4] has to be examined on two levels: governmental and social. From the regime's point of view there was pressure from outside, from Germany; and there was pressure inside, from the radical right wing. The anti-Jewish legislation could be perceived—and was by many—as an attempt to take the wind out of the sails of the indigenous Nazi movement by restricting the part played by Jews in professional and economic life (Royal Institute 1939, p. 66). Apologists of the Horthy era even try to justify exclusionary legislation by positing that the aim of the legislation was to protect Hungarian Jews from increasing pressure from Germany and from the local fascist and Nazi groups. However, the regime's first anti-Jewish law was passed in 1920 before the rise of Nazism.[5] This law was the first institutional way of marginalising Jews and it was applauded by most.[6]

The German pressure on Hungary to introduce anti-Jewish measures could be compared to that exerted on Denmark. Denmark was occupied but the Nazis set up a 'model protectorate', and this created special political conditions in which the Danish government had some freedom compared to other occupied countries. In Denmark, the 'Jewish question' became a 'kind of a symbol, a barometer of principle in theory and practice' (Yahil 1969, p. 41). To repeated Nazi demands, Scavenius, the Danish foreign minister (later prime minister), reiterated that there was no 'Jewish question' in Denmark. The Jews of Denmark were assured: 'As long as a Danish government has anything to say in this country, the Jews have nothing to fear' (Yahil 1969, p. 50). The leader of the Danish conservative nationalist party stated that the national character of the Danish people required a democratic system, and consequently 'the treatment of Jews as practiced in Germany is completely unsuitable for the Danish character' (Yahil 1969, p. 42). He was expressing popular sentiment. The chief of police at the time of occupation, a protagonist of cooperation with the Germans, said to Himmler: 'if the Reichsführer SS thinks that 5000 Jews here in Denmark constitute a problem, then of course we have a problem, but the Danish population does not consider this topic a problem' (Yahil 1969, p. 43).

Later, in 1943, when the Germans wanted to deport Jews from Denmark, the Danes became the only nation which, in a grass-roots action, supported by every echelon and stratum of society, actively saved their Jewish citizens and the refugee Jews. What is remarkable about the steadfast refusal to implement anti-Jewish legislation is not only the fusion of nationalism and democratic principles, but the complete identification with Danish Jews, to the point of making it a symbol of national pride and sovereignty.

Even though the Danish king did not wear the yellow Jewish star, as popular myth would have it, what is important is that it *could have been* true. In 1943 universities closed down to enable the students to participate in the nation's effort of first hiding and then shipping Jews out of the Nazis' way. As Leni Yahil observed; 'What is significant here is that for the Danes *national consciousness and democratic consciousness are one and the same*' (Yahil 1969, p. 42).

For Hannah Arendt, the Danish stance and the fact that the 'Jewish question' was a political and not a humanitarian question for the Danes were the outcome of authentic political sense, 'an inbred comprehension of the requirements and responsibilities of citizenship and independence'. She noted that in Italy Jews were saved because of the 'almost automatic general humanity of an old and civilised people', which withstood the test of terror (Arendt 1963, p. 161).

The question is why the old and civilised people of *other* countries did not possess the same humanity?

Denmark was used for comparison by Bibó, who wrote, that in Hungary, following the *Anschluss*, the moderate right—that is the more Western-oriented elements of the conservative regime— settled into waiting for fascism to run its course by satisfying the local and German Nazis with the anti-Jewish legislation. This could have been the right course of action, under certain conditions, noted Bibó, provided that the legislation was aimed strictly at the rescue of local Jewry (Bibó 1984, p. 142). Had that been the case, the legislation would have been kept to the absolute necessary minimum; the radical right would have been contained unequivocally and unambiguously; and the government would have extricated Hungary from the alliance with Germany. Instead, stated Bibó, the exact opposite happened. However, Bibó's conditions were already negated by the first precondition set by him: the rescue of Hungarian Jewry as a task. It can only be argued with tortuous *ex post facto* reasoning that the rescue of Jews at any point was a consideration for any segment of Hungarian society. It did not occur even to Bibó, who faced the question as the question of 'our responsibility' (i.e. the Hungarian nation), that exclusionary legislation did not have to be introduced at all; Hungary, after all, was not occupied when the first anti-Jewish law was passed.

To ascertain the nature and the direction of the exclusionary legislation, certain questions have to be asked: Was the protection of the Jews a consideration at all? Did Hungarian society want to protect the Jews? A corollary to these questions is another: in 1938, at the time of the first law, did Jews need protection? That is, did the world perceive the need for protection of even German Jews? Certainly the participants of the 1938 Evian conference did not think that even the Jews of Germany needed asylum. The ghettoisation of Polish Jewry immediately after the beginning of the war did not change the world's perception. At the time of the first two anti-Jewish laws, the protection of the Jews was not an issue at all. The laws were indicative of the prevailing official antisemitism *and* logical steps in the regime's ideological and political alignment with Nazi Germany.

Following Bibó's reasoning, further questions need to be asked: Did the presence of the Jewish community influence Hungary's foreign policy *vis-à-vis* Nazi Germany? And vice versa, did foreign policy considerations influence the treatment of the Jews? Finally, was anti-Jewish legislation a direct result of Nazi demands?

The fundamental consideration of Hungary's foreign policy was the revision of the Trianon borders and it was this that set the course. According to György Ranki, the historian who wrote extensively about the Horthy era's foreign policies, three main topics dominated the dynamics of the German–Hungarian relationship: Hungary's economic dependence on Germany; the centrality of Paris Peace border-revisions in both countries' foreign policies; and certain inner similarities in power-structures. Neither of these were linked directly to the handling of the Jewish population. Acquiring territories through German largesse affected Hungary's Jewish policies in what Ranki calls a 'Janus-faced way' (Ranki, G. 1988, p. 212). On one hand, the Jewish populace of the newly regained territories, who, throughout all the decades after the Trianon treaty staunchly regarded themselves Hungarians, greeted the re-annexation with joy; and on the other hand, each of these territorial 'successes' of Hungarian foreign policies were closely followed by anti-Jewish measures (Ranki, G. 1988, pp. 212–13). Once the territories were returned, between 1942 and March 1944, there was no further legislation.

Ranki dismisses the notion that, in the given military and geopolitical situation, the protection of Jews was dependent on the loyalty of Hungary to the Germans: 'If in 1942–43 the Hungarian government could protect the Jews, it was primarily not because of loyalty to Hitler, but because of not being fully loyal' (Ranki, G. 1988, p. 205).

After 1941, the foreign policy of the regime was influenced by considerations of the state of the war. In 1942 Hitler contemplated demanding that the Hungarian government allow the deportation of Hungarians living in German occupied territories, that they order the compulsory wearing of the yellow star and hand Hungarian Jews over to Germany as the Slovakian and Croatian governments did. Prime Minister Kállay argued that Jews played an important part in Hungary's economy and their sudden removal would affect German economic interests in Hungary as well. Kállay also resisted the demands regularly put forward in parliamentary interpellations by Arrowcross members of Parliament as well (Ranki, G. 1968, p. 660).[7]

Condemning Horthy, Braham argues that by giving verbal support to the Nazis while resisting the handing over of Hungarian Jews, in the last two years before the occupation, it was Kállay who prevented the 'Final Solution' in Hungary (Braham 1981, p. 354). Another interpretation of the anti-Jewish legislation posits that the moderate Right was trying to deflate the radical right by talking social reform, with 'superpatriotic phraseology', by introducing laws against the Jews and by using the trappings of fascist militarism (Deak 1985, p. 49).

The overall policies of the Horthy era were informed by antisemitism. Anti-Jewish legislation was introduced as a direct outcome of the preceding decades' antisemitism. Not wishing to argue Kállay's motives, and even accepting that he aimed at saving Hungarian Jewry—whether as a statement of sovereignty or as pro-Allied contingency, or even as a humanitarian act, or all of these considerations—the means of anti-Jewish legislation could not be used sometimes against the Jews and other times for them. Although it may have had the effect of placating the Germans, internally, the official antisemitism and the increasing harshness of the anti-Jewish laws further strengthened and emboldened the far right.

The Kállay government chose antisemitic means to save Jews. But it was not only the wrong—not to say immoral—means that determined the outcome of these efforts. By using antisemitism as means, the government was *continuing* the previous policy, in which the aim was the exclusion of Jews. And that is the other determining factor in the outcome. Antisemitism could not be a successful means for saving the Jews—especially not after the long decades of the political and social ethos of Jew-hatred, propagated and condoned by the regime. This is why the Kállay government's stance failed to change the outcome of the events—and is thus irrelevant for the evaluation of the second phase.

Another question to be asked is whether the presence of the Jewish community had any bearing on decisions and general political directions. There was a direct connection, albeit a negative one: for decades the 'Jewish question' had been posited as the most important social question.

The government abstained from the rigorous and full suppression of the ultra-right. In fact, the opposite was happening. There was public agitation against Jews, the press was full of antisemitic incitement and there were constant overtures to the Germans. Every year newer and newer decrees were required, more and more overtly based on racism and persecution of Jews. Regarding the 'Jewish question', the Horthy regime did not do anything it did not want to do, nor did it do anything that it perceived not having mass support for.

The exclusionary legislation perfectly fitted the general political and ideological direction which started with the counter-revolution. Instead of defusing and diffusing, the Horthy governments' policies made fascism 'respectable' and pervasive. The moderate right was propelled by its own actions and slogans towards the radical right. Thus the persecution of Jews was justified, rationalised within the already existing social political culture. The ruling élite, with its twenty-odd years of anti-Jewish behaviour and rhetoric, set the climate. One could say that ideologically the moderate right in Hungary was the same as the radical right minus social revolution. An overwhelming fear of the mob and of social change kept the moderates apart from the radicals. These two fears also determined how far the moderates were prepared to go concerning the Jews on the scale that went from economic and social marginalisation to deportation.

Ultimately, it was the anti-Jewish legislation which, by providing the legal framework, adapted Hungarian society to the brutal, ultimate exclusion of Jews: to the deportations.

Hungarian society and the exclusionary legislation

In the ambiguous policies of the Horthy regime, the process of exclusion was the regime's 'punishment' of Hungarian Jewry for their role in the revolutions. Yet the regime did not touch Jewish capital. The prevalent perception was that Jews were the cause of all malady. Bibó, the moralist, summarised Hungarian social attitudes clearly:

> For most, the 'solution' to the Jewish question was childishly simple, namely that it should be decreed that the Jews should earn less and non-Jews more . . . From here on [i.e. after the anti-Jewish legislation] a wide stratum of Hungarian society got into the habit of not relying on work and enterprise to earn a living, but, instead, to choose somebody else's established livelihood, denounce that person, investigate his grandparents, get him dismissed, claim his business, maybe get him interned and simply take away his livelihood. (Bibó 1984, pp. 148–9)

The heads of the Christian churches who were sitting in the upper house gave their support to the anti-Jewish laws. The behaviour of the churches in Hungary, on the whole, was not different from the behaviour of the churches elswhere in Europe.

The only objection raised was against the inclusion of baptised Jews: they protested against 're-Judaification'. The Catholic high clergy, being part of the landowner class, supported the conservative front whilst their mass base was undermined by the fascist propaganda. According to Bibó, the explanation for the blessing vote given in favour of the anti-Jewish laws by the churches, and their continued silent acceptance even during the days of the German occupation, lay in the fact that:

> While modern, genocidal antisemitism was already running amok in the neighbourhood, Hungarian churches still treated the issue in the same old way, because they were so pleased with the conservative government's obvious observance of European tradition and respect

towards the churches and their preferences, that the Churches did not consider it a priority to be too sharply critical of the moral nihilism of hitlerism [*sic*] and racism and thus inconvenience this congenial government, which for foreign policy considerations of its own had been forced to appease Hitlerism. (Bibó 1984, p. 154)

Bibó unequivocally states that the policies aimed at the economic containment of Jews, presented as the central national question, had strong mass support. Yet, he warns about the expression, 'the majority'. Poor peasantry makes up the majority of the Hungarian nation, and to them, according to Bibó, these were distant issues and they viewed it all with 'passive indifference' (Bibó 1984, p. 146). Lacking comprehensive historical and sociological research concerning the attitudes of peasantry, it is hard to ascertain how true this statement is. On the one hand, there was the tradition of Christian antisemitism which by nature had to be still, at least, a remembered background understanding in a largely feudal peasantry. On the other hand, precisely because of the feudal conditions, the peasantry was uninformed and their political viewpoints were undeveloped. Yet there was support for the Arrowcross party. In 1940 13 per cent of the membership were peasants (Eros, J. 1970, p. 137). The radical right did aim at the peasantry, through the populist peasant writers and through establishing parties which specifically addressed issues important to the landless rural proletariat (Braham 1981, pp. 59–60). The Scythe Cross movement (as its name indicates), for instance, appealed primarily to the landless masses. Its program, denouncing the 'usurious activities of Jews', called for the destruction of liberal and democratic movements, and incited hatred against Jews.

But peasantry notwithstanding, the 1939 election results clearly indicated mass support for the right wing. Hungarian society, including the workers, unquestionably gave its support to the anti-Jewish measures. To Bibó this mass endorsement of the exclusionary legislation was the gravest symptom of the dead-end that Hungarian society, encumbered by feudal hierarchic structures, had manoeuvred itself into in the decades following the counter-revolution. The perception that blamed Jews for the maladies of public and economic life was so prevalent and general that it was 'hopelessly impossible to contradict it'. The 'solution' sought, was 'childishly simple': Jews should earn less and Christians more (Bibó 1984, p. 147).

The anti-Jewish legislation did not happen in a historical vacuum, but within an existing cultural and social milieu, created over decades by the legal institutions and the ruling classes. Had antisemitism been unacceptable, the laws would have been unacceptable. Had the parliament passed a law forbidding anybody to keep a dog, and decreeing the compulsory starving of all dogs— there would have been a public outcry. But openly practiced antisemitism, the adjustment of two thousand years of Christian Jew-hatred to modernity, allowed the persecution of Jews. Or, as Bibó put it:

> It would have been fallacious to expect serious resistance against abuses of civil rights and equality of Jews in a country where the leadership never took seriously the principle of equality of its citizens and where most of the intelligentsia, bourgeoisie and middle class—Christian and Jewish alike—for over hundred years tolerated regimes which barely paid lip-service to the principle of equal civil rights. (Bibó 1984, p. 147)[8]

What was being done to the Jews was not only acceptable—it was more. It was social *bona mores*. It was respectable.

To Bibó, the process of execution of the laws revealed the moral deterioration of society:

> For the wide strata of middle, lower middle classes and the rising bourgeoisie these laws meant the chance to establish, without effort, a new, more desirable living, granted by the state, at the expense of the established livelihood of others, without any credible justification by some authentic and comprehensive social cause. (Bibó 1984, p. 148)

In fact, the dishonesty of these demands and policies encouraged a wide stratum not to rely on work and enterprise but instead, to steal somebody else's established livelihood by denunciation, 'getting his parents investigated, getting him dismissed, maybe getting him interned' (Bibó 1984, p. 148). These options on the one hand revealed, and on the other further exacerbated, the process of moral decline of Hungarian society. To Bibó this was a shocking illustration of 'unbridled greed and uninhibited hypocrisy or, at best, chilling ambition' in a substantial section of society (Bibó 1984, p. 149).

The peculiarities of the Holocaust in Hungary

There are two highly controversial issues of the Hungarian Holocaust. One concerns the role of the Hungarian government, institutions and society in the destruction of Hungarian Jewry. The second issue clusters around the role of the Hungarian Jewish leaders.

When the Germans occupied Hungary, on 19 March 1944, the decision to do so was precipitated by the Horthy government's secret contacts with the Allies. Randolph Braham suggested:

> Ironically, it appears in retrospect that had Hungary continued to remain a militarily passive but vocally loyal ally of the Third Reich instead of provocatively engaging in essentially fruitless, if not merely alibi-establishing, diplomatic maneuvers, the Jews of Hungary might have survived the war relatively unscathed. (Braham 1985, p. 185)

In the second phase, the exclusionary legislation worked towards the strengthening of the radical right and the process of ever increasing discrimination and persecution which adapted Hungarian society to the acceptance of the deportations. Evaluating the third phase, that of the 'Final Solution' in Hungary, the Hungarian government and society largely fit into the category of bystanders. However, with the role of the Gendarmerie and certain segments of the administration, the demarcation line between the bystander and the perpetrator is crossed.

A recent interpretation, articulated by historian Mária Schmidt, posits that Hungarians and Jews were both victims. This is not a new argument. It has been voiced by apologists for Austria and for Vichy France. Schmidt argues that Hungary itself was in an impossible situation and was more or less powerless against Germany, and Hungarians and Jews were caught in the same predicament:

> There was no way out for Hungary and of course for Hungarian Jewry. Both resorted to hope, the only refuge of the weak. They believed because they wanted to believe that they can avoid the worst. They did not succeed. (Schmidt 1990, p. 41)

Schmidt's depiction of Hungary as victim fails on similar grounds to the one which posits Austria or Vichy France as a victim. The cooperation and collaboration of the administration and of the gendarmes, the hostile indifference to the fate of the Jews and the number of denunciations all directly contradict Schmidt's contention. According to the Germans, in no other country did they get as many denunciations as in Hungary (Braham 1981, p. 925).

Arriving in Hungary with only a few hundred hundred SS men, the Germans needed the help of the Hungarian authorities and public. And they got it. In fact, a rather large segment of the population openly collaborated with the Nazis. As Wisliceny reportedly remarked: 'The Hungarians really seem to be the offsprings of the Huns. We never would have succeeded without them' (Braham 1981, p. 1011). Other German officials made similar statements. Reich plenipotentiary, Veesenmayer, said:

> The record clearly shows that the German demands could have been refused or sabotaged—they were in Bulgaria and in Romania as well as in the case of the Budapest Jews in July 1944—had Horthy and the Hungarian authorities really been concerned with their citizens of Jewish faith. The Germans would have been quite helpless without the wholehearted and effective cooperation of the Hungarian authorities. (Braham 1981, p. 374)

Ultimately, Hungarians did have a choice. They could cooperate or resist, they could be rescuers, bystanders or perpetrators. Jews had no choices. They could only be victims.

Trying to tackle the same problem but from a different point of view, Ranki sees the significance of the Hungarian Holocaust (which, in the euphemism-currency of *officialese* of the time at which he wrote, he calls '1944'), not only as a Jewish tragedy, but as an 'important milestone of the 20th century progress in which Hungarians are searching for their place in Europe' (Ranki, G. 1988, p. 202). Here Ranki touches on the questions of the Hungarian government's responsibility for the destruction of Hungarian Jews, and the impact of the policies that led to the Holocaust in Hungary on the 'image' the world has of Hungary. The role that Hungary played in the war years was far from homogeneous. Even though a member of the Axis, Hungary managed to preserve its sovereignty. In spite of growing militarisation and aggressive, overwhelming right-wing ideology, Hungary stayed a multi-party parliamentary democracy, a *Rechtsstaat*, based more or less on the rule of law. Ranki points to the progress the Kállay government made towards getting out of the war and making a separate peace with the Allies. In Ranki's evaluation, all these positive moves not only came to nothing, but the very positiveness was cancelled out by the role of the Hungarian government in the wake of the German occupation. The deportations isolated Hungary internationally, and 'deepened to a moral crisis the military and political breakdown' (Ranki, G. 1988, p. 202).

Ranki points to the famous documentary film the Germans made for propaganda purposes, which showed the brutality of the Hungarian gendarmes and the feigned horror of the German Red Cross officials, as contributing to the new image of Hungary, one that negated and dispelled the perception of the reluctant ally. The documentary, produced during the deportations from Nagyvarad, was in two parts. The first part showed the Hungarian gendarmes beating women with rifle butts and whipping children with the all-encompassing brutality the gendarmes generally displayed. The second part showed horrified German Red Cross nurses helping the deportees off the cattle-cars at Kassa, distributing water and food and leading them away. The film was shown in neutral countries but it did not convince the world any more (Braham 1981, pp. 610–12).

The picture of Hungary the West held, not without some justification, was that of a feudal–aristocratic regime, born in the White Terror, oppressive to its minorities, with unbridled revisionist demands and antisemitic policies, the first ally of Hitler. And this picture was reinforced by 'the active minority, who, on the side of the Germans, at their bidding and with their support, committed unprecedented mass-murder' (Ranki, G. 1988, p. 203).[9]

While commending Kállay, Ranki lays the blame for failure to protect the Jews on the Horthy regime, for incitement against the Jews in their propaganda. In the atmosphere created and approved by the Horthy regime the Hungarian population was more inclined to assist or passively acknowledge the murder of the Jews, rather than protect and help them. While Kállay made the right moves in foreign policy—however gingerly—he did not move away from the exclusionary policies internally. Had Kállay carried the new direction to its logical end, in rhetoric and in action, in foreign and in internal politics, had he legitimised it—the final outcome could have been different, ventures Ranki. Because of their shilly-shallying Horthy and his regime ultimately are to be blamed, even if, 'as a peculiar irony of fate, the deliverance of Budapest Jewry is owing to Horthy' (Ranki, G. 1988, p. 207). Even though Horthy did issue the order to stop the deportations, he did not do so until only the Budapest community was left, which at best puts a question mark on Horthy's motives, e.g. increasing international pressure and Germans losing on all fronts. Without the full cooperation of the Hungarian authorities on every level, political and administrative, and without the enthusiastic support of the radical right wing, the Germans would not have been able to carry out the deportations. In fact, Ranki firmly places the responsibility for deportations on the Hungarians. Since Eichmann had only a few hundred men at his disposal, 'Not only active resistance, but sabotage, or the refusal to cooperate would have slowed or frustrated the implementation of the program' (Ranki, G. 1988, p. 208).

Eichmann's worst fears concerned possible resistance from the Hungarians, because he lacked man-power and did not know local conditions (Arendt 1963, p. 125). Cooperation was essential for the German plans that deportation should be carried out by the Hungarians. But Eichmann did not need to fear. The Hungarian Gendarmerie was 'more than eager', and 'everything went like a dream'—phrases Eichmann kept repeating whenever he was talking about what happened in Hungary. There were only minor dissensions that Eichmann recalled, such as the fact that the Hungarians wanted to start the deportations with Budapest, to make the capital *judenrein* ('Jew-free') (Arendt 1963, p. 125).

Ultimately, as Feher pointed out, the hesitation to allow the Germans to murder Hungarian Jews before 1944 was not morally motivated (Feher 1980, p. 12). The Horthy regime did not take the moral stance that the Danish government took. All kinds of political considerations played a part, and Hungarian society took on the role of the bystander, with all gradations, from impotent distaste to hostile indifference and even support, unlike the Danes who became rescuers *en masse*. In dialectical interaction government policies were fortified, underpinned and supported by Hungarian society and, concurrently, antisemitism, nationalism and even fascism were fostered, nurtured and condoned by the government.

From the time of the German occupation, days were measured by tens of thousands of lives and by unimaginable suffering. Every moment was concentrated horror. Every day became horribly important and significant.

To Elie Wiesel, the tragedy of Hungarian Jewry was a 'severe indictment', because it could have been stopped: '450 000 Jews from the provinces were being taken in the sealed wagons of their trains. Day after day, night after night. Why weren't they stopped?' (Wiesel 1985, p. xiv). When Horthy was trying to negotiate peace with the Allies, deportations were stopped. According to Feher, Hungarian Jews were 'exchange objects, tokens of goodwill to be offered to Churchill' (Feher 1980, p. 12). Their saving was not a moral imperative.

Hungarian society and the persecution of Jews

With the German occupation, the implementation of the 'Final Solution' started. Let's see how Hungarian society fit into the two basic roles during the Holocaust, that of the perpetrator and that of the bystander; and whether the bystander category fits the bulk of Hungarian society.[10]

Hannah Arendt recounted how Eichmann 'could see no one, no one at all, who actually was against the "Final Solution"' (Arendt 1963, p. 103). Even more:

> His conscience was indeed set at rest when he saw the zeal and eagerness with which 'good society' everywhere reacted as he did. He did not need to 'close his ears to the voice of conscience', as the judgment has it, not because he had none, but because his conscience spoke with a 'respectable voice' with the voice of respectable society around him. (Arendt 1963, pp. 111–12)

In spite of his conclusion that Hungarian society welcomed anti-Jewish legislation, Bibó thought it not unreasonable to have expected the same society to challenge the physical victimisation. And indeed there were some who took positive action, but only a few. That some Jews survived was 'not because of the intervention of individuals or the good offices of Hungarian society, but because the brigands did not have the time or the tenacity to murder them' (Bibó 1984, p. 150):

> It would be deceptive to enumerate how many of our own acquaintances were hidden and escaped with the help of others, because most of those who were so helped were either converts, or came from the same social circle, or were married to a non-Jew, or were members of organised labour. In other words, they had the connections and the chance to escape because they enjoyed the solidarity of a closed, intimate circle. (Bibó 1984, p. 150)

And while there may have been sporadic sympathy and support, 'Jews did not and could not feel the staunch support of the entire community, of the whole country' (Bibó 1984, p. 151). Bibó here compares the behaviour of Danes and Hungarians:

> If, to take a non-combatant country, say, in Denmark, a Jew happened to have to escape into the first available building, asking help at

random, in all probability s/he could safely count on help of some sort, and, even if limitless self-sacrifice wasn't available in every house, certainly s/he could find those who identified with his situation and tried to give full support, only to a lesser degree did s/he face indifference, refusal or reticence, and only as extraordinary bad luck would s/he be denounced. In Hungary, however, had one dared at all to knock on a strange door, as a normal prospect s/he faced indifference, refusal and coolness; somewhat less probably s/he risked being denounced, and help would have been unexpected, unanticipated good fortune. (Bibó 1984, pp. 150–1)

The *sui generis* story of how the Danish government and Danish society stood steadfastly by the Jews and defied the Germans openly had an interesting effect on the Germans. The German authorities in Denmark sabotaged their own orders.[11] As Hannah Arendt noted, this was the only case where the Nazis met countrywide resistance and when confronted with this 'resistance based on principle, their "toughness" had melted like butter in the sun' (Arendt 1963, p. 157). In Hungary, on the other hand, there was a sense of righteousness and cohesion produced by the anti-Jewish measures among 'Christian Hungarians', i.e. non-Jews. As the measures became harsher—from dismissal to deportation—the 'elevation', the 'sacredness' of the goal was becoming shriller and more frenzied, single-minded and unequivocal. Every action that 'protected' the superior, noble Christian Hungarian from the nasty, evil Jew was a noble action itself—and giving way to immoral Jews was an act of immorality (Berkes 1993, pp. 69–80). The idea that Hungary and Hungarians had to be defended was partly based on history, but mostly on the conception of identity, expressed in the national anthem, and reverberating as chief component of the concept of Hungarian identity. That Hungary and Hungarians had to be defended from Jews, i.e. the Jew as enemy, was underpinned by Nazi ideology.

To Bibó it was clear that Hungarian society failed the Jewish community:

> But what is most difficult to forget is the stubbornly obtuse behaviour of those honest people, who did continue to have contact with Jews, who were compassionate, and maybe even helpful, but demonstrated odd confusion and perverse deafness regarding the ultimate defencelessness, hunted state and fear of death of the Jews and the ruthlessness, the savage brutality and the moral nihilism of their persecutors . . . those compassionate people who appended their pity

with some moral censuring that 'see, you shouldn't have, while things were still good, be like this or that', or 'see how insolent and demanding you still are', or those who declared that they are ready to help those who are 'deserving'; or the priest who readily and considerately accepted requests for conversion, but irritably castigated Jews for converting out of expediency, without conviction, or for not learning the catechism well enough; or the clerk, who politely issued some certificate, but when thus somewhat encouraged the persecuted would ask for a minor adjustment on the document, he would refuse indignantly, and say or convey that 'see, this is what you are like, to gain selfish 'advantage' you would tempt an exemplary official to commit a crime'. (Bibó 1984, p. 151)

Decency and courage are individual characteristics, wrote Bibó, but their deployment is also conditional to social fortitude. Bibó warned against the self-deluding romanticism of the illusion that only leaders of the state were responsible and the rest of the nation guiltless (Bibó 1984, p. 172). Even the churches, the perceived moral beacons of Western society, were implicated: 'apart from outstanding heroism of individual priests, nuns and others, the churches on the whole displayed the same gamut of uneven behaviour, ranging from compassion and distant incomprehension to indignant hostility as the rest of Hungarian society' (Bibó 1984, p. 165). He comes to the severe conclusion that 'in every stratum and faction of Hungarian society an identical disintegration of social morality, conventions and conditions occurred' (Bibó 1984, p. 165).

This is also the observation of another political moralist, Hannah Arendt. To her, the perceived cooperation of Jewish organisations 'offers the most striking insight into the totality of the moral collapse the Nazis caused in respectable European society—not only in Germany but in almost all countries, not only the persecutors but also among the victims' (Arendt 1963, p. 111).

Bibó blamed society, but above all Horthy and a handful of other politicians, and saw the behaviour of the rest of society as a product of their policies. Arendt put the onus of responsibility onto the individual. The relevance of obedience and compliance was explored by Arendt, Stanley Milgram and Zygmunt Bauman (Arendt 1967; Milgram 1973; Bauman 1989).

Administration and other institutions

The fate of the Jews of the re-annexed territories and those of rump-Hungary were different. The extermination phase of the

Holocaust started in 1944 for Hungarian Jews, but much earlier for the Jews who were 'returning' to Hungary as a result of the two Vienna awards, and for Jewish refugees from Austria and Slovakia—in other words, those Jews who were not Hungarian citizens. The treatment of refugee Jews was contradictory and haphazard.[12]

Implicitly, Bibó separated their treatment by the authorities. In the regained territories, the 'large majority of higher and lower ranking military administrators used the opportunity to place Jews within their jurisdiction, virtually outside the boundaries of law'. The same tendency was taking place in the labour service, where malevolence, cruelty and torture abounded well before the German occupation, supported by many higher officers. In this, Bibó saw further evidence of the ambivalence and reckless shortsightedness of the Hungarian government which, from time to time, would try to half-heartedly control the radicals while it nurtured and sought to satisfy pervasive antisemitism (Bibó 1984, p. 144).

Bibó argued that, faced with the forces of disintegration, it was up to the operative authorities within that society to uphold moral integrity, to inspire those who were unsure, to generate the feeling of social solidarity, in short, to provide moral momentum to the courageous. But, he observed, in Hungary 'the exact opposite happened' (Bibó 1984, p. 160).

This was not accidental. Fascist ideology was most widespread in the civil service. The role of the institutions in the destruction of Hungarian Jewry was vital, and thus their viewpoint and ideological indoctrination, i.e. commitment to Jew-hatred, played a significant role. The upper classes and the intelligentsia made fascist ideas, hatreds and value-systems respectable. But these notions did not simply filter down from above. Regarding Jews, there was a radicalisation process at work within all strata. What was vaguely acceptable to the government and to the upper middle classes was desirable to the lower classes—and they were the ones who implemented policies. While Horthy and his circle, or writers and journalists, did pick and choose which elements of antisemitic and nationalist ideologies they found tolerable and which they did not, the 'message', as it was understood and perceived, enabled the gendarmes and policemen, ministerial clerks and the army to carry out the deportations and to assist, at every bureaucratic and practical step, the destruction of Hungarian Jews. The same antisemitism which Bibó described earlier was at work. After all, members of the civil service were part of society.

The German occupation of Hungary in 1944 provided a good chance for pulling out of the Axis. Instead, the government resigned without protest, and Horthy appointed a new government as required by the Germans, thus legitimating German occupation:

> This step destroyed the self-respect of the Hungarian army, it rendered meaningless, indeed disastrous, all the concessions made by the Teleki and Kállay governments to the Germans in order to gain time, including all anti-Jewish decrees. It also enabled the civil service to hang onto the false belief of unbroken legality and, finally, it persuaded them to provide continuing administrative assistance, when in this phase of the war not only active resistance but even a passive or obstructive civil administration could have caused serious difficulties to the occupying forces and their stooges. (Bibó 1984, pp. 162–3)

Bibó described the deliberate delusion fabricated thereon. Horthy, the government, the army, the Arrowcross and the Germans in unison began pretending that nothing much had happened but a mere incident, a minor disagreement. Thus cooperation was validated by treating 'the impending genocide as splendid national policy' (Bibó 1984, p. 162). Ultimately, this behaviour invalidates any perception or explanation which regards the anti-Jewish legislation as protecting Hungarian Jewry. The attempts to rescue Jews under various pretexts were contradictory and ambiguous.

To Arendt, the story of 'mitigators' (those who stayed in their positions to do what they could to alleviate the harsh orders) was a postwar 'fairy tale' (Arendt 1963, p. 114). Bibó also bemoaned the absence of 'mitigators', although ideally, Bibó would have preferred people to resign and emphatically not cooperate (Bibó 1984, p. 153). Instead, the 'cultured, more European' members of the civil service in Hungary were aloof and kept 'too far away', and did not speak out against the persecutions:

> In the years of anti-Jewish legislation this better half of Hungarian civil servants strove to keep the enforcement of anti-Jewish decrees within the boundaries of law and order and in that period this was the most intelligent and appropriate approach. (Bibó 1984, p. 153)

Interestingly, Bibó did not raise the question of the legality of the exclusionary laws, only their implementation. Only from the time of the German occupation did Bibó raise the question of legality and demanded an evaluation of legality from members of the civil service, because, according to him, from then on more was needed:

> namely, to conclude the partial and later the complete cessation of political and moral legitimacy of state sovereignty, and to act accordingly. Instead, even the more humane segments of the civil service worked under the delusion that they were merely administering lawful measures of the legitimate government, and that the ensuing diverse horrors were only due to the cruelty and brutality of the executive officials. (Bibó 1984, p. 153)

Unfortunately an isolated occurrence, still, I personally know of one important exception. My mother was hidden by a lawyer, Dr Margit Kovács, who worked at the Ministry of Justice. Immediately following the German occupation she resigned. She gave the reason of having to look after her Down's syndrome child. She felt compelled to do more than just resign, so she saved my mother. Dr Kovács's behaviour was the exception. The very fact that she had to lie about the true reason for her resignation showed that her colleagues did not share her sentiments.

Bibó did not take into consideration that the anti-Jewish decrees issued after the occupation were a direct continuation of the legislation which had already stripped Jews of basic human rights, the implementation of which involved police and bureaucrats, on every level. Examining provincial police reports between 1941 and 1944, Mária Schmidt found that these documents revealed strong antisemitism within the police force, in some places 'striking hatred' (Schmidt 1987, p. 265). The civil service already administered laws and regulations concerning miscegenation and deportation of refugee Jews. According to Schmidt's research, in the regained territories, 'hostile police apparatus tried to maximise the number of Jews whose papers were considered invalid, thus condemning them to certain death' (Schmidt 1987, p. 266). Schmidt also demonstrated that 'minor government officials . . . had benefited from the discrimination against the Jews and thus favoured their removal' (Schmidt 1987, p. 267).

Yet Bibó expected that members of the civil service would suddenly draw the line. In explaining why they had not done so, Bibó attributed importance to the fact that Horthy legitimised the occupation. Thus, ultimately, Bibó did lay the blame on Horthy and the leadership. Feher found it 'realistic' that Bibó distinguished two phases, one in which the 'otherwise repressive and reactionary

Hungarian state observed at least its own laws and rules' from the second, later phase which started with the German occupation (Feher 1980, p. 8). But he argued with Bibó's expectation of civil disobedience, asking the question:

> Is this a realistic Ought? Is a postulate feasible which demands that a stratum not follow its professional moral code, but act in a way diametrically opposed to it, especially when there are no fixed, externally given criteria to make clear the turning point at which the state power has yielded the vestiges of moral authority? (Feher 1980, p. 8)

The civil service continued to behave as before: carrying out laws and regulations. They may not have liked their tasks, they may have carried them out half-heartedly, but the government officials, camp clerks, registrars, who administered the tasks relating to the deportation of Jews, 'still obeyed their superiors scrupulously, without major protest' (Bibó 1984, p. 153). Samu Stern, the leader of the Budapest *Judenrat* (Jewish Council) wrote in his memoirs that when the Council had to evacuate Jewish apartments to provide accommodation to bombed out Christians, the Jewish leaders tried to empty bigger flats, reasoning that more affluent people would not be as harshly affected. The authorities demanded small apartments because they did not want to provide too nice places for those who were bombed out (Stern 1990, p. 76). A specification like that lent a false sense of 'reasonableness', a false sense of equity and, above all, righteousness to the totally lawless appropriation of Jewish property. It was as if some kind of social justice was being meted out: Jews being punished and Hungarians getting their dues.

To Bibó it was clear that continued civil obedience was in fact obedience to criminal laws legitimising murder (Bibó 1984, p. 153). In Arendt's analysis, Eichmann, as many of his fellow perpetrators, refused to make moral judgments. Bibó saw something else: a different type of morality that justified and allowed horrible deeds to be carried out. Being an official meant executing racial purity laws and involved proceedings concerning citizenship—all life and death matters. As Dwight MacDonald observed after the Holocaust, it is not the law-breaker we must fear so much as the person who obeys the law (MacDonald 1957a, p. 35). Civil obedience produced the murderers, including the bureaucrat–murderer.

A question of evil—the ethics of obedience

Hannah Arendt's *Eichmann in Jerusalem: A Report on the Banality of Evil* is a seminal and highly controversial book. The book has three main themes: the study of the role of the bureaucrat in the destruction process, Eichmann's 'ordinariness' and the 'banality of evil'; the analysis of the trial from a legal point of view; and a strong indictment of the Jewish leadership for its role in the Holocaust. The debate centred on Arendt's condemnation of the victim. Describing and analysing the Holocaust, Arendt focused exclusively on Eichmann, the 'desk-murderer', and the Jewish leadership. Reading Arendt it is as if the Holocaust happened in a vacuum, between German Nazis and Jews. There is no mention of the role of the Hungarian or the French gendarmes, the informers and the pogromniks, the collaborationist governments or the enthusiastic allies. In spite of this, Arendt's penetrating analysis of the psychology of the middle and lower ranges of the Nazi bureaucratic hierarchy, and her articulation of the 'banality of evil', is highly pertinent to Hungarian administration and Bibó's assessment of it.

With the formulation of the 'banality of evil' Arendt firmly located the evil (as she called it earlier, in her *The Origins of Totalitarianism*, the 'radical evil') of Nazism, not in the deeds and behaviour of monstrous individuals, but in the deeds and behaviour of ordinary people. (Which is not to say that horrible monsters were not among the perpetrators.) Bauman pays particular attention to the role of not only the Nazi administrators, but those in other countries as well:

> The leaders of the doomed communities performed most of the preliminary bureaucratic work the operation required (supplying the Nazis with the records and keeping files on their prospective victims), supervised the productive and distributive activities needed to keep the victims alive until the time when the gas chambers were ready to receive them, policed the captive population so that the law-and-order tasks did not stretch the ingenuity or resources of the captors, secured the smooth flow of the annihilation process by appointing the objects of its successive stages, delivered the selected objects to the sites from which they could be collected with the minimum of fuss, and mobilised the financial resources needed to pay for the last journey. *Without* all this substantial and diverse help, the Holocaust would probably have taken place anyway—but it would have gone down in history as a different

and perhaps somewhat less frightening episode . . . (Bauman 1989, p. 118)

Without the compliance of these ordinary bureaucrats in Hungary the task of the German administration would not have been effective; in fact, it is doubtful if the deportations in Hungary would have taken place. By the time the Germans arrived in Hungary they needed the cooperation—the collaboration—of Hungarian institutions and society much more than in the earlier stages of the war. Following the revolt of the Warsaw ghetto and the Danish experience, at this last, losing stage of the war, the Germans had to take into consideration whether there was going to be resistance in Hungary and whether, with the small number of available SS, the deportations would have been feasible. Eichmann, in fact, feared Hungarian resistance to the deportations, only to be reassured by the enthusiastically eager help provided (Arendt 1963, p. 125; Ranki, G. 1988, p. 208).

Why did they comply? For some the answer is in the bureaucratic process itself.[13] Others sought an explanation in the particular nature of the authoritarian personality.[14] To Arendt, the real problem lay in the dehumanisation process of modern society. The Holocaust as a direct and logical outcome of modernity is central to Bauman's thesis:[15]

> The Holocaust confronts the historian and the sociologist with an entirely new challenge. It serves as a window through which one can catch a glimpse of such processes as have been brought into being by the thoroughly modern art of rational action: of the new potency and new horizons of modern power, which become possible once such processes have been employed in the service of its objectives. (Bauman 1989, pp. 118–19)

Bauman set out to construct a sociological theory of morality. He sees society as a 'factory of morality', which suits its own purposes, and argues with Durkheim who, working with the view that sees moral norms as social products, formulated the theory, according to which society is an actively moralising force, and social prohibition determines which actions are evil. Bauman considers the Holocaust as a challenge to this reasoning (Bauman 1989, pp. 171–3): 'Political and legal responses to the Nazi crime put on the agenda the need to legitimise the verdict of immorality passed on the actions of a great number of people who faithfully followed the moral norms of their own society' (Bauman 1989, p. 176).

Arendt also argued that with the committing of 'legal crimes', the individual is faced with the moral responsibility for resisting socialisation (Arendt 1967, p. 134).

Milgram's findings on the mechanism of obedience showed that given suitable conditions, cruelty can be committed by ordinary people. It is not inherent cruelty in the individual but subordination to authority that allows cruel acts: 'The key to the behaviour of subjects lies not in pent up anger or aggression but in the nature of their relationship to authority' (Milgram 1973, p. 168). The source of inhumanity, according to Milgram, is social relationships. He stressed the importance of the sequential nature of the action, described as 'an unfolding process in which each action influences the next' (Milgram 1973, p. 149). Bauman's picturesque description is especially apt: 'One can even define the swamp as a kind of ingenious system so constructed that, however the objects immersed into it move, their movements always add to the "sucking power" of the system' (Bauman 1989, p. 157).

Applying this line of argument to Bibó's expectations of the Hungarian civil service, the sequential aspect of the earlier anti-Jewish laws and their administration made deportations 'only' one other step. To deny the propriety of the step they were to take would have meant undercutting the propriety of the previous steps. The Hungarian civil service was sucked in by the black hole of the ongoing immorality of antisemitism—as, indeed, all of Hungarian society was. To paraphrase Bauman: they were slaves to their own past actions, trapped in 'the impossibility of quitting without revising and rejecting the evaluation of one's own deeds' (Bauman 1989, p. 158). For the bureaucrat and the gendarme there was another factor, namely what Milgram called 'situational obligations' or 'situational etiquette', implicit sets of understandings that are part of the social occasion, defined by their respective institutions. Inside the bureaucratic system of authority the focus is on 'the job to be done and the excellence with which it is performed' (Bauman 1989, p. 159). Bureaucracy concentrates on the technology of the action and not on its moral meaning. As Milgram postulated, 'it is psychologically easy to ignore responsibility when one is an intermediate link in a chain of evil action but is far from the final consequences of action' (Milgram 1973, p. 11). This aspect obviously does not apply to the gendarmes' role in deportation, which was characterised both by compliance and outstanding brutality. The gendarmes were face to face with the victim.

An additional point explaining the direct perpetrators' behaviour is to be found in Christopher Browning's *Ordinary Men*. Analysing the process in which ordinary policemen became killers and joined the *Einsatzgruppen* in August 1941, in the East, Browning found that only 20 per cent refused the orders to kill; the others, in spite of the protection offered (and received by those who refused), became mass-murderers for a few months. Browning concluded that apart from what Milgram called 'overarching ideological justification', conformity to the group made these men killers (Browning 1992, pp. 172–89). Among the antecedent conditions of obedience, Milgram also stressed the importance of 'overarching ideology': 'ideological justification is vital in obtaining willing obedience' (Milgram 1973, p. 142). Kren and Rappoport, whose research offers a particularly valuable analysis of resistance and the psychology involved, constructed a framework isolating three essential factors which make resistance possible: the probability of success, the intensity of oppression and the presence of an alternative authority system (Kren & Rappoport 1988, p. 196). This last factor (the presence of an alternative authority system) determines the extent to which resistance is justified by values and norms which contradict those of the authority system in force. This is basically understood to 'involve the ideological basis for denying the legitimacy of established authority' (Kren & Rappoport 1988, p. 197). Bibó observed:

> [I]t would have been necessary to articulate clear and lucid guidelines for resistance and altruism and thus to reach and inspire as many as possible of those who were sympathetic but ambivalent concerning the Jewish and the national issue. But the Hungarian intellectuals did not dispel any ambiguities and did not proclaim a concerted and explicit program of defiance and humanity which would have made all who strayed marginal and unimportant. (Bibó 1984, p. 157)

Not only was Hungarian society and the institutions within it imbued with an overarching ideology, i.e. antisemitism, but there was no alternative authority system. There was no articulation of values which would have questioned the values which allowed obedience. What was ubiquitous and overwhelmingly articulated for some 30 years, not only by the political circles, but by the intellectuals, did endorse and validate compliance with anti-Jewish measures.

The politics of the intellectuals

In 1938, during the parliamentary debate of the draft of the first anti-Jewish law, a declaration was published in the *Pesti Napló*, defending the equal rights of all citizens. It pointed out that the law would not improve the situation of the poor and, in a quite remarkable way, indignantly refuted the assumption that the Christian middle class could only survive if others lost their livelihood. The declaration called on institutions and 'sound and patriotic people of the whole country' to stand up against the law (Juhasz 1985, p. 55). It was signed by some of the outstanding names of Hungarian cultural and social life, composers Béla Bartók and Zoltán Kodály among them. Instead of working, as it was intended, as a rallying call for Hungarian intellectuals, the declaration attracted a negative reception and those who signed were savagely attacked from both the moderate and the extreme right. The signatories were called 'pseudo-humanist champions of justice' and the accusation levelled against them was that they were insensitive to the needs of the community. The *Magyar út* (Hungarian Way), the weekly addressing mainly the protestant middle class, sympathetic to populist ideas, deplored those who signed, especially Bartók and Kodály, who, after all, were reaching to the ancient rural sources of Hungarian folk-music and thus could not be simply labelled urbanist. By 'exposing' alleged business contacts, i.e. being bought by Jewish money, the signatories were condemned (Juhasz 1985, pp. 55–8). The next issue of the periodical described the signing as treason. This pointing to Jewish 'contacts' was one of the ways through which people were publicly discredited.[16]

By the time of the second anti-Jewish law, some half a year later, public opinion had shifted. In 1938, with the First Vienna Award, Hungary regained the *Felvidék* (Upper Province) in the northern part. The fact that this was bounty from Germany's overrunning Czechoslovakia did not sour the elation. There was no more talk of equal rights. The issue was articulated within racist parameters: could true Hungarians benefit from the exclusionary legislation? Even statements intending to be generous and noble accepted the underlying racism. Dezső Szabó, for instance, in an obvious reference to the Nuremberg laws, defined Hungarians as anybody with one non-Jewish parent (Juhasz 1985, p. 59).

The Tiszaeszlár blood libel made a comeback. A book written by the antisemite prosecutor, Bary, was published in 1938, along with a poem written by a Nazi-sympathiser poet, about the same topic:

> The court passed the judgment. The witness is
> a hallucinating half-wit,
> the libel is without foundation, the blood libel,
> the frightful suspicion.
> The court passed the judgment. The trembling men in kaftans can
> leave: they did not kill
> Eszter Solymosi, they are not guilty, they are not murderers, they did
> not bake the Easter wafer
> with human blood. The world is to realise that
> the blood, the libel is an old wives tale, to scare children.
>
> The court passed the judgment, and Jews,
> 'the persecuted', breathed relieved,
> but the 'tale', the 'myth' has been spreading
> among the poor Hungarian folk,
> the song was reverberating, and from the
> trickle of blood a river of blood has flown,
> sea, a sea of blood amassed,
> immeasurably deep and eternal,
> like the blood of Jesus,
> the god-man who redeemed the world,
> her blood, the defiled poor
> Eszter Solymosi[17]

With the many trends of intellectual political thought, Bibó believed that on the whole, the intellectuals did not support fascism and by and large were passive. Nevertheless, he charged that scholars, writers and journalists were 'conspicuously silent' (Bibó 1984, p. 157).[18] What was missing, according to Bibó, was the explicit assertiveness, the articulation of anti-fascism. Consequently there were no 'clear and lucid guidelines for resistance and altruism' and they failed to reach and inspire those who were sympathetic but ambivalent (Bibó 1984, p. 157). Bibó charged that in spite of some inadequate attempts, the intellectuals failed to act as moral beacons (Bibó 1984, p. 160).

There were factions of Hungarian intellectuals in semi-opposition, but they stuck in empty and archaic liberal phraseology. Others had a stance, which originated in conservative, Westernoriented circles. It was anti-German, and essentially aimed at lumping the radical right and Bolshevism together—and of course this was unsatisfactory too. Bibó identified a third group of intellectuals who simultaneously contrasted German and Jewish expansion with Hungarian survival and defiance. Although they challenged the Nazis, they still abetted the anti-Jewish right. Bibó articulated the necessity to distinguish between 'their genuine national pessimism and romanticism alongside the nebulous, genocidal, destructive and power-thirsty German metaphysics', but nevertheless drew attention to the 'fallacy and futility' of this romantic pessimism (Bibó 1984, pp. 158–9). Bibó himself belonged to a fourth group, which viewed the 'Jewish question' as a social question and demanded the end of all exploitation and called for national resistance. This view, in the fiercely nationalist country, where the socialist ideas represented by this group were viewed with distrust and disdain, could not rally endorsement from the masses. On the whole, as Bibó lamented, Hungarian intellectuals did not dispel any ambiguities and did not proclaim a concerted and explicit program of defiance and humanity. There was no categorical and unambiguous rebuttal of anti-Jewish sentiments, measures and legislation (Bibó 1984, pp. 52–160).

Many well-known names of Hungarian literature were often sympathetic to the anti-Jewish atmosphere and government policies. Even those who otherwise were anti-Nazis tolerated the anti-Jewish measures. Few found it abhorrent, for instance, that Jewish writers should be abused and humiliated for being Jewish. The writer who made the most significant impact in the late 1930s and 1940s, comparable to the influence of Szabó and Szekfü in the 1920s, was László Németh. Widely perceived as the intellectual leader of the third (Nazi-sympathiser) trend in the populist movement, Németh openly engaged in politics.

Ferenc Fejtő, who recognised the leading role of Németh, analysed his political stance in an article, 'Magyar narodniki' ('Hungarian Narodniks') written in 1935: 'There are those who consider Németh a fascist and many who think of him as a Bolshevik . . . László Németh, however, knows that labels do not count by themselves. Lately, we can detect some tones of sympathy, when he is talking about them [national socialists]' (Fejtő 1990b, p. 127).

Németh believed in the importance of the role of the writers:

> Great nations, which are carried by their own mass, can afford a *jardin des plantes* as their literary heritage—flowering creations next to each other. Small nations on the other hand move through centuries as

worried caravans; their writers are sentinels, and here spirit has to be judged by vigilance. (Karsai 1992, p. 93)

Intended as the words of such a vigilant sentinel, his essay, *'Kisebbségben'* ('In Minority'), published in 1939, provided the rhetoric and the ideology for the populist movement. Németh formulated two words: *'híg-magyar'* (thin, or watery Hungarian) as opposed to *'mély-magyar'* (deep Hungarians). Surprisingly, for a writer such as Németh, whose articulate usage of language befitted a writer of his standing, he ignored the fact that the opposite of thin is thick, and the opposite of deep is shallow. Maybe this linguistic inaccuracy, which caught on and became the descriptive phrase used by moderates and populists (in other words, those who were not radical Nazi sympathisers), reflected the forced falseness of an immoral ideology. In Németh's phraseology, assimilated Jews were diluted, watery Hungarians, of whom, he postulated later, in 1943, Hungarian society should be cleansed. Németh preached that the culture and existence of Hungarians needed to be protected from the Jews. In the following years, Németh kept publishing articles against Jews.

Németh gave a much-quoted, controversial speech at a meeting of populist writers, held at Szárszó in 1943, while the Holocaust was raging and knowing that some 18 000 Hungarian Jews had been massacred two years earlier. Németh warned that 'revengeful Jewry, devoid of self-criticism, had to strengthen enormously in the last four or five years' (i.e. since the anti-Jewish legislation) and he called on the literary archetype of Shylock, who is already sharpening the knife to cut out the heart (i.e. of the Hungarian nation). The logic is both vicious and circuitous. Jews are to be feared now *after* the anti-Jewish legislation. With the Holocaust in its fourth year, having exhausted the marginalisation, humiliation and economic measures with the anti-Jewish laws, the unspoken, oblique solution looming behind the words of Németh, is final.

The knife-sharpening figure of Shylock lends additional respectability and righteousness. A Shylock, who is after not just flesh, but the heart, is lethally menacing.

He elaborated on his thesis that Hungary was subject to an 'internal colonialism', meaning both the Schwabian (the German minority in Hungary came originally from Schwabia) and Jewish influence. Not surprisingly, the 'Jewish question' became the main topic of the Szárszó meeting. Németh was not pro-German. He also said at the Szárszó gathering that a German, British or Russian victory was equally bad. What he suggested was that Hungarian intellectuals unite and 'set up a radical camp' on racial and social platforms (Karsai 1992, p. 125).

Németh made a lasting impression on the middle classes. His expressions and phrases elevated antisemitism to the realm of literature and righteousness.[19]

Censorship was introduced in Hungary with the outbreak of World War II. The censors were primarily looking for matters concerning foreign policy (especially the alliance with Nazi Germany), but criticism of social conditions or government policies was also scrutinised.

The person who was the most vociferous against the populists was the poet Attila József, one of the giants of Hungarian literature. The majority of writers remained non-committal concerning the 'Jewish question'. From a survey of newspapers in 1944 the clear picture emerges that there were plenty of journalists who not only supported the deportations and brutality against Jews, but demanded even harsher measures. Following the German occupation, only those newspapers who supported the government were published. The rest were banned (Berkes 1993, pp. 69–80).

Chapter six

The process of exclusion and the Jewish community

> Budapest was still a very quiet, peaceful city
> until 1944 . . . The Jews in Budapest lived as
> in a strange hallucination. Yeshivas were full,
> with many underground bachurim [religious
> students] who came from Poland. And the
> Hasidic rabbis were travelling from Szatmar to
> Sziget and Nagyvarad. The cafés were full.
>
> Wiesel 1985, p. xiv

> And they came—they brought the message. And
> the message was not received, meaning, it was
> not absorbed: it did not become knowledge. The
> information was there but it was not trans-
> formed into consciousness.
>
> Wiesel 1985, p. xiii

> If I had known what Auschwitz was, no power
> on earth could have gotten me on that train,
> but there was no power on earth that could have
> convinced me that Auschwitz was possible and
> indeed existed.
>
> Gideon Hausner, in Gutman & Greif
> 1988, p. 443

To Wiesel the tragedy of Hungarian Jewry was unique for three reasons: 'one, the world knew; two, the victims did not; three, it could have been prevented' (Wiesel 1985, p. xi). It is well docu-mented and overwhelmingly clear that by 1944 the world knew of the Holocaust.

The third phase of exclusion was as much determined by the second one as the second was determined by the first phase. The national Christian antisemitic course of the counter-revolutionary regime led first to alliance with the Germans, and from there to the Holocaust. I am thus questioning Elie Wiesel's observation that the destruction of Hungarian Jewry could have been prevented, and Randolph Braham's suggestion, which implies that had the Hungarian government played along with the Germans for a little bit longer, Hungary would not have been occupied.[1]

Applying Bibó's analysis of the exclusionary legislation to the official policies regarding Jews in the war years, it becomes clear that the destruction of Hungarian Jews was not prevented because prevention was not intended. The intention of the exclusionary legislation and the intention of the anti-Jewish policies were just as fuzzy as the underlying ideology. The course was set with the Christian national principle and with the anti-Versailles Treaty, pro-German, pro-fascist foreign policies. It would have needed extreme luck, and extreme deftness, to evade Nazi occupation. The same applies to chance. The contradictory, ambivalent policies had to end in the botched attempt to extricate Hungary from the Axis, and in the occupation. Furthermore, the role of Hungarian institutions in the destruction of Hungarian Jewry, and the social apathy regarding the fate of the Jews, makes both chance and the possibility of prevention a non-issue. The exclusionary policies and legislation were so effective that, with the German occupation, they led to the destruction of Hungarian Jewry.

Historical overview

The antisemitic ambience of the Horthy era hardened into black letter law with the first anti-Jewish legislation. Act XV of 1938 introduced the so-called Professional Chambers to serve as a network for most liberal professions. The concept itself—compulsory membership in professional chambers, an innovation based on medieval guilds—was borrowed from the Italian model of a corporatively structured economy. The Hungarian version was designed to keep down the number of Jewish lawyers, doctors, engineers, journalists and actors. The Act stipulated that Jews could only be admitted to the local chambers when the ratio of Jews in that chamber was below 20 per cent. Salaried Jewish professionals became exposed to a compulsory process of half-yearly dismissals. The Act adopted a basically religious rather than a racial definition of Jewishness. It represented a brand of right-wing constitutional antisemitism and openly violated the fundamental principle of Act VII of 1867, which had granted emancipation.

The preparations for the second anti-Jewish law began amidst antisemitic demonstrations. During the debate of the bill there was a terrorist attack on the main synagogue of Budapest, killing and wounding several Jews.

The second anti-Jewish Act in 1939 already aimed at not simply containing Jews as a 'threat to national economy and culture', but at branding them as an alien, destructive body. Not part of the previous legislation, the 1939 Act gave a definition of who was to be considered a Jew. Article 1 of the Act stated that any person who belonged, or one of whose parents or two grandparents belonged, to the Jewish community on or before the promulgation of the law, was considered to be Jewish (Braham 1981, p. 154). A person with at least one Jewish parent, or two Jewish grandparents, even if converted to Christianity, was a Jew.[2] This was still more 'liberal' than the Nazi concept, under which having one Jewish grandparent already condemned a person as being of 'mixed Jewish blood'.[3]

The Act also authorised the government, following Nazi policies of the time, to 'promote the emigration of Jews' (Braham 1981, p. 148). Although the Act stated as its principal objective 'the Restriction of the Public and Economic Functioning of the Jews', it went far beyond economic containment.[4]

The second anti-Jewish law hit the lower middle classes especially hard. Larger businesses continued to operate with a front, a *stróman* (straw-man). But the sections of the law regarding salaried clerks were not only strict, but could be monitored easily. As a consequence, large numbers lost their livelihood altogether. Some 250 000 people were affected (Csorba 1990, pp. 22–3). The law was not fully implemented until 1944. This was partially due to the consideration that the large number of Jews in Hungary (800 000 among 14 million Hungarians, in contrast to 600 000 Jews among 60 million Germans) and their vital role in economic life, made the application of the Nazi approach to the Jewish question tantamount to economic suicide.

An interesting aspect of the second anti-Jewish law was that it introduced the system of exemptions.[5] There were several categories. Jews whose ancestors settled in Hungary before 1 January 1849 were exempted. So were Jews who were born into a mixed marriage in which both parents belonged to a Christian denomination before 1 January 1939, and the child of the marriage was baptised before reaching the age of seven; nine additional categories were for Olympic champions, university professors, war heroes, etc. The reason for some of these exceptions was due mostly to the influence of the Christian churches, which did not want those who were baptised to be treated the same way as Jews.

Following the German occupation, the system was widened. Apart from the exemptions under Hungarian law, there were a limited number of Jews who gained de facto exemption from the SS, through the so-called immunity certificates. Granting exemptions to converts served to appease the Christian churches. The SS used the exemptions to ensure the most effective implementation of the deportations, by granting exemptions to some Jews whom they needed for the time being, such as members of the Jewish Council. Horthy used his position to exempt Jews not covered by legislation. The system of exemptions worked partly through bureaucracy, involving enormous amounts of paperwork and officious authorities, and partly through corruption.

Exempted Jews were safe from official persecution and harassment, and most of the anti-Jewish restrictions did not apply to them. If their apartments or property had been confiscated, they were returned to them. They did not have to wear the yellow star. Being exempted was a privileged category: it meant entitlement to almost the same human and civil rights as Christians.

The third anti-Jewish Act in 1941 showed the increasing pervasiveness and acceptance of racial ideology. Law XV of 1941 amended the 1894 Act on marriages and it introduced miscegenation as an offence and a crime. This was Nuremberg-style legislation in every respect.

In 1939 the labour service system was introduced and it operated with increasing brutality throughout the war. Jewish men of military age (and later those who were younger) were classified as unreliable and were organised into quasi-military formations, without right to any weaponry. Originally the system was intended for all 'unreliables' such as Romanians, Serbs, Slovaks and Communists, but it was primarily used against Jews. The antecedents of the system reached back to the days of the White Terror (Braham 1981, p. 285). The basis for the forced labour system was Act II of 1939 on national defence. Section 230 of the Act provided that, in accordance with the mobilisation law, Jews were liable to be drafted into the army for 'auxiliary service', as distinguished from 'armed service'.

The Jewish labour servicemen served as army engineers, in construction projects, mine clearing operations and miscellaneous dirty work. Tens of thousands were sent to the front but many battalions stayed within Hungary. The labour squadrons which were attached to the regular army units wore army uniform, but without the insignia.[6]

The Holocaust came very late to Hungary. Through 1941, while the first phase of the 'Final Solution' was carried out by the mobile killing units, and through 1942 and 1943, while the death camps were operating at full horrible force, Hungarian Jewry lived in relative security—relative, because it could be called security only compared to the fate of the rest of European Jewry in Nazidom. Branded and increasingly oppressed, suffering growing economic hardship and taken to forced labour, nevertheless Hungarian Jews were not deported till 1944.[7]

Within days of the German occupation several anti-Jewish decrees were passed, and by early April, Hungarian Jews had to start wearing the yellow star. Eclipsed by the overwhelming terror of what followed, the yellow star nevertheless meant not only humiliation, derision and loss of rights, but fear of physical violence. Hungary was divided into zones and the ghettoisation and deportation of Jews started. By early July all Jews were deported from the provinces. When it would have been the turn of the largest and the most assimilated community (that in Budapest), Horthy stopped the deportations. After the Arrowcross *putsch* in October 1944, the *Nyilas* resumed deportations and wreaked havoc on the streets of Budapest.

In his 1982 essay, entitled 'Hungarian Holocaust', Ranki opines that the drama of the Hungarian Jews fully represented the central contradictions of East-Central European development of modernity: Jewish assimilation; the relationship between small and large countries; the dilemma of assimilation and segregation; and the historical–moral alternatives of collaboration and resistance (Ranki, G. 1988, p. 196). Ranki identifies this specificity as 'fatelessness'. According to Ranki, Western European 'Israelites' shared the fate of their nation, while in Eastern Europe they could view it as some 'eternal Jewish fate'.[8]

> Hungarian Jewry could not interpret the events either way, since from the 19th century, they consciously confessed to be Hungarians and consciously wanted to share national destiny . . . And even if they interpreted their belonging to Hungary differently—either through

identification with the ruling classes or by participation in movements aimed at changing Hungarian reality—their undertaking was always part of Hungarian destiny. Only the harsh reality of deportations, the brutality of Hungarian authorities and gendarmes made them fateless; it confronted the survivors with the conflict of having to seek identity. (Ranki, G. 1988, p. 201)

Ranki's assessment that the fate of Jews in Western European countries was part of their nation's destiny is questionable. Undoubtedly the character of the Holocaust was different in Western and Central Europe and in the East.[9] However, the fate of the Jews in each of these geographical areas was the Nazi program of total extermination, whereas their fellow-citizens' fate was that of occupation or cooperation. Although the Nazis despised some Western nations, on the whole they were deemed to be of a higher racial order than the peoples in the East. Some, like Danes or Norwegians, were classified as Aryans. However (even if considered below the Aryans, like the Slavs), in the Nazi racial order all these nations were deemed to be humans. Jews were not. The world was to be reorganised on Aryan terms, with some, such as Poles and Russians, as slaves to the Germans—but they were to live. But all Jews were to be killed. The old, the dying, the children, the babies—all. The 200 Jews of Albania were on the list of the Wannsee conference. The aspect of total extermination created the qualitative difference between the experience of non-Jews, and Jews. There were genocides and massacres committed by the Nazis, from the 'euthanasia program' to the murder of the Polish intelligentsia, from the fate of the Soviet POWs to the murder of Sintis (Gypsies) and homosexuals—but the Holocaust was distinctly different, unique. The Gypsies were murdered for being 'asocial'. Jews were to be murdered for being Jewish, as Jews and not as members of any nation. Soviet POWs could join the Nazis if they so chose. Occupied nations could cooperate or resist.

While there were some alternatives and options in the first and the second phases of the Hungarian Holocaust, in the third phase Jews did not have real choices left.

The Hungarian Jewish community and its leadership

Hungarian Jews continued to view themselves as part of the Hungarian nation, differing only in religion.[10] Of the three religious trends in Hungarian Jewry (orthodox, status quo and *neologue*), it was the orthodox and the *neologue* leadership which dominated the community. Zionist organisations and leaders emerged from the early 1940s. The movement contained many political and religious groups, ranging from the labour-oriented, secular *Hashomer* to the orthodox religious *Mizrachi* and right-wing *Betar*. The traditional leadership came mostly from the upper middle class, while Zionist leaders, like their mass-base, came mostly from the working and lower middle classes.

The traditional Hungarian Jewish leadership completely lacked young people, intellectuals and artists. It was made up of older, right-wing, rich men, 'an anachronistic group', 'out of their depth', very much like the Hungarian political leadership (Vago 1981, p. 149). There were numerous divisions within the community: by social status and wealth; by the three different confessional frameworks between assimilated, secular, and orthodox; between country and Budapest; between Zionists and non-Zionists.

With the territories re-annexed under the Vienna treaties, there was an influx of left-wing Zionists, especially from Transylvania. They were well-versed in politics and they brought a new dynamism into the Zionist movement. They aided Slovak and Polish refugees and generally engaged in rescue operations. As a result of their activities, in January 1943 an alternative leadership emerged next to the traditional leadership. They differed from the official leadership in many ways. They were mostly in their thirties and early forties, belonged predominantly to the labour wing of the movement, and came from working and lower middle-class backgrounds (Vago 1981, pp. 144–7). Around 1942–43, a third leadership group emerged: the Zionist *Hehalutz* movement. Although they were only a youth group within the movement, because of their independent rescue-activities and armed resistance, they represented the third leadership. These three groups of leadership represented three different levels of social status, political views and age. As Vago observed, the triple leadership was a natural outcome of the specific history and condition of Hungarian Jewry (Vago 1981, p. 147).

Responses to the anti-Jewish legislation

The Jewish response to the anti-Jewish decrees was a logical consequence of the long history of Jewish assimilation in Hungary and has to be viewed within that context. It was poignantly expressed

in a pamphlet which, referring to an 1848 manifesto, emphasised
the same total commitment:

> We are Hungarians and not Jews, not a different nation, because we
> are a separate denomination only when in our houses of worship we
> express our thanks and our innermost gratitude to the Almighty for
> His grace lavished on our Homeland and us, but in every other aspect
> of life we are only patriots, only Hungarians. (Manifesto of the
> representatives of the Hungarian and Transylvanian Jews on the 17th
> of March, 1848).
>   We profess this even today, the spring of 1938. (Vida 1939, p. 63)

The *Numerus Clausus* Act of 1920, which followed the
pogroms, was in clear contradiction of previous laws by defining
Jewry as a 'racial and ethnic minority', by ignoring equality before
the law and, because of this definition, also violating the Minorities
Protection Treaty to which Hungary was a willing signatory. The
Paris-based *Alliance Israélite Universelle*, and the Joint Foreign Committee of British Jews brought the issue before the League of
Nations. The Jewish leaders of Hungary publicly protested against
this 'foreign intervention' into internal affairs. They issued a declaration of protest, which was amply exploited by the Hungarian
government in Geneva, defending their case (Braham 1981, p. 31).
A few years later a Hungarian Jewish leader talked about the
'incident' in front of the League of Nations' subcommittee:

> Hungarian Jewry never asked through any means the intervention of
> foreign Jewry . . . it can be only called tragicomedy how these
> distinguished strangers [the subcommittee] treated the case of the
> Hungarian *Numerus Clausus*. The Chinese delegate, for instance, asked
> at one of the sessions that since at the universities of Budapest baptised
> Jews count as Jews, how do they ascertain if somebody is Jewish or
> not. (Csorba 1990, p. 227)

Although the question is perfectly valid, and thus in the realm of
tragedy, the reasoning clearly tells where Hungarian Jewry stood:
'To us, however much it is to our shame that hundreds and
hundreds of our students have to lead a life of penury abroad, it
hurts us just as much that this our inner pain should be discussed
in front of foreign diplomats' (Csorba 1990, p. 227).

It thus became a shame and a pain of Jews, still within the
'family'. And the source of pride was still Hungarianness: 'the grief
of our nation, the treaty of Trianon must not be the source of
rights. This sentence characterised the proud and honourable

demeanour of Hungarian Jewry, and this declaration was the shield the Hungarian government used . . .' (Csorba 1990, p. 228).

Apart from voicing their protests against the government, the leaders of the Hungarian Jewish organisations had a pragmatic approach: setting up charitable organisations and raising funds to send Jewish students to study abroad.

Hungarian Jews kept to their side of the 'assimilationist social contract'. In spite of the growing evidence to the contrary, they maintained the belief that there was still a contract and that all that had to be done was to answer the 'accusations' (which were validated by answering them). The more difficult it was to keep up the trust, the more effort went into the maintenance of what proved to be a fools' paradise, and the more difficult it became to stop and reassess the situation. A vicious circle was thus generated. With each accusation the determination to show commitment grew, new and clever ways of *proving* commitment were sought, with action, argument and with constant self-monitoring. It was a siege mentality that did not acknowledge that there was a siege.

A constant dialogue was going in which Jews took every word on face value and ignored, literally to their peril, the underlying truth: there was nothing Jews could say that would have changed the situation. There was nothing to prove. The discussion only existed in the perception of the Jews. The accusations hurled at them could not be refuted in any way because the role of these accusations was justification. They did not represent true grievances. They were merely the manifestation of hatred. This 'dialogue' was perpetuating not only the self-delusion of Jews but of Hungarian society. While these accusations were levelled at Jews, while hatred was indulged, the real issues of social justice were effectively obscured. Jews kept on inventing newer and newer arguments, newer and newer ways to prove the accusations wrong. And the more both parties engaged in this 'dialogue', the more the hatred of one side grew and the more the false dialogue (which, by its very nature could not lead to understanding) reassured Jews.

The first anti-Jewish law in 1938 was met by acquiescence. Jewish leaders took their cue from the government and engaged in trying to rationalise the law, arguing that it should take the wind out of the sails of the extremists. The Jewish leadership embarked on a campaign trying to prove the steadfast Hungarianness of the Jewish community. Pamphlets and booklets were printed, *Itéljetek* (You Judge) being particularly notable amongst them.

In neighbouring Romania, the Jewish response to the emergence of the antisemitic Goga–Cuza government was totally different. They appealed to Western powers and to the League of Nations and also kept in close contact with Jewish organisations in other countries, and were actively trying to undermine the oppressive regime politically and economically. Comparing the Jewish leadership of Romania and Hungary, Bela Vago came to the conclusion that although the survival of most Romanian Jews cannot be attributed to the ability of their leaders, neither can the destruction of Hungarian Jewry be blamed on the faults of their leadership. Nevertheless, the role of the leadership was relevant, because:

> We see in Romania the vitality of a less assimilated community that had long been harassed and imperiled. Under conditions of extreme danger, such a community and its leaders proved less vulnerable and more viable than their assimilated, self-confident, more established, more sophisticated and therefore less militant counterparts in Hungary. (Vago 1981, p. 149)

Unlike Hungarian Jews, Romanian Jews perceived themselves as a nation and strove for the status of national minority. There was another significant difference: the leadership was more representative of the community than in Hungary. As in Poland, Jewish politics in Romania was openly Jewish: the political activity of Romanian Jews was conducted on a specifically Jewish platform for specifically Jewish interests.[11] From 1928 there was a Jewish political party in existence and Zionism was also a mass movement (Vago 1981, pp. 138–45). In Hungary, where Jews viewed themselves as a religion and part of the Hungarian nation, the Zionist movement was weak by comparison. True to the Zionist *credo*, in order to fight the 'Jewish question', the movement strove for the redefinition of the self-perception which reduced Jewishness to a religion, and of the political, social and cultural status of Jews. Faced with the anti-Jewish legislation, Zionists too aimed at what they long perceived as the spiritual erosion of Hungarian Jewry: the devaluation of Jewish historical self-awareness and recognition of people-hood. While steadfastly reiterating the need for the repudiation of assimilation, the Zionists' proposals were initially no different from those of the mainstream Jewish leadership. They confined themselves to addressing practical needs as they arose: professional retraining and welfare. By the second anti-Jewish law however, the Zionists re-articulated their position. Advancing the inevitability of the recognition that the Hungarian state itself wanted to end Hungarian–Jewish coexistence, Zionists proposed mass emigration. The Zionists did organise emigration, but also tried to tackle the problem of conditions until the planned exodus. Nathaniel Katzburg saw the distinctiveness in the Zionist response in that it recognised the need to dissolve the Hungarian–Jewish 'partnership' and to prepare for emigration after the war (Katzburg 1966, pp. 168–75).

Mária Schmidt argues that the Jewish leaders knew that they did not have choices. There was nowhere to go. By this time, emigration was out of the question, so they fortified the traditional inner structures (Schmidt 1990, p. 41). The Jewish organisations looked after those who were without income, helped those in forced labour battalions and their families, provided legal aid and re-training (Braham 1981, pp. 344–7).

I believe that a differentiation has to be made between the survival strategies and tactics of the early stages of the Holocaust, that is, before the implementation of the 'Final Solution', and of the time when Jews (leadership and masses) grasped that all Jews were to die. Furthermore, the survival strategies cannot be understood without the recognition of what Lanzmann called the 'terrible loneliness of the Jewish people': that is, that there was no help coming from the outside—not from the nations amongst whom Jews lived and which were now occupied themselves, and not from the Allies or the neutral countries. In this respect again the importance of what they knew and when is critical.

After the German occupation Hungarian Jews faced the final phase of the Holocaust: deportation to death camps. By this time the Nazis had it down pat. The last phase started with incredible force, ease and speed. The Germans followed the same process of destruction as everywhere else. This included the setting up of Jewish Councils.

Some historians argue that the Jewish Councils were powerless and that the Budapest Jewish Council simply did not have the means to help the Jews in the provinces (Schmidt 1990, p. 53). Others, like Randolph Braham, argued that these leaders were living in the 'psychologically understandable illusion' that somehow the community would survive (Braham 1990, p. 12). The *'iberleben'* (survival) hope of all Jews in the ghettoes reflected the survival wisdom, learnt over and over for some two thousand years, repeated over and over after the pogroms of the Crusades, the

Inquisition, the Chmelniecki massacres and many other catastrophes that befell Jews periodically throughout history. But by 1944, the unprecedented aim of total destruction was unfolding and was already known to the world, and to the Jews of Hungary: to the leaders and to the masses.

So the first question is: was this 'illusion' the same, and did it have the same dynamics as the *'iberleben'* strategies in the ghettoes of Poland, or did it ignore compelling evidence? After all, the Jewish community in Hungary had information of the mobile killing units and of the death camps. Was it 'knowledge', as Yehuda Bauer argues? Could they have behaved differently, with their particular history of assimilation and the previous symbiosis with Hungarian society? Finally, what were the options available for the leadership?

The controversy over the role of the Jewish leadership

The debate concerning the role of the Jewish Councils was raised by survivors themselves immediately after the war. Some members of the Jewish Councils were even indicted and tried, and 'courts of honour' agonised over these issues. With the passage of time, Holocaust research re-evaluated the initial condemnations. The lack of real alternatives, the horrible conditions and the fact that all Jews were intended victims became more and more obvious. There are those who feel that because of the uniqueness and the extremity of the destruction, the generations born after the Holocaust do not have the moral justification to make judgments over those who had been forced into choiceless choices.

It has to be asked: what is the relevance of looking at the behaviour of the victim? Did it make any difference what the Jews did? There is the danger that by critically examining the victim, attention—and responsibility—will be deflected from the perpetrator. After all, if the victim can be shown to be complicit, or morally reprehensible, the perpetrator's crime is lessened. Conflating victim–perpetrator–bystander categories by drawing immoral equivalences is the first step towards Holocaust denial (Lipstadt 1993, pp. 85–103). Another aspect is the measure, the guideline for evaluating the victim's behaviour. Is objective critical evaluation possible at all? There are those, like Elie Wiesel, who argue that the 'netherworld' of the victim was a universe with its own rules, incomprehensible and inaccessible after the event. Where the choice is 'Sophie's choice' (you must choose one of your children to die, or both will be killed), is there a choice really? With this question we are entering the evil circle of choiceless choices.

The historical legitimacy of this question was raised by Raul Hilberg and Hannah Arendt. Hilberg's analysis stems from the firm conviction that the behaviour of the Jews mattered, in fact the process of destruction 'ultimately depended' on the behaviour of the victims: 'In a destruction process the perpetrators do not play the only role; the process is shaped by the victims too. It is the *interaction* of perpetrators and victims that is "fate"' (Hilberg 1967, p. 662).

According to Hilberg, a group can react five ways to force: 'by resistance, by an attempt to alleviate or nullify the threat (the undoing reaction), by evasion, by paralysis, or by compliance'. Considering each in turn, Hilberg's accusations are basically two-fold: lack of resistance, passivity and the tendency for 'anticipatory compliance' with Nazi orders. 'Institutional compliance', Hilberg called it, pointing out the sameness in the behaviour of the Jewish Councils and in the behaviour of the masses as well (Hilberg 1967, pp. 662–6). Why was this so? Why did the Jews try to 'tame' the Germans? asks Hilberg. Why did they comply so 'automatically'? Referring to two thousand years of Jewish history, of living as a minority in constant threat, Hilberg asserts that by the time the Jews realised that appeasing and placating would be in vain this time because the destruction was to be complete, it was too late: 'A two-thousand-year-old lesson could not be unlearned: the Jews could not make the switch. They were helpless' (Hilberg 1967, p. 666).

Michael Marrus points to the fact that Hilberg's analysis was based on research which used almost entirely German sources, and that the German documentation would have 'portrayed Jews according to Nazi stereotype'. Marrus joins Hilberg's critics in pointing out that Hilberg's discussion of the Jewish communities was 'remarkably thin' (Marrus 1987, p. 110).

Writing about the Eichmann trial in Jerusalem, Hannah Arendt was deeply influenced by Hilberg's interpretation. But her accusations were even more sweeping. Ignoring the role of the murderers, the real collaborators and the bystanders, individuals and institutions, Arendt condemned the Jewish leadership. For Arendt was certain that were it not for the collaboration of the Jews, the number of victims would have been a lot less: 'To a Jew, this role of the Jewish leaders in the destruction of their own people is undoubtedly the darkest chapter of the whole dark story' (Arendt 1963, p. 104).

Arendt's harsh condemnation of the role of the Jewish Council drew a lot of criticism. The notion of blaming the victim is callous and obscene, and, as Henry Feingold said, 'Something perverse occurs when victims (or witnesses) are singled out for a large share of the responsibility—even if there is an element of truth' (Bauer & Rotenstreich 1981, p. 229). With the publication of Isaiah Trunk's monumental *Judenrat* (Jewish Council), several critics pointed out that Arendt's conclusions were historically unfounded (Bauer & Lowe in Bauer & Rotenstreich 1981, p. xi; Feingold in Bauer & Rotenstreich 1981, p. 223).

I think that the key to understanding *why* Arendt said this is in the opening three words: *to a Jew*. Arendt, the moralist, expected some kind of perfect martyrdom, clear sainthood to contrast with the clear evil—perfect victim to the perfect criminal. This notion ignores the fact that Jews died as individuals for being Jewish: and that being Jewish means being a member of a people, the Jewish nation. And as people, there were weak and strong, rich and poor, religious and non-religious, dark and fair.

Mária Schmidt in a way also denies the people-hood of Jews:

> In reality, Jews as such did not exist. It was only a national socialist fabrication. There were Hungarian Jews and German Jews. Polish, French and Russian, Sephardim, Ashkenazi, orthodox, *neologue*, reform and Hassidim. Noble lords, doctors, salesmen . . . But Jews, simply like that, without any difference—did not exist. (Schmidt 1990, p. 24)

Schmidt's is the Hungarian notion which sees Jews not as a people but as a religion, i.e. Jewish Hungarians and not Hungarian Jews. But while Schmidt is talking from the vantage point of inclusion, according to the Hungarian paradigm formulated by the assimilationist social contract, a Hungarian accepting Jews, Arendt is talking from the vantage point of non-acceptance. People-hood, i.e. being a nation, validates Zionism, and Arendt, already an anti-Zionist, did not. She described Eichmann as a convert to Zionism, for instance (Arendt 1963, p. 36). Arendt did not perceive in Zionism the essential love for the nation and love for the land. She saw Zionism simply as transferring Jewish people to the Middle East. Yet the three words 'to a Jew' implicitly declare that to the rest of the world it is not the behaviour of the Jewish leaders that is the most important. For the Holocaust was the tragedy of Western society, of Western culture, of modernity—the victims were Jewish but the tragedy is shared by humankind. But in Arendt's view, any group could have been the victim.[12] And that acquires a certain relevance.

Viewing any other group as potential victims, in other words, by generalising the victim, we would ignore the very specific, unique aspect of Jews in Western society: their status of being what Ferenc Feher called the 'persecuted *par excellence*', the long history in which the Jewish people was singled out as victim *par excellence*. This status, which, viewing it only in its historical context, Arendt called the 'pariah' status in other writings, produced the total isolation of Jews during the Holocaust. In comparison to other persecuted groups, who could rely on the support of their compatriots (traitors notwithstanding), Jews were surrounded by hostile populations—and help and support were the rare exception. There was no supportive environment of sympathetic populations, no links with the Allies or governments in exile and, as Milovan Djilas pointed out, no prospect of victory (Marrus 1987, p. 141).[13] Arendt's harsh condemnation, then, must also contain the fact that her views were coloured by a self-enforced—and thus false—'objectivity', which used as a point of departure the interchangeability and thus the sameness of any group as victim.

It is also important to remember that Arendt's condemnation contained another deep conviction: that is the repudiation of the 'exception' Jew, expressed at length in her study of Rahel Varnhagen (1957). In her opinion, 'if you are attacked as a Jew you have got to fight back as a Jew, you cannot say "Excuse me, I am not a Jew; I am a human being"' (Arendt 1979, p. 334).

The Jewish leaders were exempting themselves, or at least attempting to exempt themselves from the fate of Jews. By accepting the system of exceptions, argued Arendt, they implicitly validated the rule (Arendt 1963, p. 117).

To Bibó, the system of exemptions was evidence of the moral shortsightedness of Hungarian Jewry. He called it a 'striking Jewish communal deficiency' that 'instead of united protection, how many people, especially the leaders were seeking the dubious course of individual exemptions, in a way accepting persecutions provided they were not extended to those who were exempted . . .' (Bibó 1984, p. 164).

It is hard to disagree with Arendt and Bibó on the issue of exemptions, although again and again one has to remember that no matter from what moral height we view these actions, in each and every case the exception meant the possibility of saving their lives. In other words, the system of exception was corrupt—but to expect refusal is to expect heroism. And one lives in bad times when the only way to be decent is by being a hero.

Arendt called it the 'gravest omission' of the trial of Eichmann that the question of the cooperation of the Jewish leadership was not raised. Without the efficiency of the Jewish organisational structures the Holocaust would not have been as severe, she claimed (Arendt 1963, pp. 110–11). Arendt essentially condemned the Jewish leaders of Hungary.

The title of Mária Schmidt's book about the Hungarian Jewish Council is *Collaboration or Cooperation*. She comes to the conclusion that it was neither. While cooperation is the working together towards a common goal, collaboration contains the meaning of betrayal. Could one call the actions of the Jewish Councils cooperation? No, because the Nazi goal was the murder of the Jews. The goal was not shared. Was it then collaboration in the sense, for instance, of the collaboration of the gendarmes, of betrayal of treachery? (This is the sense implied by Arendt.) But even collaboration contains that meaning of working together towards a common goal.

The poet Abba Kovner, who was a survivor himself and whose name is inseparable from the Vilna ghetto uprising (which started with his passionate manifesto), asked the question:

> [W]hat was collaboration? People were brought to the pits. They were told to remove their last bit of clothing and they did. And then one of them was out of the line and the other ones told him to move back into the line because 'you are making all of us unhappy'. Is that collaboration? Is is choice? Is it power? (Bauer & Rotenstreich 1981, p. 251)

This last question of Abba Kovner is the crucial one. Every Jew was a victim without power. They were faced with choiceless choices. As Abba Kovner said: 'We were all defeated, the dead and the living' (Bauer & Rotenstreich 1981, p. 251).

The Hungarian Jewish leader most often singled out for condemnation, but sometimes for praise, is Kasztner. Kasztner was a Zionist leader, who, on behalf of the Hungarian leadership, tried to negotiate with the Nazis. These negotiations, the so-called 'Europa plan', were started much earlier, by the Slovakian Jewish leaders.[14] By 1944 the complicated talks included the Allies. There were many ramifications to these negotiations, but ultimately they came to nothing. However, Kasztner succeeded in getting permission for 1600 Hungarian Jews to leave. The Hungarian leadership had to select those who would go. Kasztner was bitterly criticised, culminating in a trial after the war in Israel, for selecting rich, 'paying persons' and his own family and friends. Although Kasztner was found not guilty by the court, he was assassinated in 1957 in Tel Aviv.

Arendt scathingly recounted that after the war Kasztner was proud of having saved prominent Jews, 'as though in his view, too, it went without saying that a famous Jew had more right to stay alive than an ordinary one' (Arendt 1963, p. 117).[15] Yet Arendt's condemnation notwithstanding, the Kasztner case demonstrates the impossibility of the choices facing Jews.

The Hungarian Jewish leadership during the Holocaust

Randolph Braham, whose authoritative book *The Politics of Genocide* is the most comprehensive work on the history of the Holocaust in Hungary, addressed the issue of the Hungarian Jewish leadership several times. His evaluation went through some changes. What he calls 'the first dispassionate and fully documented overview, carefully differentiating between facts, claims, and assumptions' regarding the role of Hungarian Jewish leaders was presented by Braham in 1975, at an international conference on 'The Holocaust: A Generation After', in New York. Some six years later, in *The Politics of Genocide*, published in 1981, Braham, in line with his earlier findings, 'tentatively' concluded that the Hungarian Jewish leadership was 'remarkably aware' of what was happening to Jews in Nazidom, yet they failed to inform the masses authoritatively, and as a result the Jews of Hungary were uninformed, unprepared and disunited. In an entire chapter, unambiguously entitled 'The Conspiracy of Silence', Braham painstakingly researched and documented 'who knew what and what did those who knew and were able to act do'. He clearly articulated his position:

> The Hungarian Jewish leaders, like their co-religionists elsewhere, and the leaders of the world at large, were unwilling or unable to

understand both the extent and the speed of the destruction that was
taking place in Nazi-dominated Europe. Their false optimism was
based on the continued survival of the Hungarian Jewish community
in the midst of the cataclysm that was engulfing the neighbouring
Jewish communities. When coupled with their incapacity to accept
the worst, the result was ultimately a disaster. (Braham 1981, p. 724)

By 1985 his position softened. In an essay in *The Holocaust in
Hungary: Forty Years Later* (which he co-edited with Bela Vago),
Braham essentially saw the failure of the Hungarian Jewish leaders
as a result of the 'symbiotic relationship' between the Hungarian
national and Jewish élites during the Golden Age (Braham 1985,
p. 190). The Jewish leaders viewed the antisemitism that surfaced
during the White Terror and which, although toned down, persisted
all through the inter-war years as a temporary aberration, assuming
at each turn that this was to be the last one. The assimilation-accul-
turated Jewish leaders operated on the basis of the assumption that
Hungarian Jewry shared the fate of the Hungarian people. Total
and absolute loyalty to Hungary motivated not only the rejection
of a 'Jewish line', but contact and cooperation with Jews outside
of Hungary. Braham assessed the role of the leadership during the
relative 'normalcy' until the German occupation as quite effective
in serving the community. Their belief that the community in
Hungary would escape the Holocaust 'while tragically mistaken,
was not irrational' (Braham 1985, p. 190).

In the 1988 publication of his paper delivered at an earlier
conference, Braham re-examined the 'conspiracy of silence' thesis.
He analysed the position taken by John Conway, who argued that
the decision to maintain the silence was due to the assessment of
the Hungarian Jewish leadership that their best course of action
was to enter into secret negotiations with the Germans. Braham
found this 'linkage theory' dramatic, and though possessing 'considerable merit', based largely on conjecture. Still, Braham himself,
after examining the rescue attempts, centred his condemnation on
the Allies, also pointing out the passivity of the Red Army (Braham
1988, pp. 447–66).[16] In a discussion following another session on
Hungarian Jewry, Braham exonerated the Jews of Hungary:

Before the occupation they could have done a lot but they were so
certain that the Russians were approaching fast, and everyone knew
that the Germans had already lost the war. They were protected by
the conservative aristocratic government. All these reasonings were

> valid at the time. Moreover, who in his right mind would have
> believed that Germany would invade a fellow Axis partner and ally?
> (Gutman & Greif 1988, p. 444)

And once they did invade, there was not much the Jewish community could do with most of the men already conscripted into forced
labour service.

'Sheep to the slaughter'?—the community

The circle has to widen: one must look not only at the leadership
but at the whole community. The refusal of German Jews 'to
confront real life, a tendency to block out or repress reality' bears
an uncanny resemblance to the reaction of Hungarian Jews
(Bolkosky 1975, p. 184). This description is entirely true not only
all through the Horthy years, with Hungarian Jews hanging on to
the illusion of a still functional assimilationist social contract, but
also of the whole horror-filled year of 1944. In Amsterdam and
Czestochowa, in Bialystock and in Lodz, Jews were hoping against
hope that whatever the horror befalling other communities, their
fate would be different, for a variety of reasons (Schmidt 1990,
pp. 25–6).

For Hungarian Jews to doubt that the Hungarians would
protect them would have been tantamount not only to suddenly
questioning their trust in the Hungarians, but also to admitting
that the integration into the Hungarian nation did not work, that
assimilation on the nationalistic line had failed.

But what about the non-assimilated Jews of Hungary? Why did
not the people of Sziget believe Elie Wiesel's beadle, who came
back with the horrible tale of massacre?[17] Lacking power and thus
real information, they fell prey to the same dynamism as the rest
of the Jewish population of Europe had done earlier. Their information scanty, the religious communities were more involved with
the religious aspects of their life than the secular. Their reality could
cope with the threat of pogrom, that is, the periodical random
violence limited to a few communities, but certainly not this
product of modernity, this all-encompassing, industrialised,
institutionalised evil which meant to eradicate all Jews, all of the
House of Israel, the whole of '*Am Yisrael*' (the Jewish people). At
any rate, the 'secular' worries were mostly in the hands of the
largely assimilated Jewish leadership of Budapest, who hobnobbed
with the nobility and politicians. They were for many a source of

pride and achievement because their high visibility was seen as proof of acceptance and emancipation. They were thus a source of assurance and reassurance that the Jews of Hungary were safe and at home.

In keeping with the Nazi policies regarding the Holocaust, deliberate deception was exercised once the Germans invaded. László Endre, the Arrowcross Secretary of State, wrote at the time:

> The leaders of the Jewish Council have to be summoned, and told that deportations are only from theatres of military operations where there is a lot of spying and sabotage. These Jews [referring to Jews in Carpatho-Ruthenia] are not assimilated, a lot of them infiltrated, consequently their removal is in the interest of the honest Hungarian Jewry. If the rest of them behaves, the deportations will stop. (Ranki, G. 1988, p. 204)

In addition, Hungarian political life was also confused and contradictory. One of the idiosyncrasies of 1944 Hungary was that while deportations had already started in the northern provinces, in Budapest the government was debating whether Jews with the yellow star should be allowed to keep dogs, or buy tobacco.

However, Yehuda Bauer argues that the secret was not so much a secret. It was rather that both the Jewish leadership and the Jewish people were psychologically incapable of absorbing information:

> To say that Hungarian Jewry had to rely on their leadership for information regarding the 'Final Solution' is to misread the whole historical process. This mistake has at its root the confusion between 'information' and 'knowledge'. The information was there all the time, including information regarding the ways in which the Nazis were misleading and fooling their victims. The point is that this information was rejected, people didn't *want* to know, because knowledge would have cause pain and suffering, and there was seemingly no way out. (Bauer, Y. 1978, p. 106)

This is borne out very powerfully by Elie Wiesel, in *Night* (1981). Polish refugees told their story, Hungarian soldiers and Jewish forced labour men returning from the east told of the massacre at Kamenets-Podolsk.

Ultimately, as Vago argued, it was not the leadership that shaped Jewish reality but the reverse (Vago 1981, p. 149). Even though the leadership was not democratically representative of the community, it was representative of the deep divisions within the community.

Bibó also was critical of the victim. He concluded that 'Hungarian Jewry fell for the moral distortions' and shortsightedness in two ways: by accepting the system of exceptions and by observing lawfulnesss. Although Bibó does not separate the two, I deal with them separately because there were different dynamics at work. As to obeying the letter of the law, Bibó remarked: 'amazingly, the majority of Jews did not resolve to hide and to forge papers and while the aim of the persecutors was more and more obvious, still as a body, Hungarian Jewry submitted to the familiar civil authorities even when non-obedience would not have been too risky' (Bibó 1984, p. 164).

Bibó used the word *megszokott*: familiar or customary, or regular or accustomed, to describe the nature of the authorities. This surely must be one of the main reasons why Jews, Hungarian Jews as well, obeyed the authorities. These were authorities they were used to. They were law-abiding citizens. The authority was, literally, authority. A good citizen, in fact most citizens, would not even contemplate disobedience: it would have been tantamount to criminal behaviour. As the conductor on the tram shouted out the commands for expected behaviour, 'move further in', nobody questioned this for fear of becoming the centre of attention, of risking that the tram would be stopped, the police would be called, and then s/he would have to face all the passengers' wrath. Only criminals went against the law and the authority imposing it. Questioning the authority is tantamount to questioning the law of the land—and that, together with morality, is the basic structure of social behaviour. This total and absolute submissiveness to authority started at childhood ('do not step on the grass'), continued at school, (no pupil would dare to enter the teachers' room without explicit permission—and even then with trepidation), and included the absolute, unquestioning acceptance of any text (the book is always right), and the authority of the text was not questioned. In fact, all learning meant accepting knowledge as it was taught. Questioning was not encouraged. Critical thinking and a critical approach simply did not form part of even tertiary education. Law as text remained unquestioned, unchallenged, so too the authority representing the law, the embodiment of the law and ultimately the state. It requires something strong: inner morality, integrity, a sense of justice, pluralism, to question the legality or the morality of the law and, even more, to act on the challenge. Henry Friedlander's words also fit Hungarian Jews: 'German Jews were so caught by their legalism, by their legalistic tradition that they reported voluntarily for deportation, unlike Jews from communities in which this kind of legalism did not exist. If those people had not persisted in the fiction that an actual legal order existed, they would have been forced to think of escape' (Friedlander in Bauer & Rotenstreich 1981, p. 248).

To Bibó, the reason why Hungarian Jews obeyed the orders of their murderers was a symptom of over-assimilation into Hungarian society which lacked vital democratic norms. One can but agree with Bibó. Apart from an exaggerated sense of legalism, both Hungarian and German society had other vital features in common: authoritarian political structures and lack of democracy.

All through the Horthy era Hungarian Jews were supportive of the government and its policies. They were resigned to the selective antisemitism of the ruling classes and hoped that it would be a kind of insurance against the increasingly virulent racism of the fascist parties. The good citizenship of the Hungarian Jews was not a sensitive barometer: on the contrary, it deceived them into believing in enduring, guaranteed security.

Keeping to the assimilationist contract and believing that ultimately they were part of the Hungarian state and society, to the last minute Hungarian Jews thought that Hungarians were rescuers. But Hungarians turned out to be perpetrators and bystanders.

Chapter seven

The aftermath

Six hundred thousand Hungarian Jews, well over two-thirds of Hungarian Jewry, were murdered during the Holocaust.[1] Apart from those who returned from camps, the survivors were largely of the assimilated community of Budapest. The returning Jews found their assets gone, confiscated, looted, synagogues and community institutions, such as libraries, schools, etc. desecrated, demolished. Even cemeteries were vandalised. Although there was a veritable array of legislation, there were no tangible results of restitution or compensation.

But economic hardship was of lesser severity than the loss of family and life as they knew it. In forging a new life, two basic conflicts in perception emerged. Both perceptions persisted and influenced both Jews and Hungarians, and especially their perceptions of each other, over the next 50 years. One of the controversial issues was how Hungarians and Jews viewed and perceived liberation. The other was the presence of Jews in the Communist party.

The German defeat was and is experienced and perceived differently by Hungarians and Jews. 'Liberation' is a loaded, controversial word in Hungarian. Historically, it denotes 1945, but only Jews and Communist official vernacular use/d it.[2] Although many Hungarians were relieved and even happy that the German occupation was over, and, as the election results of 1945 showed, there was quite a surge of support for the leftist parties, there was the inescapable experience of losing both the war and the regained territories.[3] Hungary was vanquished. The Soviet army defeated the Hungarians. At this stage, of course, it was not yet clear that the Soviet army would not leave and that the February 1945 Jalta conference created a new geo-political reality: 'Eastern Europe' under Soviet hegemony. Nonetheless, for the Hungarians—even those who were not supporting the Germans and who were hoping for a German defeat—1945 meant another occupation: that of the Soviet army.

For Jews, however, Soviet victory did not mean losing the war. It meant victory for the good side. It meant liberation and escape from the Nazi and Arrowcross murder-machine. Philosopher Ágnes Erdélyi wrote:

> For me, and for the other surviving Jews it is obvious that we were saved from certain death by the Soviet soldiers—not by anyone else. But this experience does not create a link, rather, it separates us from the others. They [non-Jews] could perceive the fact that liberation was brought by the Russians in many ways. They could be happy or they could view it as a national tragedy; they could be ashamed that they could not achieve it themselves, the less timid could speculate that maybe it would have been better if not the Russians but the English, or the Americans had come. We could only perceive it one way: we survived because the Russians *came*. They [non-Jews] could have been liberated under luckier circumstances . . . For most of us, nothing, not even what happened later could have erased the fact that, then, the Russian soldier was our liberator. (Erdélyi 1991, p. 223)

Erdélyi's description is true of most Jews, at least until the post-Communist years, when the Soviet occupation was reappraised, along with the until then unadmitted and unresearched evidence that many Jews, freshly liberated from forced labour or returning from camps were taken by the Russians for forced labour in the Soviet Union.[4]

This different, in fact diametrically opposite way of perceiving historical events, was not a first in Hungarian history, and in a way it was related to the other conflict: that of the Jews in the Communist party. Both conflicts of perception had historical echoes in the 1919 White Terror. That was the first time that Hungarians and Jews felt differently about an event concerning Hungary. Many Hungarians blamed Jews for what they called the Red Terror and Jews suffered pogroms during the White Terror. Yet, as described in the previous chapter, the antisemitic atrocities of 1919 did not stop Jews from supporting the Horthy regime and rejoicing in its 'successes', namely the return of territories. But what at that time remained unprocessed information for Jews, not only never fully recognised, but suppressed and forgotten, now, after 1945, looked like an obstacle separating Jews from Hungarians. Strangely, it was the other conflict, which could be titled 'Jews and Communism', that—at least for Jews—seemed to dissolve the conundrum.

Surviving Jews could not and did not fool themselves any more that they were an integral and fully accepted part of Hungarian society. This illusion was shattered in the Holocaust, when Hungarian society largely stood by, disinterested, and watched without sympathy while Jews were deported and brutalised. However, it was not only the passive bystander role of society which destroyed the trust. It was also the active participation in the brutalities by many of its members, not only the murdering Arrowcross thugs, but the Horthy regime's gendarmes and *keretlegények,* the soldiers who 'commanded' the forced labour battalions. (The word is untranslatable to English, because the concept does not exist. They were brutal and murderous and thousands of Jews died at their hands even before the German occupation.)

In the pitiless experience of the Holocaust, nationalism turned out to be not only a bitter disappointment as a conduit for assimilation, but an enemy of the Jews. For many Jews the answer was dissimilation and that road led to Palestine, where Jews were fighting for a land of their own, where they would not depend on the goodwill of a 'host' society. Indeed, non-Jewish Istvan Bibó described Zionism and emigration as a way out of the Holocaust and the failed assimilation (Bibó 1984, p. 261). But there was another way which allowed the maintenance of assimilation through a different conduit: and that led to the internationalism and classless utopia of Communism. Or, as Bibó so vividly put it: to 'dissolving in the smelting furnace of social change' (Bibó 1984, p. 256). The Soviet Union fought the Nazis and liberated the Jews. Marxist ideology promised the disappearance of antisemitism. The platform, especially of the Communist party, promised a total break with the ideals and values of the Horthy regime. And with this we arrive at the other conflict between Jews and Hungarians: Jews flocked to the Communist and Social Democratic parties:

> How could I grapple with the awareness that my people is hated in this country—at least was hated yesterday? That they accepted with indifference worse than hatred the murder of my people and my survival? I did not grapple with it, I was not strong enough to face the bare facts. It was preferable to understand that Jewish suffering was part of the millennia-long injustice afflicting society, it was better to believe that with the abolition of social inequities and class

oppression, antisemitism would disappear too. Without question I
knew I had to be a Communist. (Márványi 1991, pp. 238–9)

A study, published in 1995, proposes an additional reason for
Jews joining the Communist party: the author points to the 'joy
of hanging' for a group of 'pseudo-revolutionary fascist Jews', for
whom this was the first time that they could join any kind of power
enforcement organisation: in other words the article proposes that
this was the Jewish chance to become oppressors themselves (Szabó,
R. 1995, p. 36). Róbert Szabó's argument is based on Bibó's
differentiation between the fascist personality and the revolutionary
personality. According to Bibó, the revolutionary personality will
subject morality to the ideal, whereas the fascist personality will
use the ideal to dispense with morality (Bibó 1984, p. 282).[5] But
Bibó did not use his analysis of the fascist personality to explain
why a group of Jews joined the Communist party. Rather, Bibó
came to the conclusion that because of its antisemitic content,
Nazism (or as he called it, fascism) only corrupted Hungarians.[6]
Because antisemitism was the ideological heart of Nazism, it could
only reach non-Jews and degenerate the politics and morality of
Hungarians (Bibó 1984, p. 280). Although Bibó mentioned the
possibility of revenge as a motivation for joining the Communist
party, he emphasised that this is problematic as an explanation (Bibó
1984, pp. 284–5). Szabó's assertion is based on the concept of
vengeful Jews, rather than the analysis of reality. The surviving Jews
left retribution to the authorities.[7] And if by becoming authority
themselves they assisted the capture and punishment of war criminals, they were part of the organisation and did not act on their
own behalf.[8]

Between 1945 and 1948, until Hungary became firmly and
openly part of the Soviet bloc, the changes in assimilation patterns
revealed two developments: a new sense of identification through
Zionism and emigration to Palestine on the one hand, and assimilation through joining the Social Democrats and the Communist
party on the other.[9]

Becoming socialists or Communists allowed Jews not to face
the role Hungarian society had played in the persecution of Jews.
The antisemitism of the Horthy regime and the Holocaust could
be viewed as the outcome of capitalist imperialism, and with the
promise that in the new society there would be no antisemitism,
Jews who chose to stay in Hungary did not have to face the treason

of their neighbours. Deportations and genocide could be viewed as the crime of class, of fascists and Nazis.

The original assimilationist contract had undeniably failed and Hungarian nationalism had turned against the Jews in a spectacularly shocking manner. Now a new contract was constructed, based on the universal revolutionary tenets of Marxist ideology. Through the building of a new, classless society, Jews yet again could participate in an exhilarating new project: this time the creation of a just society. The Jews who went to Israel subordinated their personal needs to the creation of a state of their own—but they did not have to give up their identity and roots. The Jews who stayed in Hungary experienced the elation of building a new society—but those who joined the Communist party had to give up their Jewishness. It seemed for a while that communist ideology had achieved what Christians had wanted for two thousand years.[10]

The exhilarating task of building a new society bore some resemblance to the building of a new nation in the nineteenth century. Hungarians and Jews, it seemed, could join again in a common goal, could fuse in the elation of the new and the shared work for the shared goal. As in the nineteenth century nationalism was the cohesive force and the tool, now Marxism with its allusions of internationalism united Hungarians and Jews and served for the latter as a new, successful assimilatory vehicle. Certainly, there was a lot of support from non-Jews for the left, which, until 1948, meant both the Communist and the Social Democratic parties (Kovacs 1985, p. 209).[11]

The new project also needed a new identity. This new identity meant a denial of Jewishness. It was described in a recent study, entitled 'How did I find out that I was Jewish?': 'It was never mentioned at home that we were Jewish, because we were Communists, not Jews' (Erős et al. 1985, p. 133).[12]

The denial, or rather, the non-admission of being Jewish was widespread and not only among Communist party members. The mainspring of the denial–avoidance was an unwillingness and an inability to deal with the past, with the Holocaust.[13] The fact that this was a new society, with new rules and new laws, meant that the Holocaust could be swept under the carpet by viewing it as part of the old regime.

For most Holocaust survivors there was a long period of 40 years until they began talking about their experiences. For Hungarian Jews there was an additional reason for silence: the fact that up to the last minute Hungarian Jews trusted Hungarians. The failure of assimilation could be resolved by a new, successful assimilation, where nobody uttered the word 'Jew' or 'Jewish' officially.

Thus, after the liberation, a new assimilationist contract was forged, this time between the Communists and the Jews. The party promised the disappearance of the 'Jewish question' and demanded that Jews shed their Jewishness. It was more than conformity and more than total acceptance and support of the party-line. Similar to medieval times, when Christianity strove to convert Jews, and to modernity, when the price of emancipation was assimilation, now party ideology demanded sole identification as Communists and not Jews. The leaders of the party did exactly that, and when the Communist purges started, Jews were not excepted. Jews were persecuted as 'bourgeois' just as much as non-Jews, in fact more, due to the higher number of Jews in businesses.

According to some estimates, approximately one-seventh of adult Hungarians became members of the Communist party after 1945 (Karady 1984, p. 178). The rest of Hungarian society viewed this development with little sympathy. Although antisemitic prejudice needs little or no factual support, the old accusation of Jewish predominance in the Communist party seemed to be reaffirmed. Antisemitism did not disappear: it just used additional and adapted rationalisations, depending on which strata of society it came from.

A year and a half after the war ended, in 1946, there were violent antisemitic incidents and pogroms, which were reported in the press.[14] These pogroms occurred in small towns and villages, where a few surviving Jews had returned and tried to get back their pillaged goods. The property claimed was often no more than household items, in other words not of real value, but nevertheless still valuable to those who had returned and to those who had taken it. A survivor talked of 'eiderdown' antisemitism, because often the property in question was a feather doona (Miháncsik 1995, p. 230). Atrocities were occurring all over Hungary, but predominantly in the villages. The reasons for this village and small-town violence were manifold. Perhaps the most important was that, while all Jews were deported in the provinces, deportations were stopped when it would have been the turn of the Jewry of Budapest, and were not resumed until October. Consequently, more Jews who were believed dead returned to rural areas and to small towns than to Budapest.

That these violent outbursts occurred at all is an indication of the strength of rural Jew-hatred, which had been fed by decades of official antisemitism, by religious and lay leaders, and even by the Communist party.[15] The two main sources of peasant antisemitism were religious teachings and the ideological exploitation of poverty and social injustices by the Horthy regime. The strength of religious antisemitism was manifest in the fact that the blood libel resurfaced in many instances. The radical right, and now the Communists, used anti-Jewish stereotypes and anti-Jewish sentiments as an explanation for economic injustice, as the populists had done. Antisemitism, nurtured and promoted by the Horthy regime, adapted to the new situation. The 'old style' (i.e. religious, racial and political) antisemitism found open expression in the pogroms and antisemitic incidents, but new features became more and more prevalent. One of these features was the class-antisemitism of the Communist party, whose anti-Jewishness was not on racial or religious grounds, but was an expression of its anti-capitalism.[16]

The reclaiming of plundered property was just one source of aggravation and rationalisation of Jew-hatred. Middle-class Hungarians, especially, viewed with irritation the development that Jews, who for decades had not held positions of power, were now prominent in political jobs and in the public service. Going against received wisdom and perception, Bibó argued in 1948 that, in spite of the conspicuous numbers of Jews in the public service and in politics, Jews had less power than ever in the modern era (Bibó 1984, p. 285). Bibó maintained that Jews do not hold positions of power *qua* Jews. He went even further and warned that the position of Jews in the Communist party was not very secure:

> While the openly antisemitic counter-revolutionary state needed cataclysmic and shameful legislation to divest Jews of their positions in the economy, today, if, for the good of the party, the leaders of the [Communist] party deem it necessary that a number of positions should be filled by non-Jews, they do not need special legislation to do it, without even uttering the word 'Jewish'. (Bibó 1984, pp. 288–9)[17]

Written in 1948, this was based on an analysis of the ideological structure and internal policies of the Communist party, rather than facts. Already at this stage there were signs of left antisemitism. The accusation of 'Jewish revenge' surfaced along with the attacks on 'Jews and money'. Jews were admonished not to monopolise claims on suffering, or, more sanctimoniously, were cautioned not to lose moderation in demanding retribution, and were called on to forgive and forget (Bibó 1984, p. 140). The Communist party's newspaper, *Szabad Nép* (Free People), preached to returning Jews to understand Christians living in apartments earlier confiscated from Jewish owners. Populist writer József Darvas, later to become one of the leaders of the Communist party and powerful for decades to come, gave an election speech in the summer of 1945, reported fully in the newspaper *Szabad Szó* (Free Word):

> There is a stratum here, who were subjected to inhuman suffering by blind hatred. This stratum now claims privileges because of their suffering. We acknowledge their suffering, we know very well what they had to endure, we did everything to help them ourselves at the time of their plight [the beginning of the official myth of resistance], but we must stress that if anybody is entitled to compensation because of suffering—that is the working Hungarian nation. [These last three words sound just as stilted in Hungarian as in English—yet it was a phrase used for five decades to come.] We opposed the racial persecution of the past, now we oppose racial privileges. (Darvas 1945, p. 2)

There were certain other ambivalences regarding the Communist party and Jews—almost from the time of liberation. Not only Jews flocked to the Communist party. The so-called *kisnyilasok*, that is, the former rank and file of the Arrowcross party, were encouraged to join.[18] In the same speech, quoted above, Darvas said: 'There is a stratum, the former *kisnyilasok* who were propelled by revolutionary zeal towards the Arrowcross, who were falsely promised bread and land. We have to be forgiving with them' (Darvas 1945, p. 2).

And so the Communist party was not the haven Jews wished it to be. Not only were its ranks filled with *kisnyilasok*, not only were many of the antisemitic populists among its leaders, but the party directives from Moscow were also anti-Jewish.[19] Marxist anti-capitalism was open to the antisemitic imagery of 'Jewish capital', the Jewish capitalist. This in fact, was the main theme of the antisemitic pogroms in 1946.[20]

Apart from its anti-capitalist direction, the new, emerging face of left antisemitism was anti-Zionism. Indeed, already in those three years when Hungary was still open, and the Zionist movement was free to operate, and Jews were free to leave for Palestine (even though they were not free to arrive there due to British anti-refugee policies), and even though when the time came, the Soviet bloc supported the establishment of the independent state of Israel, there was palpable anti-Zionism coming from the left, especially the Communist party. The Communist party's official organ, the *Szabad Nép*, warned:

> Now, when the whole country, irrespective of religion, is working for the recognition of Hungarians as a nation, the Zionists don't have anything better to do than the fight for Jewry in a not even recognised nation . . . It is not yet ten month ago that the Red Army put an end to the wickedness with the yellow star, the massacre under the flag of racism . . . there are those who want to put up the yellow star again. (Szabó 1995, p. 42)

This was the time when, prompted by what he saw as neo-antisemitism, Bibó wrote his *Zsidókérdés Magyarországon 1944 után* (Jewish Question in Hungary after 1944).[21] In these first three years until 1948, the year of the Communist takeover, many publications, including testimonies, memoirs and reports, appeared. After 1948, there were publications in Israel and in other countries, with France and the United States leading the list. After the long silence imposed by orthodox Marxist historiography, Hungarian historians and writers also started to publish works concerning the Holocaust. But even now nothing surpasses the lucid analysis and the underlying normative morality of Bibó's essay.[22]

There are three phases in Bibó's account of the twentieth-century development of the 'Jewish question'. The first phase started with the White Terror in 1919. Bibó saw the anti-Jewish legislation as the beginning of the destruction of Hungarian Jewry, in which the next stage was the German invasion of Hungary. The second phase was characterised by the collective responsibility of Hungarian society for the deportation and murder of Hungarian Jews. The period immediately following the Holocaust was the third phase. In this era Bibó identified two crucial issues: the need of Hungarian society for soul-searching and for facing responsibility, and for the Jews the examination of Jewish perspectives and a review of assimilation. Bibó saw both as vital for Hungarian democracy. In fact, it was clear to Bibó that the validity of democratic norms in Hungarian society depended on how these issues were handled, and that the measure and success of democracy depended on how collective responsibility was dealt with.

After the war he perceived with growing concern that the Jewish identity of the survivors who chose to stay in Hungary did not intensify. Even more alarming he deemed the total and absolute avoidance of self-examination demonstrated by the cultural élite concerning the Holocaust, during which they were passive bystanders at best. To Bibó this behaviour spelt danger. He was concerned that by missing this outstanding historical and psychological moment for self-reflection, absolution would be too easy and too quick, and the chance for recognition and analysis of the roots of antisemitism would be forfeited. He saw that, after the end of the war, antisemitism was rekindled.

Without facing the 'Jewish question', Bibó argued, democracy could not be attained. As political philosopher Ferenc Feher emphasised, using Habermas's much later coined terminology, 'domination-free communication' was a crucial constituent of Bibó's model of democracy (Feher 1980, p. 9). Feher made the inescapable comparison with another 'worthy defender of the Jews': Sartre (Feher 1980, p. 11). Yet, not surprisingly, Sartre, coming from a different direction (that of the radical left existentialist) called the democrat a 'sorry champion' of the Jews in his *Portrait of the Anti-Semite*:

> For a Jew, conscious and proud of being a Jew, who insists on the fact that he belongs to the Jewish community, without at the same time ignoring the ties which bind him to a national collectivity, there is not such a great difference between the anti-semite and the democrat. The former wants to destroy him as a man, so that only the Jew, the pariah, the untouchable will remain: the latter wants to destroy him as a Jew, in order to preserve in him only the man, the universal and abstract subject of the rights of man and of the citizen. (Sartre 1948, p. 47)

According to Sartre, by denying collective identity, the democrat defends the Jew as a person, but annihilates the person as a Jew (Sartre 1948, pp. 45–6). Bibó did not do that. He examined every option for Jews from various modes of assimilation to religious or nationalist Jewish identity—without preaching assimilation either from the Hungarian nationalist inclusionist standpoint or from the Marxist stance of class. Neither was Bibó a 'philosemite', a sentimental protector of Jews as 'pet victim'. Rather, Bibó followed his own moral normative which had human dignity as its centrepiece.

Bibó's moral stance and commitment to democracy suggests another comparison: to Rosa Luxemburg and 'the humane spirit of

her Marxism' (Wistrich 1990, p. 18). Rosa Luxemburg had deep
respect for individual freedom and for democracy. She wrote:

> Lenin is completely mistaken in the means he employs. Decree,
> dictatorial force of the factory overseer, draconian penalties, rule by
> terror, all these things are but palliatives. The only way to rebirth is
> the school of public life itself, the most unlimited, the broadest
> democracy and public opinion. (Wistrich 1990, p. 19)

Yet, Rosa Luxemburg, herself Jewish, could not, and did not
transcend the Marxist view of antisemitism. Luxemburg believed
that both antisemitism and the inferior status of women were but
social details which would be taken care of by the advent of
socialism. In the meantime there was no point in paying any special
attention to it. Wistrich argued that Luxemburg's uncritical acceptance of the Marxist doctrine regarding these issues stemmed
directly from her Jewish background.[23] Bibó, unhampered by such
a background, but with the same commitment to Marxism, morality
and to democracy, followed the route all the way. The result is the
comprehensive treatment of the 'Jewish question'. His analyses, his
deductions and forecasts are not only still relevant and potent, but
assumed a new relevance in the post-Communist era.[24]

After the Holocaust, indignant denial of responsibility produced
a distortion of Hungarian national identity very similar to the
reaction to Trianon. A vital part of self-hood is the incorporation
and integration of the past.[25] With the condemnation of Hungarian
Jews, the sense of historical continuity suffered. Denial strengthens
guilt, mystifies, and leads to loss of self-esteem and dignity. The
losses of Trianon were not as destructive as the reaction to it.
Summing up the situation, Bibó wrote:

> After the liberation, the first shock having passed, increasingly
> palpable re-emerging antisemitism surrounds the survivors.
> Concerning this issue, official and semi-official, social and moral
> bodies made various declarations, the essence of which can be
> summarised by two simple theses. One thesis is the statement that
> the majority of Hungarians was far removed from the horrors
> perpetrated by the Germans and their stooges and that the worthier
> members of Hungarian society did everything in their power to
> prevent them. The other is the condemnation of the renewed
> antisemitism, and the statement that it should be vigorously opposed.
> Wherever any well-intentioned organisation tries to say something
> morally lofty, humane and reassuring, ultimately, notwithstanding the
> pains taken, they can't go beyond variations on these two themes;

and somewhere deep down everybody feels that both statements are meaningless and convey nothing, or rather, that they evade something. (Bibó 1984, p. 139)

Dialogue was thus prevented. It never started in the following decades either.

In order to be able to carry on and in order to start a new life after the war, Hungarians and Jews had tried to forget what happened. The problem was that both tried to forget a different experience. Jews tried to forget that they had been rejected, victimised, brutalised, and murdered, while the majority of Hungarians tried to forget that they were bystanders, or worse, perpetrators of these crimes. This mutual effort of forgetting, but trying to forget diametrically opposite events, characterised and in certain ways determined not only the three years immediately after the Holocaust, but the following decades and especially the post-Communist era.[26]

Chapter eight

Nationalism, antisemitism and assimilation

The link between assimilation and modern political antisemitism was nationalism. The case of Hungary highlights that both inclusion and exclusion used the agency of nationalism. Through the specificities of the Hungarian–Jewish experience, have also analysed the relationship between traditional Christian anti-Jewishness, modern political antisemitism, and how, once allied with anti-liberal conservatism, nationalism accommodated and reinforced the hatred of Jews. Another theme which has run through the book is the relationship between hatred, political ethos, and the state and legal institutions.

The creation of the modern nation–state was underpinned by the ideals of popular freedom and sovereignty. Nationalism in the nineteenth century was firmly linked with Enlightenment ideals, and thus was a doctrine of liberty and independence, enabling modernisation. The universality of the liberal ideals demanded that emancipation should be non-selective. Equality meant the equality of all.[1] It meant that Jews, who had been placed outside the European community all through the middle ages, had to be brought into society, integrated, included. As Ernst Gellner established, the role of nationalism was indispensable in the creation of a homogeneous culture, which in its turn was indispensable in education, without which the modern industrial nation could not develop. With emancipation, Jews were 'invited' through the agency of this homogeneous culture—language, traditions, mores and customs—to be part of the modern state. Thus, in this period at least, assimilation and nationalism are closely linked. Assimilation is a prerequisite of the homogeneous culture, nationalism seeks to assimilate, and, at the same time, nationalism is the assimilatory vehicle.

In Hungary, not only the homogeneity, but important aspects

of national culture had to be created, especially language. The quest for modernisation developed simultaneously with the creation of the national language and culture. In fact, the same people who fought and struggled for independence from the Habsburgs, for a sovereign, modern state and industrialisation, were also actively involved in the cultural birth of the Hungarian language. The fight for the creation of the modern nation ran parallel to the linguistic renewal. The role of language had an added dimension of relevance in Hungary. The fact that Hungary consisted of multi-lingual nationalities created the demand for these minorities to Magyarise. Self-determination was perceived by Hungarians as a Hungarian prerogative in their part of Europe.

In nineteenth-century Hungary, similarly to the rest of Europe, the 'Jewish question' first emerged in the context of liberalism, which dictated the emancipation of Jews, and in the context of nationalism which simultaneously demanded assimilation and was the vehicle of assimilation. The liberal, inclusionary approach made emancipation dependent on assimilation, while the antisemitic, exclusionary approach questioned the ability and the willingness of Jews to assimilate and thus was against emancipation. Thus, while the ethnic minorities were subjected to forceful Magyarisation, unquestioned by any segment of Hungarian society (except maybe by a few liberals), Hungarian Jews had to fight for the right to assimilate and continually prove successful assimilation.

The paradox of assimilation

This presented a paradox of assimilation peculiar to Hungary. For the ethnic minorities it was an imposed obligation, unwanted and resented. For Jews assimilation was a disputable right, something to fight for and defend, its success proven constantly.

The difference between the Jews and the ethnic minorities was, firstly, that historically they were assigned different status within society (Jews were on the periphery of Christian society, not part of the social hierarchy, while other ethnic minorities had their place within that hierarchy). Secondly, although they shared the social oppression of the underprivileged and the discrimination against the non-Magyars, Jews were exposed to religious discrimination. Thus, three levels or grades of discrimination and oppression are discernible. On the first level was the Magyar peasant; on the second level the non-Magyar peasant who also had to put up with national discrimination; on the third level the Jewish lower classes, who, on top of all that, were subjected to religious discrimination. While the non-Hungarian nationalities were expected to change their nationalities, i.e. become Magyar, in speech and in sentiment, Jews also had to change or at least reform their despised and reviled religion, especially its publicly visible aspects. Thus for Jews the demand to assimilate was really a double call: to become Magyar, *and* to reform their religion and to abandon Jewishness, or at least some aspects of Jewishness. With this demand we arrive at the paradox of emancipation.

The paradox of emancipation

The paradox of emancipation was the impossibility of the demand of assimilation. Emancipation means making equal, of being set free of legal, social and political restraints. But, in fact, Jews were really emancipated for what they promised to be: fully assimilated, that is, non-Jews. In other words, emancipation was granted to the Jews not to participate fully as Jews, but as a first step for the process to become non-Jews.

In Hungary, there were specific political and social imperatives, which made the emancipation of Jews vital. In the process of industrialisation and economic modernisation the role of the middle class is crucial. In Hungary, this middle class had not even started to develop at the beginning of the nineteenth century, and only had faint echoes at the time of the Compromise, when, becoming equal partners in the Austro–Hungarian Monarchy, explosive modernisation started in Hungary. The extraordinarily multitudinous nobility not only took on nationalism in their quest for national independence but also promoted industrialisation. Jews were instrumental to both the industrialisation of the economy and building, indeed largely becoming, the middle class.

Hungarian specificities

The Hungarian ruling aristocracy eagerly facilitated the development of middle-class and industrial and economic modernisation, but at the same time they were committed to the preservation of feudal structures. This resulted in three other Hungarian specificities:

1 Unlike in other parts of Europe, there was no existing middle class to serve as model for assimilation. Thus, wealthy Hungarian Jews tried to emulate the aristocracy.

2 Connected to this phenomenon was another specificity: the considerable numbers of Jews who became ennobled. The ennoblement of comparatively large numbers of Jews signified the importance of Jews in the Hungarian economy. It also signified their acceptance and recognition on pre-modern, aristocratic terms in the feudal and autocratic structures of the Monarchy.

3 The explanation of high Jewish participation in the socialist movements partly lies in the fact that modernisation was the project of the modernising aristocracy who not only provided the assimilatory model and niche, but the boundaries of the project. Because of the aristocracy's wish to maintain certain pre-modern structures, modernisation stayed unfinished and limited in Hungary. Modern urban resentments against the semi-feudal agrarian structures were felt and articulated by Jews who wished to carry modernisation further. At the end of the Liberal Era, this conflict was articulated by the radical circle of Jászi, and it culminated in the relatively large numbers of Jews in the 1918–19 revolution, and, articulated differently, it reemerged in the Horthy era, as the populist–urbanist conflict of the middle classes.

The 'over-representation' of Jews in the revolutionary movements after World War I stemmed from the role of the Jews in the modernisation of the country and, ultimately, was also connected to assimilation through nationalism. Jews were needed to fill up the middle class and their social acceptance was contingent on the aristocracy who, as demonstrated by the ennoblement of Jews, did accept the Jews. However, most of the Jewish population did not become industrial magnates and bankers and there was no social acceptance of working-class or rural Jews. Neither the proletariat nor the peasantry accepted Jews. Indeed, Christian Jew-hatred and anti-capitalist antisemitism was widespread among these classes. They were joined in these sentiments by the increasingly impoverished gentry, who resented both the rich capitalist Jews whom they perceived as usurping the gentry's former status as second in riches to the aristocracy, and the success of Jews in the liberal professions (who, by this time, largely constituted the liberal professions). These Jews faced not only social non-acceptance, but a wall of resentment and antisemitism. The secularised lower middle-class and working-class Jews, alienated by their poverty or modest wealth from the prosperous industrialist Jews, found the universalism and classlessness of Marxism (and socialist ideas generally) an appealing and accommodating ideology. Appealing, because socialism echoed the messianic teachings of Judaism, and accommodating, because it promised the atrophy of antisemitism. By being only concerned with social class and promising to build a classless society, it offered the ultimate assimilation.

Another sociological–political characteristic of the Hungarian empire made the process of Magyarising Jews vital: the fact that Hungarians needed Jews to make up the ethnic balance in the multinational Empire. With the Magyarisation of Jews, Hungarians constituted the numerical majority amongst the ethnic minorities. The emancipation and assimilation of Jews, therefore, became vital not only for modernisation but because of the nationalities question as soon as the Empire was established. Hence the essence of the assimilationist social contract was that Jews should Magyarise.

Jews took on Hungarian language and culture with remarkable speed and enthusiasm. The construction of a new identity, necessitated by changed social and legal status, used Hungarian nationalism to an extent that is only comparable to German Jewish identification.

Hungarians and Jews had two common projects: the *construction of a new, modern identity*; and, by taking on the crucial task of industrialisation, and the equally crucial Magyarisation, the *creation of a modern nation–state*. But although both shared projects seemed to be in the collective national interest, the assimilationist social contract was 'negotiated' with the upper echelons of the nobility. Since the interest of the state, of the nation, was articulated and determined by the aristocracy and the liberal stratum of the gentry, the assimilationist 'contract' was endorsed and authorised not by the whole of the nation but by the upper classes only.

In Hungary, where feudal structures stayed largely intact, the aristocracy and the upper levels of the gentry who served in the civil service, constituted the ruling class. The increasingly large segment of impoverished gentry, the newly developing proletariat and, certainly, the peasantry did not benefit from modernisation in the same way as the aristocracy or the new middle class. Consequently they did not view modernisation with the same enthusiasm. However, the strong state protected the Jews from sporadic antisemitic violence and it also thwarted the development of an indigenous antisemitic movement. Although Istóczy's antisemitic platform was part of a European trend, Jews were still needed. Industrialisation and economic modernisation in Hungary was not advanced enough to accommodate the ideology of modern political antisemitism.

This did not mean that in this period there was no antisemitism at all. Even when the ruling state policy was inclusion, Christian Jew-hatred lived on underneath, albeit because of its suppression by the otherwise modernising state, not 'modernised', that is, not becoming modern political antisemitism with a racial content. The Tiszaeszlár blood libel was in essence the paradigm. The medieval concept met enlightened defence, the sporadic anti-Jewish excitement met the police, and the modern political antisemitism of Istóczy did not become a mass movement or even have the effect of changing the nature of antisemitism, but fizzled out in parliamentary disinterest and even scorn. In spite of Istóczy's attempts, for quite a while, Hungarian antisemitism remained essentially medieval, religious, anti-Jewish sentiment. In Hungary, not only were conditions not yet ripe for political antisemitism, itself a phenomenon of modernity, but the regime's interests and policies were contrary to it.

The demise of liberalism by the end of the nineteenth century changed the nature of nationalism. By the beginning of the twentieth century, it became allied with conservatism and other anti-modernity ideologies, such as the *Völkisch* movement. Nationalism not only ceased to be an agent of modernisation, but turned against it. And, as before, when it was a liberal doctrine and an agent of modernisation, Jews were directly affected. Nationalism, which brought emancipation and acted as a vehicle of assimilation, now, in turning anti-liberal and anti-modernity, turned against the Jews and became an agency for antisemitism. Even in countries where there were political enemies outside of their country, the enemy within was the Jews.

The transition from inclusion to exclusion signalled the victory of political antisemitism. The powerful ideology of nationalism became a conduit, an agency of antisemitism. In France this was manifested spectacularly with the Dreyfus affair, in Germany and Austria with the rise of the *Völkisch* movement. In Hungary it came somewhat later. The Tiszaeszlár blood libel case was defeated by the liberals and the strong state. But World War I, and, even more decisively, the revolution and the Trianon peace treaty, changed the whole sociological and political landscape in Hungary too. The switch from inclusion to exclusion, from protection to pogrom, seemed to happen overnight.

The rise of political antisemitism in Hungary was connected to changes of three basic factors, the very factors which earlier made the role of Jews indispensable: modern economy, middle class and ethnic balance. Modern economy was built at a spectacular speed in Hungary. Within a few decades the success of industrialisation was measurable not only in national wealth and rate of economic growth, but in the rise of the burgeoning middle class, whose interests clashed with the already established Jewish middle classes. The end of the war brought not only defeat, but the end of the empire. As the Monarchy was dismantled Hungary truly became a nation–state: there were almost no minorities left. Not only were Jews not needed to tip the ethnic balance any more, but the new, truncated Hungary, full of ethnic Hungarians, made the Jews stand out as different even more. Now the resentment already brewing under the surface could freely bubble up to the surface. Antisemitism was not oppressed any more by the strong state—the state having been transformed—and, encouraged by the new political structures, animosity against Jews strengthened and became more widespread. Within the new borders, even the section of gentry, which until now earned its livelihood and, maybe even more importantly, occupied positions of power as civil servants, found that their role was gone with the rest of the empire. They were now ready and eager to take over the role of capitalists and professionals from the Jews, as the 'Christian Hungarian middle class'. All these changes came practically overnight with the Trianon Treaty. But even before signing the treaty, there were the revolution and the seminal pogrom of the White Terror. The combined traumas of loss of war and loss of empire were aggravated with yet another fissure of continuity through the 1918–19 revolution. The fact that for centuries Jews were the traditional scapegoats, the victims *par excellence*, and that rampant political antisemitism from the surrounding countries was exerting an insidious influence, easily combined with these historical traumas. Thus, modern political antisemitism in Hungary emerged as a mixture of traditional Christian anti-Jewishness, the influence of antisemitic movements in neighbouring countries and of specific historical events.

What made the White Terror a seminal event in these developments was its subsequent ideological justification and, indeed, glorification. The same people who conducted or condoned the pogroms were well established within the regime that came to rule Hungary for the next decades. Antisemitism became an integral part of the ideology and policies of the Horthy regime. The exclusionary policies of the Horthy regime reflected the times.

After the pogroms and the anti-Jewish *Numerus Clausus* Act, antisemitism became central to all social and political discourses. In fact, the pressing social problems were presented, and willingly perceived, as problems caused by Jews. Unlike its allies, Germany and Italy, Hungary did not become a full fascist state—although it shared the right-wing authoritarianism, the same border-revisionist foreign policies and the desire for revenge.

In the first decades of the century, Hungarian antisemitism was initially more informed by anti-liberalism than by racism. But with the development of the Christian national principle, which declared that only the Christians are Hungarians, Hungarian patriotism and nationalism became interchangeable, or rather, fused with antisemitism. This was underpinned by vehement anti-Bolshevism. The regime and the nation agreed on the 'Jewish question'. This, together with the pro-German foreign policies, provided fertile ground to proliferating fascist and Nazi groups.

Although it increasingly used racist terminology and had racist overtones, the essence of Hungarian antisemitism was nationalism. While Italian fascism was nationalist without being antisemitic and racist antisemitism was at the heart of Nazism, in Hungary nationalism and antisemitism fused in a particular way, so that during the Horthy era one stood for the other, and they were not only interchangeable but also interdependent.

Unoccupied and sovereign until 1944, Hungary willingly and eagerly enacted anti-Jewish laws which withdrew basic human rights and curtailed the economic activities, especially of lower middle class Jews. But the Jewish economic preponderance, developed in the former Liberal Era, persisted, and it was clear that the regime needed Jewish industrialists to maintain the economy. This situation, coupled with a wish to maintain sovereignty, kept the Horthy regime from surrendering Hungarian Jews.

The answer to the inevitability of the Holocaust in Hungary concerns the role of Hungarian institutions and of the Hungarian government and the role of the Hungarian people as active participants and passive bystanders in the destruction of Hungarian Jewry. It is the very cooperation of Hungarian institutions and the overwhelming and mostly hostile indifference of Hungarian society that holds the key to the inevitability of the Holocaust.

In light of the consistent pro-German and anti-Jewish policies of the Horthy regime, from its inception to its demise, the attempts to wriggle out of the alliance had to fail. The pro-German and anti-Jewish ethos was too fundamental to the regime and to society. So, in this sense, the outcome was inevitable. The long decades of ethos and policy building could not be offset by the feeble see-saw politics of a few months. The regime, born in the pogroms of the White Terror, ended in the Holocaust. The state-sponsored and population-supported antisemitism between the two events, enunciated by politicians and articulated by the intelligentsia, hailed and unquestioned by any sociologically relevant strata of society, legislated over a number of years, increasingly harshly and viciously, was an integral part of the political ethos and social *bona mores*. With it, Hungarian society 'graduated' from the acceptance of the sporadic violence of 1919 to the acceptance of collaboration in the deportations by Hungarian society.

There was a causal connection between policies of the Horthy regime, the widespread social support of the irredentist foreign policies, the economic containment of Jews, the sending of Jewish men into forced labour battalions, the indifference, often glee, with which Hungarian society viewed deportations and the destruction of Hungarian Jewry. In other words, the ideological, historical, political and social developments inevitably led to the Holocaust in Hungary.

After the Holocaust, both nationalism and antisemitism went underground. In exact reversal to the Horthy regime, neither were political *bona mores*. The assimilationist contract developed between the Communists and the Jews was adhered to at least for a decade. It contained a total absence of the word and idea of 'Jewish', and the suppression of 'bourgeois' antisemitism by the regime; a broad acceptance of Communist ideology and all trimmings of Jewishness abandoned by the Jews. Members of the Communist party or not, Jews yet again widely participated in the building of a new society—this time convinced not by nationalist but internationalist slogans and being part not so much of a nation but of the 'dictatorship of the proletariat'. Yet antisemitism, in the guise of anti-capitalism, was very much present in left-wing ideology.

Postmodern antisemitism

Modern antisemitism links with larger, more general ideologies. Having been part of religious teachings for two millenia, in modernity, antisemitism became an ingredient of militant nationalism and of left internationalism. Antisemitism was (and is) used as a political *tool* to show *commitment to an ethnic group*, as for instance Hungarian or Romanian antisemitism between the wars, and Arab antisemitism in recent decades. As in the past, antisemitism is still used in the political struggle against 'modernist oppression', for instance, by militant African–American antisemitism or by numerous third world struggles. Non-Western antisemitism is especially observable through the issue of Holocaust denial. What is the meaning of the Holocaust for non-Western culture? For the third world? It could be perceived as an issue for Western civilisation, after all it 'belongs' to Western civilisation.[2] Yet, already in 1959, Adorno observed: 'Today the fascist fantasy undeniably blends with the nationalism of the so-called underdeveloped countries' (Adorno 1986, p. 123).

By linking the Holocaust to the state of Israel, Holocaust denial transcends the obvious Nazi, neo-Nazi (including skinhead) groupings and surfaces in the non-Western world. This is behind the strange political alliances. Nazis found haven in Arab countries and (neo-)Nazis and Islamist terrorists found common ground in their hatred of Jews and Israel. Unreconstructed Nazis, who seek to reclaim the 'honour' of Nazism by denying the Holocaust and arguing that it was a Jewish 'invention', supported Saddam Hussein and opposed the Gulf War.[3] Books on Holocaust denial (alongside *Mein Kampf*) are printed and sold in Damascus and Cairo and are promoted and distributed by the Ku Klux Klan. Holocaust denier Butz was invited to speak to Louis Farrakhan's Nation of Islam. In 1992, the world anti-Zionist conference was scheduled to have Farrakhan, the Black Muslim leader, alongside infamous deniers of the Holocaust such as Robert Faurisson, Fred Leuchter and David Irving and representatives of the paramilitary Russian *Pamyat*, of *Hezbollah* and *Hamas*.[4] What all these diverse groups had in common was the hatred of Jews.

But there are other aspects of this phenomenon. Modernisation is a Western concept. In Western society the problems of modernity appeared as connected, or at least connectable, to Jews and Jewish issues. The third world perceives Western modernisation as a threat to identity which now has to be reclaimed and developed in spite of the influence of Western culture. For those who are reclaiming their own identity (and not only Moslems or fundamentalists) it is a ready-made connection to use those ideologies (or parts of those ideologies) which attacked modernity through Jews.

In a post-colonialist context, Jews are perceived as symbolising the white enemy, the white slave-trader and keeper; colonialism and colonialists; the pornographer and the perverter of culture; American imperialism and corruption in the Middle East. If modernity equals Western culture (traditions, morals and imagery), attributing the ills of modernity to Jews allows non-Westerners to still identify with some Westerners through a 'shared' hatred. Stressing this mutual hatred also helps to trump up support. The 'shared' hatred also serves as a kind of legitimation: if we share the enemy we must be on the same side. Holocaust denial is the platform where the radical right of Western societies and some elements of the third world meet.[5] But why the Jews again? Is it the sheer strength of Western culture which is inherently diffused with antisemitism and that postmodernity after all is still informed and determined by modernity?

The hatred of Jews went through being a religious, racial or class issue, but while all three left their residues, ultimately it is connected to the nationalist issue.[6]

Nationalism and identity in Hungary

Both antisemitism and assimilation are essentially linked to nationalism, and in its different phases, nationalism was a conduit for assimilation and for antisemitism.

Initially, Hungarian nationalism was assimilationist and not antisemitic, although the first signs and stirrings of modern antisemitism appeared in the Liberal Era. After World War I, with the necessity to adapt national identity to the vastly changed situation, nationalism changed. Influenced also by the trauma of revolution and discontinuity, Hungarian nationalism became anti-liberal, like most, more 'advanced' European nationalisms already had by the end of the nineteenth century. This phase of nationalism, adopting modern political antisemitism, was emphatically anti-assimilation. In the discontinuities of the revolution and of the changed status from empire to inconsequential humiliated small country, continuity was found in the conservative content of the ethnic

Hungarian identity. Racial tenets informed official policies and ideology. The earlier aristocrat–bourgeois alliance, which aimed at modernisation, was superseded by a bureaucratic–populist direction, which aimed at maintaining the economy, suppressing the Jews and refusing social change. The three aims were 'fortuitously' linked: social justice was presented as the 'Jewish question', this pleased the racist right and the populist left. The national interests of Christian Hungarians became anti-Jewish and anti-assimilation. As nationalism and antisemitism fused on the platform of Christianity, the alliances and enemies were clear: Nazi Germany and fascist Italy were allies, and the West, especially France, England and America, were the enemy along with the Bolshevik Soviet Union. And Jews were the enemy inside. The Christian national principle set the Horthy regime's political course and led to collaboration in the deportations as the last ally of Nazi Germany.

The link between Hungarian Jewish assimilation and nationalism becomes even more pronounced when viewed in the context of the shared project of nation-building. Economic and social modernisation and the construction of a modern national identity were shared projects for Hungarians and Jews in the nineteenth century. The connecting tissue was nationalism. With the loss of the Empire, and the discontinuities and traumas of the revolution, Hungarians had to reconstruct their identity. This time however it was not a shared project: Jews became outcasts. The new Hungarian identity centred on the Christian middle classes. Jews shared the nationalist grief of losing the territories, but neither their sincerity nor their commitment was wanted. The assimilationist social contract was broken, the alliance was over, although Jews went on adhering to it. They stayed Hungarian patriots and kept on fulfilling their commitment. After World War II, Hungarians and Jews, yet again, participated in the same project: this time the building of a new society. This new project, with the underlying socialist ideology, became the new assimilatory vehicle.

The role of Jews in the revolution of 1918–19 and following World War II were interconnected historically. That is, the accusation of being responsible for the revolution and the vehement anti-Communist stance of the Horthy regime was one of the motivations of post-Holocaust participation in the socialist parties. They provided the opposite ideology to nationalist particularism and to antisemitism. It was not only the anti-Bolshevism of the Horthy regime, but the very Christian national principle which proved to be the propelling force *away* from everything that the regime stood for and *towards* socialist movements.

For Jews, in the pitiless experience of the Holocaust, nationalism turned out to be not only a bitter disappointment as a conduit for assimilation, but an enemy.

Was assimilation successful in Hungary? If the measure of success is social integration and social acceptance—Hungarian Jewish assimilation was a success in the Liberal Era and became a failure in the Horthy regime. If the measure of success is the construction of a national identity, Hungarian Jewish assimilation was and is a success story, from the time of the Liberal Era, through to the years of Communism. If, however, the measure of success is modern identity, that is, a new, multi-layered plural identity, Hungarian Jews became too Hungarian and suppressed their Jewishness too much to be truly plural.

The Hungarian experience raises the question of relevance of the state policies and institutions in the success of antisemitism as a political movement. Antisemitism becomes pervasive when it is attached to, or constitutes part of, a larger, more general ideology. In the middle ages this ideology was religion, in modern times it is nationalism. In pre-modern times all institutions and all of society shared the same ethos based on the unified ideology of religion. In modern times, with the separation of church and state, ethos became a pluralised social construct, in which both state and religious institutions played a role. The Hungarian experience suggests that the state and state policies do play a vital role: by supporting or suppressing antisemitism, the state exercises immediate control *and* it influences political ethos.

Thus, until the twentieth century, antisemitism did not become a mass-movement in Hungary, and, in spite of Istóczy's ingenious and vigorous attempts, old-fashioned Jew-hatred did not graduate into modern political antisemitism in Hungary. There were four interconnected reasons:

1   *The late development of modern conditions* meant that the ills of modernity appeared later and were less obvious.
2   The effect of the *lack of middle class*, especially the lower middle classes, which form the mass-base of antisemitic movements, was twofold. In Hungary, where there was no third estate prior to the modernisation, these middle classes developed alongside industrialisation, that is, significantly later than in the West.

When it did develop, it was predominantly Jewish. The *déclassé* gentry was still living and thinking in the feudal paradigm for decades to come, propped up by their role in the public service.

3 *The state policy of Jewish assimilation and suppressing anything that would interfere.* The alliance between the Hungarian ruling class and the Jews was based on the needs of both. Hungary needed a modern economy, a middle class and a Hungarian majority among the nationalities. Jews wanted to become part of society, to achieve equality. The terms of the unwritten social contract reflected these requirements. Jews were largely emancipated as individuals and the Hungarian state suppressed antisemitism. Jews built the modern economy, largely made up the new middle class, embraced assimilation and Hungarian nationalism. Anything that threatened the assimilation of Jews was threatening the social contract and thus the modernisation of the economy. It was in the interest of the state not to condone political antisemitism and suppress its development, although this suppression did not have to be vigorous or constant.

4 *The perception of antisemitism as potentially undermining existing social order.* Paradoxically, the authoritarian Hungarian regime, steeped in feudal institutions, upheld liberal principles much longer than any other country at end-of-the-century Europe. Precisely because the regime was authoritarian and democratic institutions were weak, yet the state suppressed social unrest. While in pre-modern Czarist Russia, state-controlled antisemitism was one of the weapons against social unrest, in modernising Hungary liberal principles did not allow the exploitation of antisemitism.

All four reasons have the agency of the state in common. Thus they demonstrate the role of the state, of government policies, of the ruling classes and the institutions in the success of political antisemitism. Political antisemitism as an independent ideology was virulent in Austria and Germany by the end of the nineteenth century. Antisemitism as a sole political platform did not survive long in these countries either. It attached itself to, or was absorbed by, nationalism, and through nationalism became the ideological heart of Nazism. In Hungary it was through the double agencies of nationalism and Christianity that antisemitism was articulated, and antisemitism became a measure of a good Christian Hungarian. Without the Horthy regime's condoning the various forms and expressions of antisemitism and formulating and upholding its own as state-ideology, antisemitism would have stayed an undercurrent.

Hatred as political ethos, the law and the state

The eruption of active, murderous antisemitism is rooted in society: in political culture and in legal institutions (inasmuch as they are simultaneously instrumental in the development and practice of political culture and are integral parts of it).

While legal institutions and the law have enormous relevance, the ethos of society is decisive. Laws and legal institutions can be changed abruptly, the working of the civil servant, the administration, the bureaucracy will follow the 'law', as has been explored and analysed by Max Weber, Hannah Arendt, and the Hungarian Istvan Bibó. But if the political ethos does not allow hatred, xenophobia, prejudice, racism, discrimination, the political and social climate will not follow the law. It is civil society and political culture that is the real safeguard and the prevention.

Because antisemitism changes and accommodates the times, according to what is deemed *acceptable* and desirable, its underlying presence and its constancy are of importance. This is where *policies*, state and political interests play a role in giving shape, defining the form, but the content is the constant, the hatred, the image of the 'other' as the 'enemy' and this content in its turn is a social construct: part of culture and of subculture, *constructed, in the sense of engineering as well*, in every society by those who have the transmission of culture in their hands. In medieval times this was the church, in the modern state it is education, information and entertainment, with the overall understanding of society of what is moral, what is permissible and desirable, by the majority. So not only policies and legislation are of crucial relevance but so is the whole of the legal system (law, the legal institutions, the judiciary, public administration); social behaviour of the dominant classes, or rather, whichever class or strata is emulated by the majority; the teachings of the academe; the media; entertainment; literature, theatre, because they all continually shape the content and the form. Antisemitism is part of morality—for the individual, for a society, for a culture and for a state. *The crux is the acceptability of hatred*, in all its various forms, as prejudice, and the expression of it as discrimination, racism, murder. How society handles this hatred, how much credibility, desirability, social standing, righteousness it lends to it, becomes the history of modern antisemitism, from the social to genocidal—and back to social.

Genocide, and its precondition, murderous hatred, does not erupt in a vacuum. Its preconditions are in culture, in social and political ethos, and in social and legal institutions. Generally, the law has enormous relevance but laws and legal institutions can be changed. Anti-Jewish legislation was passed in countries with differing legal systems. But if the social political ethos does not condone hatred, xenophobia, prejudice, racism, discrimination, then political and social climate can resist even the formation of the law. (Denmark is an example.) Democracy is not a deterrent, as the Vichy regime demonstrated in the first country of Enlightenment. Conversely, fascist Italian soldiers helped Jews in Yugoslavia and initially neither Italy nor Hungary pursued deportations.

In Hungary, both inclusion and exclusion were determined and shaped by incomplete modernisation. While the economic modernisation was spectacularly successful, feudal structures stayed intact and this, coupled with the anti-liberal turn in political ethos, resulted in the process of exclusion, culminating in the Holocaust. From the point of view of Jewish national identity, assimilation was complete. So complete that the long decades of antisemitism and exclusion did not shatter it, and after the Holocaust, assimilation continued. The fusion between antisemitism, Christianity and nationalism, however, had the effect that for Jews nationalism lost its appeal and gave way to radical leftism and to Marxism as an assimilatory agency. The assimilatory drive and wish stayed the same: Hungarian Jews continued regarding themselves as Hungarians. After the Holocaust, with the demise of fascism and Nazism, antisemitism ceased to be a legitimate political agenda and ideology.[7] Nationalism itself for a while seemed to be an issue of the past for Western culture and only relevant for the self-determination of African and Asian nations. We are currently witnessing a revival of tribal nationalism, especially in Eastern Europe.

Modern antisemitism evolved with modernity. However, for modern antisemitism to become a movement, something more was needed: the support of the state, overtly or covertly. None of the states where political antisemitism became a movement was a full democracy and, in each, modernisation was incomplete. Hungary was an authoritarian state, but during the years of the monarchy, unlike its Austrian counterpart, the authoritarian state suppressed antisemitism. The Hungarian experience seems to suggest that the development of antisemitism as a political movement and the proliferation of modern antisemitic ideology is dependent on the state.

Examining the role of the state, the question arises: can hatred be controlled by the state, by legislation? In Western societies and in democratising post-Communist countries this question is articulated as a freedom of speech issue: should hate speech be curtailed? The countering argument is that in the 'market place of ideas', these hatreds and ideologies are freely countered, without the interference of the state or legislation, which could only interfere by limiting freedom of speech, one of the fundamental freedoms of democratic societies. Yet this freedom is not an absolute, even in the most developed Western democracies. Free speech is curtailed by the observance of the laws relating to defamation, blasphemy, copyright, sedition, obscenity, use of insulting words, official secrecy, contempt of court and of parliament, incitement and censorship. In countries where democracy is not a well-established political and legal tradition, for instance in post-Communist countries, the question seems to be dictated by two contradictory needs. On one hand, with the tradition of hate-ideologies, such as xenophobic tribal nationalism, there is the need of protection from these ideologies and hate-speeches. On the other hand, democratic institutions have to be built and strengthened, and freedom of speech, one of the pinnacles of democracy is especially cherished after decades of silence.

But even more far-reaching and explosive is another aspect of state control: the manipulation of hatred by the state. In the Former Yugoslavia, Turkey, or in some of the former Soviet republics for instance, ethnic conflicts and disputes are clearly used by political leaders in a violent and odious fashion. Slobodan Milosevic in Serbia and Franjo Tudjman in Croatia, are quite explicit in using nationalist ideologies for political reasons and to produce a highly slanted version of history. As both nationalism and the nation are constructions, Serb and Croatian nationalism and the Serb and the Croatian nation are reconstructed through hatred and ethnic cleansing.

The different varieties of nationalism do not necessarily divide simply by geography; often one kind of nationalism evolves into another. French nationalism for instance went from political to predominantly cultural or even ethnic nationalism. The French revolution aimed at making citizens out of serfs, while a hundred years later, the notion of Frenchman was defined on ethnic/cultural lines. Polish nationalism also went from political to ethnic/ xenophobic. Hungarian nationalism certainly went through enormous changes.

Nationalism can be the ideology for both inclusion and exclusion. In this respect the differentiation between ethnic and civic or cultural and political, Eastern and Western nationalism acquires additional relevance. The dichotomy can also be a question of chronology, or rather, of historical progression. One kind of nationalism can turn into another one. What defines nationalism is its relationship to modernity. Where nationalism seeks to modernise, or is part of a modernised state, that is, a Western-style democracy, it is inclusionary and the nation is defined in political terms. Where (or when) nationalism is against modernising, the nation is defined in ethnic terms and the result is exclusion.

Nationalism, modern identity and political antisemitism are essentially modern phenomena. This book explored, through the Hungarian experience, how hatred of 'the other' becomes part of national identity and the process of institutionalising exclusion. Neither hatred as part of national identity nor institutionalised exclusion are confined to the time and place of this book. The massacre-ridden, bloodied break-up of the former Yugoslavia, the genocide of the Tutsis and the Hutus, and even the world-wide strengthening of supremist right-wing radicalism, all use hatred as part of group-identity and they have to be understood within the dynamics of institutionalised exclusion.

In the process of exclusion, state and political interests and policies define the form, but the content is hatred, the image of the 'other' as the 'enemy'. Policies and legislation are of crucial relevance, but so is the whole of the legal system (law, the legal institutions, the judiciary, public administration), the social behaviour of the ruling classes (or rather, whichever class or stratum is emulated by the majority), culture, including academe, the press, literature and theatre. All of these continually shape the content and the form.

Antisemitism and racism are not only political and social, but also moral issues. For the individual, for a society, for a culture and for a state, the question is the acceptability of hatred, in all its various forms, as prejudice, and the expression of it as discrimination, racism, murder. How the state and society handle this hatred, how much credibility, desirability, social standing, righteousness it is afforded, will ultimately determine if murder, massacre or genocide are acceptable or even desired goals. What I attempted to do in this book was to explore these issues using the social history of the Jews in Hungary. The case of Hungarian Jews, with both inclusion and exclusion as clearly and strongly defined policies, with the role of political and social institutions, ethos and culture clearly observable, provided a poignant illustration of the *changing* politics of nationalism and the process of exclusion to the point of genocide.

Notes

Note: Direct quotations from original Hungarian texts have been translated by the author.

Introduction

1 It is important to note, however, that the strength of anti-Jewish teachings was such that Enlightenment philosophy itself carried on the Christian tradition of the hatred of Jews and thus the seeds (germs?) of political antisemitism were already sown.

2 The anti-modernity of fascism and Nazism needs clarification. Both fascism and Nazism wholeheartedly embraced modern technology. The essence of fascist and Nazi anti-modernity was connected to ideology: it is the Enlightenment ideals—that is, the foundation of Western democracy—that were attacked, and are the fundamentalists' focus of antagonism.

3 In early medieval time Jews were often invited to urbanise, and to fulfil certain tasks, such as shopkeeping, running pubs, etc. (e.g. in Poland). However, this did not mean integration into medieval society, in spite of the jobs being part of the life of the community (Katz 1978, pp. 10–22).

4 Modernity also brought a transformation of Judaism, or rather, brought about certain, very powerful trends within Judaism. The Jewish enlightenment movement, *Haskala*, sought to reform Judaism.

5 He contends that the fact that both liberalism and nationalism are tied to the historical epoch of modernity is no accident, and that the real connection between them should be traced back to the modern paradigm of thought from which liberal ideology stems (Nodia 1994, p. 11). The link between them is democracy: 'The liberal attitude towards nationalism is mediated by the liberal attitude toward the state' (Nodia 1994, p. 14). Francis Fukuyama agrees that nationalism and liberal democracy are two sides of the same coin. The potential for major contradiction lies between nationalism and liberalism. As

long as the nationalism is tolerant, it can coexist with liberalism. National identity belongs to the private sphere, argues Fukuyama, rather than forming the basis of legal rights (Fukuyama 1994, p. 26).

6 Of course, there is antisemitism on the left as well. But antisemitism on the left is really contradictory to left principles, if not to left policies or individual sentiments. Antisemitism on the left has to be articulated through the anti-capitalist stance and not through the racial, chauvinistic content of antisemitism. It is comparable, and even akin to, populist antisemitism inasmuch as the culture of antisemitism fastens itself on the capitalist, exploitative 'Jew', but the ideological target is really exploitation. The articulation of left antisemitism stems from the writings of Marx, especially his *Zur Judenfrage* (On the Jewish Question), where he presented the negative stereotype of the Jew as the personification of capitalism. Robert Wistrich (1991), in *Antisemitism: The Longest Hatred,* investigates the dynamics of left and right antisemitism. Because of the wide historical scope of the book, arching from ancient times to post-Communism, Wistrich's evaluation and analysis of left antisemitism is much more balanced than the one offered in this book. The time frame and the geographical specificity of this book only raises the necessity of discussing nationalist, right-wing antisemitism, and only Chapter 7, which deals with the years immediately after the Holocaust, touches on the relevance of antisemitism on the left.

7 Even the national membership can be subject to an exaggerated hierarchy. During World War II, for instance, Germany introduced different categories of citizenship: *Hochdeutsch*, *Volksdeutsch*, etc.

8 For example, until women could vote, they could be only passive citizens, fulfilling only the first part of Kupchan's definition of political participation.

9 Hugh Seton-Watson wrote: 'I am driven to the conclusion that no "scientific definition" of the nation can be devised' (Seton-Watson 1977, p. 5).
Hegel called them 'residual fragments of peoples' (*Völkerabfälle*), a derogatory term, which has its equivalent in Hungarian: '*népmaradékok*'. Marx and Engels argued that non-historical nationals either cannot develop bourgeoisie, or cannot develop a state on their own. Consequently the natural alliances sought by these nations are with the reactionary old order. This partly explains the vehement denunciation by both Marx and Engels of eastern European national communities, especially the southern Slavs. Otto Bauer softened the harshness of Marx's and Engels' position by arguing that non-historical nations can become historical nations with capitalist development (Bauer, O. 1988, pp. 155–74). Engels' derogatory position towards the Slavs is powerfully expressed in 'The Magyar struggle' (1977, vol 8).

10 It is important to note, however, that the politics of inclusion notwithstanding, the Liberal Era was characterised by considerable

oppression and hatred. The Hungarian poet, Endre Ady, wrote after the turn of the century: 'In Hungary it is a patriotic thing to hate Germans, Serbs, Romanians, Slovaks, isn't it?' (Barany 1971, p. 285).

11 Schoolchildren of all denominations recited daily the Hungarian Creed, which deliberately echoed the form and the words of the prayer *Credo*: 'I believe in one God, I believe in one Fatherland, I believe in one divine eternal truth, I believe in the resurrection of Hungary. Amen.'

12 Anti-Jewish sentiments in ancient times are outside the scope of this book.

13 Since there is no such thing as 'semitism', antisemitism itself is the thesis to which there is no anti-thesis, and therefore the usage of a hyphen is not only superfluous but misleading.

14 Bibó's *Zsidókérdés Magyarországon 1944 után* (The Jewish Question in Hungary after 1944) was first published in 1948. Bibó's numerous works were translated into German, but to a much lesser extent into English. Were it not for Ferenc Feher's brilliant article, titled 'Istvan Bibó and the Jewish Question in Hungary: Notes on the margin of a classical essay', published in 1980, and copious references in essays written about post-Holocaust relations between Jews and Hungarians and on antisemitism, Bibó's superb analysis would be virtually unknown in English. Influenced by Marxism, Bibó understood history in terms of conflicts. Bibó saw that any theory that tries to view antisemitism only in modern times is incomplete, because it leaves out an important psychological reason, the 'existing moral devaluation of Jews', which is critical for the understanding of both the components of antisemitism and the ordeals suffered by Jews (Bibó 1984, p. 183). The origins of this moral devaluation stem from the situation of Jews in medieval society. This, according to Bibó, was simple: Jews constituted a 'ritual community', which Bibó uses in the meaning of 'ethnicity'. The position of Jews in Western civilisation was determined by two issues: a theological and a social one. The relevant theological point was that although Jews were the first to be preached to, they did not and would not recognise Jesus as Messiah. This underlying belief was—wrongly, as Bibó states—embellished with the gory details so important to medieval imagery, thus producing not only the embodiment of 'the alien' but of 'the heathen', evoking images of sacrilege and of wickedness.

15 Leon Poliakov's classic *The History of Antisemitism* is an example (1965, 1973, 1975, 1985).

16 The main tenets are contained in the infamous *Protocols of the Elders of Zion,* still the source-book of the fundamental accusations against Jews.

17 The method was simple. Assimilated Jews often changed their names to sound Hungarian, Polish, Russian, or English. They could be 'unmasked' by referring to the original, Jewish name. This practice

occurred even in the benevolent Kádár years, albeit in a covert fashion. In the late 1960s, a friend of mine applied for a job in foreign affairs. During the interview one of the questions asked was: 'Comrade, what was your family's original, Jewish name?'

18 One may add a fourth possibility, one which evolved since the establishment of the state of Israel (hence after Bibó wrote his treatise): antisemitism in the guise of the—at least for a while—more respectable anti-Zionism.

19 This is what one might call the first phase of modernity: the period in which the old structures still persist, before the establishment of social–political institutions with which the implementation of the 'project' begins.

20 Responses to modernity:
　1 negation
　2 emancipation
　　a assimilation–nationalism–socialism
　　b self-emancipation (Zionism)
Conversion was always a way into non-Jewish society, and remained an option. Peter Berger, in *The Sacred Canopy* (1969) gives the following responses to the challenges of modernity:
　1 surrender
　　— conversion
　　— radical universalism
　2 defiance (ultra-orthodox)
　3 accommodation (religious responses, e.g. reform, neo-orthodox, reconstructionist, etc.)

21 The mystical Hasidic movement was a popular movement which spread through the Jewish communities in Eastern Europe during the eighteenth and nineteenth centuries. These communities were the oppressed and poverty-stricken, and Hasidism offered a spiritual alternative to the intellectual elitism of the scholarly rabbis. The movement engendered a serious rift within orthodoxy: the traditional opponents (*mitnagdim*) of Hasidism deplored and often excommunicated the followers of the movement.

22 Some of the religious off-shoots: reform, neo-orthodoxy, reconstructionism and others.

Chapter one

1 The education system was also responding to the demands of the industrial age. The number of elementary schools rose significantly (according to Hanak, from 13 000 to 17 000). The proportion of illiterates dropped from two-thirds to one-third of the population. With the number of teachers doubled, the standard of education, including secondary and tertiary education, improved (Hanak 1988, p. 145).

224   THE POLITICS OF INCLUSION AND EXCLUSION

2 *Vide* the popularity of Georg Ritter von Schönerer and his vulgar, fanatic antisemitism, and the Christian social movement's antisemitic demagogy in Austria. Georg von Schönerer was an antisemitic Austrian politician, whose national socialist ideology was woven from anti-liberalism, anti-capitalism and anti-clericalism. He stood for a radical, racist pan-Germanism. Adolf Stöcker, the chaplain to the court of the German emperor, was the leader of the antisemitic movement in Germany. He articulated the slogan: 'The social question is the Jewish question'. Hitler later described Schönerer as his forerunner.

3 Peter Hanak called the half century that followed the Compromise the 'age of founding': 'Modern Hungary was founded by the generation of Széchenyi, Kossuth and Deák. They were followed by new founders, with spades, industrial tools and business sense. This last group founded banks and factories, built railways and water-mains' (Hanak 1988, p. 142).

4 The winter months (usually January) were the time for festive pig-killing. Pig-breeding became so widespread that only the poorest did not kill. The custom even entered folk wisdom through the saying: 'It is not compulsory to kill the pig, only a custom', admonishing the diffident who wait to be asked to join, that joyous occasions are not to be enforced.

5 As these settlements did not possess industry, the workers were taxed at the place of their work, that is, Budapest. Consequently, infrastructure only developed inside the administrative boundaries (Szelényi 1990, p. 177).

6 Of these, 600 families possessed estates of over 1500 acres and over 180 had *latifundia* of over 15 000 acres (Hanak 1988, p. 154).

7 The word 'gentry' needs a little clarification. The same word is used in Hungarian as in English, but there is a difference in meaning. In England the word stands for a much wider section of the population than just the lesser nobility. Gentry, as it was and is understood in Hungary, was in fact narrower than the sum of the lesser nobility. The nucleus of Hungarian gentry were the landowners, but their clan extended to the towns, where they held gentlemanly positions of administration, keeping strictly to themselves in social life and in career-choices. The French *petite noblesse terrienne* would be the closest term. Although for centuries their civic and juridical status would be the same as that of the higher nobility, i.e. the aristocracy, by the nineteenth century the differences between gentry and aristocracy increased (Lukacs 1988, pp. 87–8). In Weber's terminology, Hungarian gentry would constitute a 'status' group.

8 The Hungarian gentry was beautifully depicted in many of the fine novels and short stories of Kálmán Mikszáth. One of his short novels is about a lavish gentry wedding, held with evident pomp and luxury. But as the weekend wedding is finished, family jewels, grand dresses and *Lipiczaner* horses turn out to be borrowed, presents of money

and endowment worthless, and bearers of the dazzling names return to their mundane jobs on Monday morning. But the real twist comes as the newcomer to the county (gentry himself) finds out that everybody else knew all along that it was all sham—but kept up the pretence with great flair and gusto, and could hardly wait for the next social occasion to repeat the whole performance (Mikszáth 1910).

9 During the agricultural crisis the middle-sized properties were the ones most affected, whilst the peasants suffered comparatively little. The large proprietors were able to command the credit which enabled them to tide over the period. This was not so with the smaller or middle-class proprietors (Kohn 1961b, p. 131).

10 In 1900, ten million out of the thirteen million of the farm population owned no land whatsoever (Kohn 1961b, p. 59).

11 For the definition of nation, Gellner gives two interdependent parameters: sharing the same culture (where culture means a 'system of ideas and signs and associations and ways of behaving and communicating') and the mutual recognition of this sharing by members of the nation (Gellner 1983, p. 7).

12 Széchenyi was concerned that the great numbers of Jews would change the Hungarians, so that Hungarians would end up with Jewish characteristics and habits. He phrased a much-quoted simile about ink disappearing in the ocean, but the same amount of ink spoils the bowl of soup. Kossuth's position on the ethnic minorities was based on supporting civil rights but denying self-determination, because these peoples lacked 'historical personalities' (Ignotus 1972, p. 56).

13 This Habsburg monarch, Joseph II, who never convened the Diet, is still remembered in Hungary by the name of *'kalapos király'* (king with a hat), because he refused to be crowned as the King of Hungary (thereby giving further rise to questions of legitimacy).

14 The functional equivalent of the rule of law is the legal ideal of the *Rechtsstaat* system, in which state and bureaucracy traditionally play a dominant role.

15 Hugh Seton-Watson charts the history of language and shows that the nineteenth century was a golden age of vernacularising lexicographers, grammarians, philologists and littérateurs (1977). See also Anderson, *Imagined Communities* (1993, pp. 67–82).

16 Some of the legislation leading up to making Hungarian the language of the law: Act IV of 1805 allowed Hungarian at lower levels of adjudication (but did not make it compulsory); Act VIII of 1830 ordered that all judgments—including the *'Kúria'* (equivalent of the Supreme Court)—had to be worded in Hungarian and the same Act made Hungarian the single language for the bar exams (Ranki, V. 1971, p. 61).

17 In the first half of the nineteenth century three distinct literary languages were formed in the Balkans: Slovene, Serbo-Croat and Bulgarian. The first stirrings of Turkish nationalism were signalled by

the appearance of a lively vernacular press in Istanbul in the 1870s. Both Finns and Norwegians asserted their national independence through 'philological revolution' (Anderson 1993, pp. 72–7).

18 Still, the Hungarian national anthem was not written by Petőfi, the inspired revolutionary, whose life and death became one with Hungarian independence and liberalism. It was written by Kolcsey, a sentimental pessimist. The words talk of the nation being 'torn by ill-fate' and sighs, 'this people amply atoned already for past and for future'.

19 Such was the appeal of *kuruc* nationalism, that when a historian helped along the short supply of original *kuruc* songs by simply inventing them, the forgery did not even tarnish his reputation (Deak 1992, p. 1046).

20 There were other times when this attire was particularly fashionable, for instance, during the inter-war years, and now in post-Communism. Folklore was also used in the Communist years. The Hungarian Folk Ensemble (*Magyar Népi Együttes*) was the famous state-sponsored dance group which enjoyed enormous popularity, and which was just as manipulated as the folklore of former eras when great ladies went to the Budapest opera in gold- and pearl-embroidered 'peasant' dresses.

21 To wit, one of the most popular operettas bore the name the '*Csárdás*-queen'. The main characters are the popular actress, who dances and sings the *csárdás*, and her love, the handsome count who belongs to the real aristocracy—although his mother was the *Csárdás*-queen of her own youth. Operetta was the most popular art-form, both in Vienna and in Budapest. In operettas the only conflicts were between lovers and by the third act they were always solved.

Chapter two

1 This notion of Arendt's does not explain modern political antisemitism in Russia, where the majority of Jews were not assimilated or secularised.

2 *Systemica Gentis Judaicae Regulatio* (Regulation Concerning the Jewish People), *MZsSz* 1896, no. 4, pp. 367–74.

3 The Jews of Hungary wholeheartedly supported the 1848 revolution and the war of independence. Jews volunteered for military service, and they played a prominent part. According to some estimations, there were 20 000 Jews in the revolutionary army (Gonda 1992, p. 317). Haynau, the infamous oppressive bureaucrat whose era became synonymous with terror and tyranny, wrote about Jewish participation: 'Their sympathies and evil acts fostered the revolution, which, without their assistance would never had been so wide-spread' (Vida 1939, p. 15). Because of their participation the military authorities imposed a huge collective fine on the communities (*Magyar Zsidó Lexikon* 1929, p. 1090).

4 Even Napoleon did not link emancipation to religious reform.

5 This law extended certain paragraphs of Act LIII of 1868 to include the 'Israelite religion'. These sections ordered that children should follow the religion of their parents; that nobody can be forced to participate in others' rites; everyone had to belong to a denomination; that services of chaplains be made available in military institutions and hospitals; and that parochial and community schools were to receive assistance (Handler 1980, p. 22; *Magyar Zsidó Lexikon* 1929, p. 734).

6 By July 1883 Tiszaeszlár Jews were relocated to neighbouring villages for their safety, because of growing antisemitic sentiment (Handler 1980, p. 244). The synagogue was abandoned and vandalised. 'On the inner walls the names of visitors had been scratched' (*The Times* 18 July 1883, quoted by Handler 1980, p. 244). Tiszaeszlár became a tourist attraction.

7 Assimilation was not the sole option. Cultural autonomy, propagated by Simon Dubnow (1860–1914), and later Zionism, were alternatives for participation in modern society. However, neither of these alternatives, nor the political movement of the *Bund*, was an option accepted by Hungarian Jewry in the Liberal Era.

8 Some Hungarian folk-customs, for instance, were palpably influenced by Judaism. Like the Jews of Egypt in the biblical story of Passover, the sheep slaughterers in Szeged smeared the blood of a slaughtered lamb on the doorpost of their homes, to ward off evil from their first-born (Handler 1980, p. 24).

9 The demand to assimilate, to become Hungarian in speech, culture and behaviour, and to modernise Jewish religion to fit in more with Christian culture, was in fact the modernised form of the old medieval religious demand to give up Jewishness.

10 At the end of World War I, Hungarian diplomats signed the peace treaty at the beautiful palace of Marie Antoinette at Trianon.

11 Even Baron Jozsef Eotvos, the liberal political and cultural reformer of the post-*Ausgleich* era, envisaged the eventual conversion of Jews to Christianity (Katzburg 1966, vol. 1, p. 140).

12 Jászi likened the Hungarian peasant attitude 'to the Confucian type of philosophy, which was based on agriculture, order and tradition' (Jászi 1961, p. 173).

13 'In medieval Hungary witches were sentenced, for a first offence, to stand all day in a public place, wearing a Jew's hat' (Handler 1980, p. 196).

14 A good example of this strange and artificial political association was Csernátony, former secretary of Kossuth, who returned after twenty years of exile. An ardent, chauvinistic nationalist, who hated and suspected everything Austrian, he listed the 'causes' of antisemitism. According to him, Jews were characterised—even after emancipation— by work, thrift and solidarity. They were guilty of the practice of usury, with which they contributed to the impoverishment of the

Magyars, and of spreading German culture and language (Handler 1980, p. 27).

15 He stressed a distinct Jewish race. He declared that the Jews were aliens and cosmopolitans and had retained their exclusive national and racial characteristics (Handler 1980, p. 31) .

16 'During the whole period of the great trial Hungarian society was overcome with such agitation as if they were ready to start a religious war against the Jews', as Károly Eötvös, the counsel for defence, wrote twenty years later in his memoirs (Eötvös 1968, p. 12).

17 See Katz 1980, pp. 34–47; Hertzberg 1986.

18 See Wistrich 1990, pp. 86–101.

19 Karady lists one more unique feature, the large number of Jews both in absolute numbers and proportionally (Karady 1993a, p. 35). I did not include this. Although the number of Jews in Hungary is of great relevance to the reception and the status of Jews within society, I do not think the numbers affected or characterised assimilation.

20 The proportion of secondary school graduates was one of the highest in Europe, 28 per 100 000 inhabitants, as opposed to 18 per 100 000 in France (Karady 1989, pp. 285 312).

21 According to the *Encyclopaedia Judaica* the 1869 census figure was 542 000; but the *Magyar Zsidó Lexikon* cites the figure 553 641. There are further discrepancies, with the *Judaica* giving lesser numbers. Since the *Lexikon* relies on the official census figures, it seems to be more reliable in this instance than the *Judaica*.

22 Around the turn of the century at least two-thirds of Jews belonged to the lower middle and the working classes, and one-fifth to the liberal professions; between one-fourth and one-half of Hungarian doctors, lawyers, journalists were Jewish (Barany 1974, p. 79).

23 See Karady, on the dynamics and characteristics of changing Jewish-sounding names to Hungarian (Karady 1993b, pp. 40–4).

24 First in Pozsony (Bratislava), one of the traditional homes of mob antisemitism, but soon in Budapest as well, Zionist organisations appeared. From 1910 the movement was wide enough to organise by district in Budapest (Gonda 1992, pp. 176–7).

25 In Austria, assimilation was modelled on the *Beamtenadel* and the *Bildungsburgertum* (ennobled bureaucracy and educated middle class). Austrian Jews were barred from access to the traditional upper and middle classes. The nationalism that formed identity was defined by state–patriotic identity, by attachment to the Habsburg dynasty and the state (Hanak 1984a, pp. 242–3).

26 The *Magyar Zsidó Lexikon* (Hungarian Jewish Encyclopaedia) lists 302 Jewish nobles. The editors of the *Lexikon* included families who had converted to Christianity. In addition, McCagg cites Kempelen, B., *Magyarországi zsidó és zsidóeredetü családok* (Jewish and Jewish-origin Families of Hungary), Budapest, Viktória nyomda, 1937–39 (McCagg 1972a, p. 18, fn. 9). Using the two sources, McCagg established that

between 1800 and 1918, Hungarian Jewish nobility comprised of thousands of individuals in 346 different families. About 220 of these were created after 1900 (McCagg 1972a, p. 127).

27 The time of *Ausgleich* (the Compromise) which was also the time of emancipation, between 1882 and 1887, the upsurge of political antisemitism, and between 1895 and 1897, when the Jewish religion itself became a received religion (McCagg 1972a, pp. 120–30).

28 In spite of the fact that organisationally the orthodox maintained their autonomy, the law did not recognise them as separate. Decree 1191 of 1888 ruled that: 'It is beyond doubt that the congress, the orthodox and the *status quo ante* Israelite denominations, both from the state's political point of view and the Jewish point of view, are to be considered as belonging to the one and the same religion' (*Magyar Zsidó Lexikon* 1929, p. 669).

Chapter three

1 Hannah Arendt, for instance, consistently used the epithet 'fascist' to describe Horthy (Arendt 1963, pp. 123, 159).

2 Among other measures, universal suffrage was introduced, together with legislation to guarantee the freedom of press, assembly and association and plans were made for nationalisation of certain key sectors of the economy (Hanak 1988, pp. 180–2).

3 Count Bethlen became prime minister in the period 1921–31. Gömbös, while also actively leading one of the clandestine right-radical parties, took over and was prime minister until his death in 1936.

4 Béla Kún was Jewish, joined the Communists during the war, when he was captured. Eighteen of the 29 members of the Revolutionary Council were Jewish.

5 They comprised 20 per cent: out of 72 officers, 15 were Jewish (Vida 1939, p. 51).

6 In 1932, for instance, four members of the illegal Communist party were accused; the two Jews, Sallai and Fürst, were sentenced to death; the other two were not.

7 Other sources give the number as 590, out of which 44 (7.4 per cent) were Jews (*Magyar Zsidó Lexikon* 1929, p. 220).

8 1514 C.E. The defeat of the Hungarian army at the battle of Mohács signalled the advent of 150 years of Turkish rule. Hungary was divided into three parts, Transylvania staying formally independent, the middle triangle under Turkish occupation, and western Hungary as part of the Habsburg empire. The saying, 'more was lost at Mohács' is still used. In the battle, not only the king died, along with a huge number of nobles and peasants, but the country's independence was lost. Two empires, the Ottoman and the German–Roman, took over Hungary, and the Habsburgs stayed on even after the Turks left.

9 This was, in a way, a reflection on the difference in attitude produced

by two different legal systems: the adversarial, in which the eloquence of the argument and the points raised are the basis of decision, as opposed to the non-adversarial system, where there is a supposed objective justice, and the 'judge' is trying to glean that—eloquence and arguments notwithstanding.

10 In 1938, with the First Vienna Award, Hungary regained the *Felvidék* (Upper Provinces), in the north. The fact that this was bounty from Germany's overrunning Czechoslovakia did not sour the elation.

11 Hungary had the most overexpanded civil service and bureaucracy in Europe. Thirty-nine per cent of the yearly budget was spent on administration (Nagy-Talavera 1970, p. 69).

12 After 1867, the year when Hungarian Jews were legally emancipated, the 'liberal' professions (such as medicine and accountancy), not being respectable and sought after, presented a natural opening for Jews.

13 This prompted the 1920 *Numerus Clausus* Act. The motivation for the legislation was, on one hand, to 'punish' the Jews for the alleged part played in the Red Terror, but more importantly to decrease the number of Jewish intellectuals.

14 After a post-war, limited agrarian reform, the large and medium estates still accounted for over 50 per cent of land. About 46.5 per cent were smallholdings.

15 At the end of the eighteenth century, after the liberation of Hungary from 150 years of Turkish rule, Empress Maria Theresa invited Schwabians to settle in Hungary.

16 In a memorandum submitted to the Horthy in 1938, the army demanded measures to reduce Jewish influence in the press, in cultural life and in economic activities. Most peculiar was the demand for increased taxation and control of the big firms and 'juster distribution of land', along with measures to protect the poorer classes (Macartney 1961, p. 213).

17 Szálasi, the head of the Arrowcross party, was arrested several times; the Scythe Cross party's leader and 80 followers were tried and imprisoned; this party, like the Hungarist party, was dissolved in the 1930s.

18 Procedural legitimation, including both democratic law-making and judicial review, prevails over the internal structural components of the rule of law system (Sajo 1990, p. 342).

19 For instance, when Gömbös became prime minister he knew he had to renounce his earlier antisemitism—at least nominally. He paid lip service to moderate positions, because this was expected of him.

20 The acronym stands for *Magyar Országos Véderő Egyesület*.

21 The name Turanian was an allusion to the supposed racial origins of the ancestors of the Hungarians and did carry anti-German connotation, since in legendary times the Turanians and the Aryans fought epic battles.

22 In 1940 the social composition of the membership was: 13 per cent

were peasants, 36 per cent middle class, and nearly 50 per cent army officers. The top leadership were professional counter-revolutionaries of lower middle-class origin (Eros, J. 1970, p. 137).

23 In Romania the extreme nationalist 'Legion of the Archangel Michael', with its shock troop, the Iron Guard, stood as much for militant Christianity as for violent nationalism.

24 The Catholic People's party, with its conservative–clerical ideology underlined and emphasised this focus. It also introduced the accusations of Jewish cosmopolitanism, rootlessness and rationalism, which were presented as alien to the Magyar nation.

25 Szekfü's controversial *Rakóczi in Exile*, published in 1913, created public outrage and resulted in his ostracism. His evaluation of Rakóczi went against the romanticising public perception of nationalistic history. He presented the hallowed *kuruc* prince as powerless and embittered. He was denounced as a traitor by the press and by politicians. Only Jászi and his radical circle supported Szekfü.

26 In 1934 Szekfü published the history of the generations following, in *Trianon óta* (Since Trianon). While *Három Nemzedék* was instrumental in the forging of the antisemitic anti-liberal thinking of the Christian middle classes, *Trianon óta*, in a sharp turnabout, reflected Szekfü's growing concern about fascism. Still, he expected Jews to change to eliminate antisemitism, but he argued the omnipresent belief that if Hungary regained the territories that were lost with the Trianon Treaty, all would be well.

27 Not surprisingly, Szekfü condemned Petőfi, the beloved national martyr-poet. Petőfi was a revolutionary and a liberal: two unwanted attributes in post-Trianon Hungary. Anti-liberalism and anti-revolution demands that Petőfi's Christianity should be denied: 'The Hungarians of the forties [1840s] are not Christian any more' (Szekfü 1989, p. 62).

28 Carsten, Paxton, Linz, Sternhell, to name a few.

29 Carsten's *Rise of Fascism*, Stuart Woolf's *European Fascism* and several works by Eugene Weber and George Mosse.

30 Pan-Turanism was the driving ideology under the banner of which the Young Turk movement perpetrated the genocide of the Armenians, who were perceived to be in the way of the unification of Turkic people (a Christian 'island' in the Islamic sea).

Chapter four

1 The reform of Judaism as a condition was dropped after the *Ausgleich*, but it was expected and encouraged.

2 The concept of received religion (*recepta religio*) meant freedom of worship for the 'lawfully received' religions. Judaism became a lawfully received religion in 1895.

3 Another form of voluntary assimilation was Magyarising names. The custom of changing Jewish-sounding names to Hungarian was

widespread in the Golden Age; however, it was banned during the Horthy years.

4 Calculations based on Table VII, Changes of religion affecting the Israelite religion, 1896–1942 (Zeke 1990, pp. 194–5).

5 In Karady's calculations it was actually fifteen times (Karady 1993a, p. 47). I used Zeke's tables, which show the breakdown by years (Zeke 1990, pp. 194–5).

6 These numbers do not include those who were returning to Judaism.

7 No. XV of 1941 Supplementing and Amending Law No. XXXI of 1894 Relating to Marriage and the Necessary Racial Provisions Relating to It.

8 Zionism as a Jewish revolution is explored at length by Robert Wistrich in *Between Redemption and Perdition* (1990).

9 'At first, the quest for political self-determination tended to predominate [and] nationalism retained a flexibility [and] embraced a variety of political, social and religious attitudes. Toward the end of the nineteenth century, however, the supposed supremacy and cultural autonomy of the nation challenged this flexibility . . . [nationalism became] a civic religion' (Mosse 1993, p. 1).

10 In 1944, Hannah Senesh, who by then had been living in Palestine, was parachuted by the British behind enemy lines to assist captured Allied airmen. She was caught in Hungary by the police, was tortured, tried and executed a few months before Budapest was liberated.

11 A short story in *Egyenlőseg* told a tale in which the Jewish lover of the hunted Hungarian journalist gives the signal to escape from the Czechoslovak police by putting the *Chanukah* candle in the window (Csorba 1990, p. 243).

12 Although there were major social differences, all came from urban middle-class families, ranging from wealthy banker (e.g. Lukács's father), doctor (e.g. Jászi), to lesser village officer (e.g. Béla Kún's father) (McCagg 1972b, p. 83).

13 After the first anti-Jewish law, it was openly demanded that the Social Democratic party should be 'de-Judaised'. Although one of those who demanded it was expelled from the party, feeling the groundswell of antisemitism and not wanting to embarrass the party, Jews resigned from the leadership (Borsányi 1992, p. 151).

14 Bernat Back and Samu Biedl (Száraz 1984, p. 321).

15 As in medieval Europe, in Islamic countries assimilation has only been possible through conversion to Islam.

16 The 'little Entente' was a mutual defence arrangement between Czechoslovakia, Romania and Yugoslavia, in place between the two world wars.

17 Theodor Herzl, the father of Zionism, and Max Nordau, one of its most important early ideologists, were both born in Hungary but lived in Vienna and in Paris.

18 The so-called 'engineers' *aliyah*', named after the overwhelming number of engineers in the group.

19 Published in the *Zsidó Szemle* (Jewish Review) Zionist paper, in 1934 (Csorba 1990, pp. 263–4).

Chapter five

1 On the debate, see Tim Mason (1981), Christopher Browning (1985), Michael Marrus (1987) and Colin Tatz (1991).

2 Act IV of 1939, s(1) states:

> In the application of this Act, a person is considered Jewish, if the person, or at least one of the parents, or at least two of the grandparents at the time of the promulgation of this Act belong to the Jewish *religious community*, or before the promulgation of this Act belonged to the Jewish *religious community* and all the offsprings born to those specified after the promulgation of this Act. [*emphasis added*]

The Nazi definition also contained the expression 'religious community', and, even more explicitly fusing religion and 'race', included marriage to a Jew and conversion to Judaism.

3 The introduction of forced labour service for Jewish males in 1939 also removed tens of thousands of men from the labour market.

4 The expression '*zsidó törveny*' (Jewish legislation) is regularly used by all Hungarian writers. These laws institutionalised antisemitism, thus they were anti-Jewish. By omitting the 'anti' qualification, there is a certain air of respectability accorded to them. The continued use of this euphemism validates and legitimises these laws and is indicative of the aspect of apologia characteristic of much of the Hungarian scholarship concerning the Holocaust. Holocaust historiography in the West calls the laws anti-Jewish.

5 The *Numerus Clausus* Act (XXV of 1920), created closed numbers for admission of Jewish students to tertiary institutions. Allegedly the law was necessary because of the hardships created by the Trianon treaty. Almost a decade later, at the time of passing Act XIV of 1928, which revised the *Numerus Clausus* Act, it was stated: 'Our Jewish compatriots, however, must not lose sight of the fact that the national catastrophe that befell us led to the shrinking of all our living conditions and made necessary many painful restrictions' (Braham 1981, p. 42).

6 University students rejoiced and the Act 'greatly contributed to the radicalisation of institutions of higher learning' (Braham 1981, p. 30). University students everywhere in Europe participated enthusiastically in fascist and Nazi movements and this was so in Hungary as well.

7 Kállay said in a speech: 'I have to contradict those who see no other problem in this country other than the Jewish question. In our homeland there are a lot of grave problems next to which the Jewish question is insignificant' (Kállay 1954, p. 123).

8 Bibó, ever striving to be objective, included the Jewish middle class in his condemnation—sternly unsusceptible to the irony that all through the Horthy era Jews were condemned for revolutionary activities and strivings.

9 Ranki quotes Horthy's words about the anti-Jewish measures: 'these measures many times were executed with such unjustified brutality and inhumanity, which was not prevalent in the German Reich especially against economically useful or irreplaceable Jews who were needed for their skills' (Horthy, cited in Ranki, G. 1988, p. 203).

10 Daniel Goldhagen (1996) asserts that German society *en bloc* wanted the genocide of the Jews. Without getting engaged in the considerable debate that emerged surrounding Goldhagen's thesis, the following discussion explores Hungarian society as bystanders, and only segments of society (such as the members of the Arrowcross party and the Gendarmerie) as perpetrators.

11 The German plenipotentiary, Werner Best, leaked the information of the impending deportation to the Danish underground (Yahil 1969, pp. 147–95).

12 According to some estimates, in 1943 there were some fifteen thousand Jewish refugees on Hungarian territory, legally and illegally; six to eight thousand from Slovakia, three to four thousand from Germany and Austria, two to two and a half thousand from Poland, the rest from Czechoslovakia and Yugoslavia (Bihari 1990, p. 39). The numbers fluctuated, however. There were those who left Hungary and then entered again (oral history from Olga Horak, Sydney). With the occupation of Poland, some 140 000–150 000 Poles escaped to Hungary, among them 5000–15 000 Jews, with the full knowledge of the Hungarian government. They were allowed to leave and join the Polish military in exile. However, a few stayed in Hungary, were put into a camp at Vamosmikola, where they were living in relatively good conditions till the *Nyilas coup* in October 1944 (Bihari 1990, p. 39; Braham 1981, pp. 103–4). Jews who were entering illegally were often caught and interned. The successive Hungarian governments were 'quite punctilious' in protecting Hungarian Jews, both at home and abroad, from physical danger. This protection was extended to Jewish nationals caught by the Germans (Braham 1981, pp. 255–71).

13 For instance, Eugene Kamenka and Alice Tay saw the answer in 'bureaucratic mentality' (Kamenka 1973a, p. 128).

14 Adorno, in the famous study of the authoritarian personality, focused on the individual and the individual psyche (Adorno et al. 1950). Because of that, a circular logic appeared: 'To Adorno and his colleagues, Nazism was cruel because Nazis were cruel; and the Nazis were cruel because cruel people tended to become Nazis' (Bauman 1989, p. 153).

15 At the 1975 New York conference, 'The Holocaust, a Generation After', the relationship between modernity and the Holocaust was debated. According to Richard Rubenstein: 'The Holocaust was not

a break in civilisation but an expression of it, as are Leicas, Mercedes, and intercontinental ballistic missiles' (Bauer & Rotenstreich 1981, pp. 257–8). Shlomo Avineri disputed this. Although it was 'somehow part of the culture of modernity', the Holocaust has to be understood in terms of 'retarded modernity'. Avineri also disagreed with the notion which regards the Holocaust 'as a necessary, immanent expression' of Western civilisation, 'as if there were a deterministic element in modernity that necessarily leads to genocidal policies' (Bauer & Rotenstreich 1981, pp. 262–3).

16 Another means of discreditation was exposing the Jews 'hiding' behind Hungarian names. The pre-Magyarised names of (often even converted) Jews were dug up and supplied in brackets. This was such a widespread tactic that Frigyes Karinthy, the master of Hungarian humour, satirised the practice in his enormously popular *Így Írtok Ti* (This is How You Write). In a mock theatre 'review', titled 'Unbiased Criticism', he wrote of one of the Hungarian classics: 'In their national (Neumann) theatre (Schwarz), which they tried to force on our poor magyar (Mayer) audience'; the plot 'falsifies racial psychology'. The mock review describes the main characters, Adam (Adler) and Eve (Epstein), as 'the sickeningly sentimental eastern figures, who will be surely recognised as Schwarz and Mrs Kohn from the esplanade' and who 'travel in time and space as the international Jewish salesmen, for whom the train is cradle and homeland', and so forth in similar manner. But next comes the correction, after 'it turns out that not at all! not even his grandfather!' (i.e. is Jewish): 'There were a few confusing printing errors in our article yesterday. The absent-minded printer set "Jewish garbage", instead of "greatest Hungarian treasure", "kosher stink-bomb from Budapest", instead of "real work of art" . . . We dismissed the Jewish typesetter who caused the offence' (Karinthy 1963, pp. 399–400).

17 My translation from the original text of József Erdélyi, as found in Karsai 1992, pp. 90–1. V.R.

18 A notable exception was Szekfű, whose influence cannot be overestimated in the development and the dissemination of the antisemitism and anti-liberalism in the first decade of the Horthy era, but who, by the mid-1930s, became a leader of moral resistance to Nazi Germany.

19 György Száraz, writing in a later and different epoch, wrote that the 'diluted *Magyarism*' of Jews 'provoked national irritation' (Száraz 1985, p. 17). The usage of the terminology constructed 50 years earlier shows the historical dimensions and the enduring quality of these notions. Németh himself continued writing and participating in Hungarian literary life all through the Communist years.

Chapter six

1 Elie Wiesel wrote: 'I could tell you many stories because, after all, I am a Hungarian Jew. And to this day I try to understand what

happened. If ever there was a tragedy that could have been prevented, it was that one' (Wiesel 1985, p. xiv).

2 The Nazi definition was also a mixture of the racial and religious concepts. An Aryan could become a Jew, in spite of 'blood', by converting to Judaism or marrying a Jew. The definition of '*Mischlinge*' (mixed blood) according to the First Regulation to the Reich Citizenship Law (14 November 1935) s (2) (a): who was a member of the Jewish religious community at the time of the promulgation of this law, or was admitted to it subsequently; (b) who was married to a Jew (Arad et al. 1988, p. 80). The definiton of the Aryan was also elastic, with the glib usage of the word 'honorary', as in the case of the Japanese and the Arabs. Delegations of Syrians and Iraqis attended the Nuremberg rallies. The Grand Mufti of Jerusalem was Hitler's honoured guest for long periods and toured Nazidom. There were Arab volunteers in Germany, wearing the German uniform, with an armband: '*Frei Arabien*' (Pryce-Jones 1989, p. 205). The racism of Nazi policies was extraordinarily inconsistent. Nazism used racism as an organising principle but the *ideology* of the Reich was National Socialism. The two in many ways overlapped, Nazism had its roots in and utilised racism. Habermas also argues against the historical perspective which tries to prove that 'the murder of the Jews was exclusively a consequence of the radical doctrine of race' (Habermas 1992, p. 79). The fusion of religious, political and racial antisemitism explains the quasi-religious fervour of Nazi antisemitism. Racial-hygienic legislation against 'elements of lesser racial value' on the other hand, was more a manifestation of the absolute power the Nazi state wielded than an ideological imperative. The lack of systematic approaches toward the mentally ill, homosexuals and the Gypsies was due to the fact that there was no ideological imperative concerning the fate of these groups, 'just' the arrogant barbarism of a corrupt and violent state.

3 First Regulation to the Reich Citizenship Law, 14 November 1935.

4 Under the legislation, Jews were forbidden to acquire Hungarian citizenship; no Jew could vote unless he proved that his family was domiciled continuously in Hungary from 1867. It also sought absolute elimination of Jews from all positions in the public sector, and imposed severe restrictions on the economic functioning of Jews in the private sector. The professional chambers were forbidden to have more than 6 per cent Jews (under the 1938 Act it was 20 per cent); Jewish artists and journalists were banned from positions of responsibility; Jews were barred from acquiring agricultural property, and so forth.

5 Act IV of 1939, ss 1(1), (2), (3) [a]

6 A German army report from the front recorded an incident: a German police sergeant was approached by a member of a Jewish labour

battalion, who said: 'Sergeant, I am a Jew, and you can't do anything to me because I am a Hungarian soldier' (Hilberg 1967, p. 519).

7 With the notable exceptions of the massacres of Kamenets Podolsk and of Újvidék (Novi Sad).

8 It is interesting that Ranki, himself Jewish, uses the word 'Israelites'. Even acknowledging the necessity of avoiding the use of the same word over and over, it still has the connotation of assimilationist terminology.

9 Raul Hilberg draws his 'semicircular arc' (with Auschwitz at the centre) and distinguishes the fate of European Jewry as different in the North (Norway and Denmark), in the West (the Netherlands, Luxembourg, Belgium, France and Italy), the Balkans (where he further differentiates between Serbia and Greece and what he calls 'satellites *par excellence*' meaning Croatia and Slovakia) and finally the 'opportunistic satellites': Bulgaria, Romania and Hungary. What happened in this semicircular area was again different to what happened in Poland and the German-occupied Soviet Union (Hilberg 1967).

10 Following the Treaty of Trianon, the assimilation trends of former Hungarian Jews had changed in the Succession States, especially in Czechoslovakia and in Romania. Their Jewishness meant recognising the distinctness of Jews as a nation. This did not change their loyalty to Hungary in any major way. Of the very few scholarly works on the former Jews of Hungary are the already cited works of Bela Vago and Nagy-Talavera, and Kovacs, E., *A Kassai Zsidósag Etnikai Identitása a Két Világháború Között* (The Ethnic Identity of the Jews of Kassa Between the Two Wars), unpublished masters thesis, ELTE, Budapest.

11 Between the world wars, there were many Jewish political parties in Poland. The three major ones, the General Zionists, the *Agudat Yisrael* and the *Bund*, pursued distinctly different policies, and had totally different ideologies. The Zionist party, in terms of representation in the Sejm, the Polish parliament, was the strongest political force and was committed to protecting the interests of the Jews within Poland. The *Bundists* were socialists and the *Agudat Yisrael* represented the orthodox community and opposed both the Zionists and the *Bundists* (Mendelsohn 1974, pp. 203–19).

12 In this there are similarities with Eastern Bloc historians especially, e.g. Schmidt, who quotes the writer Márai as a chapter heading: 'Yesterday the Jews, today the Schwabians, tomorrow the ones with flat ears . . .' (Schmidt 1990, p. 18). During the Holocaust this illusion was fortified by the joke: 'The bicyclists are next.' 'Why the bicyclists?' 'Why the Jews?' The joke also implied a supposed randomness of the choice of the victim.

13 See also Kren & Rappoport 1980, pp. 196–7.

14 The negotiations themselves have to be understood in the context of rescue. The Relief and Rescue Committee, known as the *Vaada*, run by the Zionists, was established in 1943. Initially its work consisted

mainly of helping Jews of neighbouring countries. The *Vaada* actively smuggled refugees across the border to Romania, in an ongoing operation called *tiulim* (excursions), and saved many lives (Braham 1988, p. 107). It had close contact with representatives of various Jewish organisations outside Hungary, including the Slovakian 'Working Group', which initiated the Europa plan. In early 1944, when the Germans occupied Hungary, Kasztner was the de facto head of the *Vaada*. Trying to avoid or at least mitigate the impending murder, and following the footsteps of the Slovakian working group, the *Vaada* started talks with the Nazis (Braham 1981, pp. 932–76; Marrus 1987, pp. 184–92; Hilberg 1967, pp. 542–7).

15 It was pointed out many times that, when consulted, Rabbi Shapiro of the Kovno ghetto said in 1941: 'If a Jewish community (may God help it) has been condemned to physical destruction, and there are means of rescuing part of it, the elders of the community should have the courage to assume the responsibility to act and rescue what is possible' (Marrus 1987, p. 134). The Talmud says: 'He who saves a single life it is as though he has saved the entire world' (*Sanhedrin*, Chapter 4). Maimonides taught a thousand years before the Holocaust: 'If heathens said to the Israelites, "Surrender one of your number to us that we may put him to death, otherwise, we will put all of you to death", they should all suffer death rather than surrender a single Israelite to them. But if they specified an individual, saying "Surrender that particular person to us, or else we will put all of you to death", they may give him up, provided that he was guilty of a capital crime . . . If the individual specified has not incurred capital punishment, they should all suffer death rather than surrender a single Israelite to them' (*Mishneh Torah: The Book of Knowledge,* translated by Moses Hyamson, Jerusalem, 1965, Chapter 5; Precepts, p. 40b).

16 Authors who are especially critical of the role of the Allies include David Wyman (1984) and Martin Gilbert (1991). As the title of his book, *The Myth of Rescue: Why the Democracies Could Not Have Saved More Jews from the Nazis,* indicates, W.D. Rubinstein, on the other hand, totally exonerates the Allies (1997).

17 'He was a poor beadle, a *Shames*. We couldn't believe him. So we also *knew*, but why should we believe a poor beadle?' (Wiesel 1985, p. xiv).

Chapter seven

1 At the time of the German occupation Hungary had 762 007 Jews, as defined by the 1941 racial law. Approximately 63 000 Jews already had perished before the occupation in forced labour service, at the hands of the *Einsatzgruppen* at Kamanets Podolsk, and some at the hands of the Hungarian army (Braham 1981, pp. 1143–4).

2 The date was used instead: '1945'. Similarly, for decades, the usage of the official name 'counter-revolution' was circumvented by saying '1956' instead.

3 Not only the elections (which were at this stage relatively democratic) show sympathy for the left. A large segment of society viewed the political and social changes after 1945 favourably. The peasantry enthusiastically supported the Communist party policies of land distribution and the workers greeted the first nationalisations (Kovacs 1985, p. 208).

4 Many Jews who were serving in forced labour battalions were taken to the Soviet Union. Many did not return until the late 1940s or early 1950s, and many perished and never arrived back. The liberating Soviet army, already in those early days, committed many politically motivated atrocities, along with the war-related ones. Scores of people, not only Jews, were taken for a 'little work' and ended up in Siberia. An active and well-known rescuer of Jews, Raoul Wallenberg, was captured and forcibly taken to the Soviet Union, never to come out again (Braham 1981, pp. 1090–1). In 1948, before the Communist takeover, a book was written about Wallenberg and his life, heroic deeds, and mysterious disappearance. The book was not republished until 1988, when the thawing climate allowed such an account of Soviet actions to be published (Lévai, J. 1948, reprinted, 1988, Maecenas, Budapest).

5 In *The Authoritarian Personality,* Adorno and his colleagues constructed two measurement scales: the 'E scale', a measure of ethnocentrism, defined as a consistently hostile frame of mind concerning aliens, and the 'F scale' as the measure of personality structures that incline individuals towards fascist ideology (1950). The two scales were found to be highly correlated: high scorers on ethnocentricism scored high on the F scale, leaning towards fascism and away from democratic ideology. The authors deduced a typology, the syndrome of associated personality factors characteristic of high and low scorers, concluding that evidence allowed generalisations, particularly regarding high scorers. They define the components of the authoritarian personality as conservatism, conventionalism, dogmatic moralising, distorted view of reality, erroneous comprehension of cause and effect, authoritative subjugation and autonomy-deficient dependence, and manipulative, stereotyped sexuality. The generic basis to the authoritarian character is a general political–economical conservatism, which essentially translates social problems into psychological ones, or rather, offers emotional solutions to social conflicts, scapegoat hunting and rigid resistance towards attempts to change.

6 Although, there were some Jews even in Hungary who sympathised with Mussolini because of his anti-Communist policies and ideas and in Italy a number of Jews joined the Fascist party—while Jews were still allowed.

7 Under the Armistice Agreement of January 1945, war crimes trials started almost immediately in Hungary. A system of tribunals was set up, under the 'people's jurisdiction': the lower level, people's court

(*nepbirosag*) and the higher court of the National Council of People's Tribunals. Each tribunal consisted of a professional judge and his deputy, both appointed by the Ministry of Justice, and five lay judges, representing the five political parties of the time. The appellate courts were composed of five professional judges, each nominated by the five parties (Braham 1981, pp. 1163–4). The defendants were represented by counsel, and the trials were public. The trials continued even after the Communist takeover—albeit with different judges and appointments. There was a trial in 1967, the so-called Zugló Arrowcross trial (*Zuglói nyilas per*), and the last trial was in 1970 (Braham 1981, p. 1168).

8 Jewish vengeance is a recurring accusation. Hannah Arendt addressed it regarding the Eichmann trial. Commenting on the argument against the possible partiality of Jewish judges, that they were judging their own case, she wrote: 'It is difficult to see how the Jewish judges differed in this respect from their colleagues in any of the other Successor trials, where Polish judges pronounced sentence for crimes against the Polish people, or Czech judges sat in judgment on what had happened in Prague or Bratislava' (Arendt 1963, p. 238).

9 It is important to note that there were many Jews who left Hungary (or refused to return), but did not or could not go to Palestine, which at this stage was still a British mandate and, apart from a meagre quota, uncompromisingly banned Jewish immigration. There were others who stayed in Hungary and did not become members of either of the leftist parties, but assumed that the elections would be followed by democratic processes.

10 In the last few decades, especially since the 1967 Arab–Israeli war, the children and grandchildren of those Jews in the Communist party have begun to search for their roots. Jewish identity and consciousness started to shift. This is powerfully documented by the research of Ferenc Erős et al. (1985).

11 After 1948 Hungary became a one-party state and an unambiguous Soviet satellite.

12 Some other interviews: 'Our family was very close, with strong traditions, which my grandmother transferred into love of the party after 1945, because she felt, that only the party saved her from Auschwitz, not god' (Erős et al. 1985, p. 135). 'I hardly knew anything about my parents' life . . . We talked about the Soviet Union, about Communism, about everything, but not about Jewishness. My father is a committed Communist, so is my mother . . . they talked about everything, but never the family or tradition' (Erős et al. 1985, p. 138). 'I don't know anything about my father, his family, his Jewishness, because he became such a Communist. My mother also joined the party early. I read a letter of hers, which she wrote to my grandmother around 1946–1948, in which she wrote how good it is that my grandmother joined the party and that she is so happy that

she doesn't have to be ashamed of her mother and can keep contact with her' (Erős et al. 1985, p. 136).

13 'My parents tried to forget those years. They wanted to forget their early adulthood, the years of war, and with that they blocked out also the years before the war . . . I didn't even know what 'Jewish' meant until I was thirteen' (Erős et al. 1985, p. 134). 'I was a teenager when I picked up words, like *Yid* and dumb Jew . . . I used these expressions without knowing my own background and then my mother and father enlightened me. They never mentioned it before' (Erős et al. 1985, p. 139).

14 At the Kunmadaras pogrom, for instance, three people were killed, eighteen wounded seriously (Vörös 1994, pp. 69, 79). For more about the pogroms, see Kovacs 1985, p. 228; *Encyclopaedia Judaica* pp. 1105–6; Braham 1981, pp. 1155–9.

15 See especially the research of János Pelle on peasant antisemitism (1991, 1992) and of Éva Standeisky on the Communist party (1995). See also Varga (1992); Vörös (1994).

16 It was complicated by Stalinist antisemitism, but its presence was not yet palpable in these first three years.

17 This was especially true after 1956. The underlying tenet was the assertion that the Stalinist–Rákosi crimes were largely the responsibility of the Jewish functionaries. The Kádár regime firmly controlled open antisemitism and at the same time maintained the unmentionability of Jewishness. Even at Holocaust memorial services, the word 'Holocaust' or 'Jewish' did not appear.

18 The late Professor Róbert Dán's father, a member of the Social Democratic party, was arrested in the Communist purges of 1948. At the ÁVH, the Hungarian equivalent of the KGB, he was greeted by one of his interrogators: 'Well, you dirty Jew, I have you in my hands again!' (Personal communication with Professor Róbert Dán.)

19 The purges in Russia in the mid-1930s was distinctly anti-Jewish. The blackest era of Soviet Jewry was to come between 1948 and 1953 (Wistrich 1991, pp. 175–6).

20 Anti-Jewish attacks followed the speech of Rakosi, the Communist party secretary, against black-marketeers, a euphemism for Jews at the time. At a Budapest factory, the workers demanded the dismissal of all Jewish employees. There were antisemitic incidents in at least five towns and villages (Braham 1981, p. 1157).

21 The essay is in four parts. The first part deals with the Holocaust and the responsibility of Hungarian society and policies. The second chapter, entitled 'Jews and Antisemites', is a historical overview of the development of antisemitism from medieval times. The third chapter, entitled 'Jewish Assimilation and Jewish Consciousness' deals with the double issue of assimilation and Jewish identity including national consciousness and Zionism; and the fourth part scrutinises all the previous issues—examining the period between 1944 and 1948.

22 Bibó consciously avoided the pitfalls of later historiography, which—
when it acknowledged it at all—treated the Holocaust as either an
outcome of the German occupation and thus essentially part of
German history, or as class conflict in which fascists persecuted
anti-fascists. Bibó viewed the whole of the Horthy era as a forerunner,
and examined each and every layer of Hungarian society from the
time of the first anti-Jewish law to the Arrowcross *putsch*.

23 'Her denial . . . was not simply the theoretical application of Marx's
teachings . . . her internationalism was also a product of an imposed
situation of national dispossession [Polish and Jewish] which ultimately drove her to a transcendent, quasi-mystical embracing of the
concept of a proletarian 'fatherland'. Estranged like Karl Marx from
her Jewish background, she found in international socialism not just
a religion but a new political home' (Wistrich 1990, p. 21). Arendt
also stressed the importance of Luxemburg's assimilated Jewish background and certain traditional Jewish virtues in her 'axiomatic' and
'almost naive contempt for social and ethnic distinctions' (Arendt
1973a, p. 47).

24 With the composites of religious, nationalist, racial and left-wing,
antisemitism, 'catering' to every political and social conviction, resurfaced with vehemence after the implosion of the Communist empire.
After the Holocaust, in the years of Communism it was the populist
aspects of Hungarian nationalism which survived. Having been formulated and propagated by writers, it was through them that populist
nationalism was present—albeit in a controlled form—in the Kádár
years. In the post-Communist era, during the four years of Christian
National rule, there was a deliberate attempt to rehabilitate the Horthy
regime and restore a sense of continuity by equating the years of
Communism with foreign rule, and even rehabilitating the ethos of
the Horthy regime. Similar to the contradictory Horthy regime, the
ruling National Democratic party and its allies, the Christian Democrats and the Small-Holders party condemned antisemitism in the
name of liberalism and democracy, but allowed vocal antisemitic
rhetoric even within its own ranks. However, the second free election
in 1994 brought the defeat of the Christian Nationalists, in spite of
the nationalist rhetoric. The election was decided on predominantly
economic issues. Yet it is important to ask whether the revival of the
Horthy era's nationalist ethos activated danger signals. After all, the
Horthy era was oppressive to peasants and to the working classes.

25 The historical treatment of Nazism was closely bound up with the wish
to build a self-confident German national identity. Exploring the relationship between the historical interpretations and identity, Wolfgang Benz
showed how many Germans exercised 'assorted defense mechanisms to
ward off the past rather than confront it' (Benz 1988, p. 1).

26 In the orthodox years of Stalinism, the slogan of the time set the
direction: 'full face to the future'. The war years along with the

Holocaust were viewed, reassuringly and conveniently, as the sins of the ruling classes of a by-gone era, when 'fascists persecuted anti-fascists'. By de-Judaising the victim, it also denied the 'otherness' of Jews while it ingeniously shifted all responsibility onto the Germans and the 'cursed' old regime. As the dramatic moral corruption and devaluation of the Stalinist years greyed into everyday existence, the Kádár regime firmly controlled open antisemitism and at the same time maintained the unmentionability of Jewishness. The Holocaust was not taught in history. Even at Holocaust memorial services the word 'Holocaust' or 'Jewish' did not appear. The historicisation of political life and the re-evaluation of the past started in the last decades of the Kádár era. With the lifting of taboos on history, the 'Jewish question' resurfaced. The insinuations and incidents during the election campaign of 1989–90 were the first manifestations of this. Antisemitic letters to the editors; admonitions and accusations by cultural, religious and political figureheads; and Holocaust denial are the main patterns that developed. In the parliament, an MP, a former general of the Horthy army, said that the 'Hungarian army was fighting a just war', because 'defending my country against Communism is a just cause'. He proudly acknowledged: 'We entered the war to show our gratitude to the Germans . . . ' (i.e. for the territorial gains of the two Vienna awards) (*168 ora*, 7 August 1990, pp. 7–8). This stance was defended by a leading right wing writer and ideologue, who accused Communists and Jews of being the cause of that: 'For 45 years we have had to live as guilty nation, losers, last satellite, humiliated servant-nation' (*Magyar Fórum*, 24 October 1991, p. 1). Catholic Bishop Endre Gyulai said: 'The more they bring up the long-ago Holocaust, the more antipathy is aroused against them. The more they are capable of forgiveness, naturally acknowledging what is necessary, that is, a certain 'I don't forget' attitude but not retribution, the better the situation will be. The more they push, the more hostile sentiments against them will be' (*Pesti Hirlap*, 7 December 1992, p. 13).

Chapter 8

1 With the exception only of America, where not only did the Declaration of Independence not include slaves but the Constitution recognised slavery.
2 Already, during World War II, there were linkages: El-Huseini, the Imam of Jerusalem, rushed to Berlin, where, as an 'honorary Aryan', he urged Hitler to kill all Jews. After the war Nazis found refuge in Arab countries. Among the more notorious Nazis, Alois Brunner and Franz Stangl stand out, both finding haven in Syria. Brunner was responsible for the deportation of over 100 000 Jews from Slovakia, Vienna and Salonika.
See, for instance, 'ZOG's war in the Middle East' in *Perseverance*,

vol. 30, no. 11, 15 November 1990, pp. 4–5; also in the same issue, 'Kuwait, a detonator?', pp. 3–4. The acronym ZOG stands for Zionist Occupational Government, meaning Israel. The word 'perseverance' was the call of the Hungarian Nazi Arrowcross party. The journal was registered by Australia Post until 1991, when it ceased publication. The standard fare of *Perseverance* was Holocaust denial and Israel-bashing.

3 Faurisson is a former professor of literature at the University of Lyons–2, whose writings centre around the thesis that the gassing of Jews is a 'gigantic politico–financial swindle whose beneficiaries are the state of Israel and international Zionism' (Lipstadt 1993, p. 8). Leuchter is a self-appointed engineer and gas-chamber 'expert' who wrote an infamous 'report' based on 'scientific tests' conducted by him at Auschwitz and Majdanek, proving that the gas-chambers there could not have been used for killing. Irving started as a writer of popular historical books. He became more and more extreme, openly associating with (neo)Nazis and the Ku Klux Klan. He is best known for his early book, *Hitler's War*, in which he expounded that Hitler did not know about the 'Final Solution'. Irving declared that he is conducting a 'one-man intifada' against the official history of the Holocaust (Lipstadt 1993, pp. 8–13, 160, 179).

4 'The Holocaust is the Jewish flame of Olympus, maintained by a world-wide financial power with the aid of the media . . . How can you tell Palestinians to commit to memory the dramas of the past, when they are living through far more unbearable ones? What difference is there between a gas chamber and a cluster bomb that falls on an Arab house on a night of Ramadan?' (*Algerie-Actualité* no. 1127, week of 21–27 May 1987, quoted by Finkielkraut 1992, p. 79, fn. 22). The imagery is all Western: Greek mythology, the Olympic games, the nineteenth-century Czarist forgery of *The Protocols of the Elders of Zion*, and it reaches into the twentieth century through the reference to the power of the media which, after all, is in the hands of the Jews. Classic, modern and postmodern concepts in one sentence. The next sentence tries to relativise, and diminish the Holocaust and the third sentence turns the victim into perpetrator, into victimiser. But, of course, it is not the Holocaust survivor who fights in today's Israeli army—maybe a survivor's grandchild. To those who know their history, comparing the horror of a cluster bomb to the totality of evil and cruelty that sought to destroy and torture all Jews inevitably weakened the relevance of the cluster bomb (not at all a desirable outcome); the ignorant, or those who think the Jews deserved their fate anyway, will not perhaps give more sympathy to the Palestinians, but will use them and their cause simply against the Jews.

5 So much so, that as Jews used to be a pariah-people, for a few decades Israel became a pariah-nation and Jewish nationalism, Zionism, was declared racism.

This did not mean that antisemitism disappeared. Both the left, especially the Soviet empire, and the right found the perfect solution: anti-Zionism, masquerading as valid political criticism. It is by no means my claim that policies of Israel cannot be criticised without antisemitism. Israel is a democracy (the only one in the region) and whichever party is elected finds hot and articulate opposition within the country. Government policies can be (and should be) criticised without questioning and undermining the right of the Jewish people for self-determination (i.e. Zionism). The ideal of self-determination, in spite of the spectacular failure and dissolution of many of the countries constructed by the Versailles Treaty, still is universally accepted and respected. Yet the right of Jewish people to self-determination has been disputed and Zionism has been condemned as racism for many years by the infamous UN resolution (now repealed). The rhetoric of 'Zionism = racism' or 'racist Zionism' still surfaces on many political forums. Anti-Zionism as antisemitism has been explored by several authors, especially by Robert Wistrich (1991).

Bibliography

Adorno, T. 1986 'What does coming to terms with the past mean?' *Bitburg in Moral and Political Perspective* ed. G. Hartman, Indiana University Press, Bloomington

Adorno, T. and Horkheimer, M. 1986 *Dialectic of Enlightenment* 2nd edn, Verso, London

Adorno, T. et al. 1950 *The Authoritarian Personality*, W.W. Norton, New York

Almog, S. ed. 1988 *Antisemitism through the Ages*, Pergamon, Oxford

——1990 *Nationalism and Antisemitism in Modern Europe 1815–1945*, Pergamon, Oxford

Anderson, B. 1993 *Imagined Communities: Reflections on the Origin and Spread of Nationalism* rev. edn, Verso, London

Andics, E. ed. 1964 *A magyar nacionalizmus kialakulása és története* (The Development and History of Hungarian Nationalism), Kossuth, Budapest

Arad, Y., Gutman, Y. and Margaliot, A. eds 1988 *Documents of the Holocaust* 3rd edn, Yad Vashem, Jerusalem

Arató, E. 1964 'A magyar nacionalizmus kettős arculata a feudalizmusból a kapitalizmusba való átmenet és a polgári forradalom időszakában' ('The dual face of Hungarian nationalism at the time of transition from feudalism to capitalism and bourgeois revolution') *A magyar nacionalizmus kialakulása es története* (The Development and History of Hungarian Nationalism) ed. E. Andics, Kossuth, Budapest

Arendt, H. 1957 *Rahel Varnhagen: The Life of a Jewish Woman* rev. edn, Harcourt Brace Jovanovich, New York

——1963 *Eichmann in Jerusalem: A Report on the Banality of Evil*, Faber & Faber, London

——1967 *The Origins of Totalitarianism*, George Allen & Unwin, London

——1968a *Men in Dark Times*, Harcourt Brace Jovanovich, New York

——1968b 'Walter Benjamin 1892–1940' *Men in Dark Times* H. Arendt, Harcourt Brace Jovanovich, New York

——1973a *Men in Dark Times*, Penguin, Harmondsworth

——1973b 'Rosa Luxemburg 1871–1919' *Men in Dark Times* H. Arendt, Penguin, Harmondsworth

——1979 'On Hannah Arendt (A Conversation)' *Hannah Arendt: The Recovery of the Public World* ed. M. Hill, St. Martin's Press, New York

Bányai, L. and Kis, A. 1990 'Tortenelmi bevezetes' ('Historical introduction') *Hét Évtized a Hazai Zsidóság Életében* (Seven Decades in the Life of Hungarian Jewry) eds L. Lendvai, A. Sohár and P. Horráth, MTA Filozofiai Intezet, Budapest

Barany, G. 1968 *Stephen Szechenyi and the Awakening of Hungarian Nationalism 1791–1841*, Princeton University Press, Princeton

——1971 'Hungary: From aristocratic to proletarian nationalism' *Nationalism in Eastern Europe* eds P. Sugar and I. Lederer, University of Washington Press, Seattle

——1974 '"Magyar Jew or Jewish Magyar?" Reflections on the question of assimilation' *Jews and non-Jews in Eastern Europe* eds B. Vago and G. Mosse, John Wiley & Sons, New York & Israel Universities Press, Jerusalem

Bauer, O. 1988 'A nemzetiségi kérdés és a szociáldemokrácia' ('The question of the national minorities and social democracy') *Elméleti viták a nemzeti kérdésről: A nemzeti kérdés lenini elmélétenek kialakulása* (Theoretical Debates on the National Question: The Development of the Leninist Theory on the National Question) ed. I. Mate, Kossuth, Budapest

Bauer, Y. 1978 *The Holocaust in Historical Perspective*, Australian National University Press, Canberra

——ed. 1988 *Present-Day Antisemitism*, The Hebrew University of Jerusalem, Jerusalem

——1994 *Jews for Sale?* Yale University Press, New Haven

Bauer, Y. and Rotenstreich, N. eds 1981 *The Holocaust as Historical Experience*, Holmes & Meier, New York

Bauman, Z. 1989 *Modernity and the Holocaust*, Polity Press, Cambridge

Benz, W. 1988 'Warding off history: Is this only a problem for historians and moralists?' *Holocaust and Genocide Studies* vol. 3, no. 2, pp. 137–50

Berend, I. 1985 'The road toward the Holocaust: The ideological and political background' *The Holocaust in Hungary: Forty Years Later* eds R. Braham and B. Vago, Columbia University Press, New York

Berend, I. and Ranki, G. 1972 *A Magyar Gazdaság Száz Éve* (A Hundred Years of Hungarian Economy), Budapest

Berend, I. and Ranki, G. 1985 *The Hungarian Economy in the Twentieth Century*, St Martin's Press, New York

Berger, P. 1969 *The Sacred Canopy: The Social Reality of Religion*, Faber & Faber, London

Berkes, T. 1993 'Napilapok a zsidókérdésrol' ('Newspapers about the Jewish question') *Világosság* no. 6, pp. 69–80

Bethlen, I. 1988 *Emlékirata 1944* (His Memoirs 1944), Zrinyi, Budapest

Bibó, I. 1984 'Zsidókérdés Magyarországon 1944 után' ('The Jewish question in Hungary after 1944') *Zsidókerdes, Asszimilácio, Antiszemitizmus* (The Jewish Question, Assimilation, Antisemitism) ed. P. Hanak, Gondolat,

Budapest (quotations from Bibó have been translated from the original text by the author)

Bihari, P. 1990 'A magyarországi zsidóság helyzete a zsidótörvényektől a deportálásig' ('The situation of Hungarian Jewry from the Jewish decrees to deportation') *Hét Évtized a Magyar Zsidóság Életében* (Seven Decades in the Life of Hungarian Jewry) eds L. Lendvai, A. Sohár and P. Horváth, MTA Filozofiai Intezet, Budapest

Bolkosky, S. 1975 *The Distorted Image: German Jewish Perceptions of Germans and Germany 1918–1935*, Elsevier, New York

Borsanyi, G. 1992 'Zsidok a munkasmozgalomban' ('Jews in the labour movement') *Világosság* no. 2, pp. 145–51

Braham, R. ed. 1966 *Hungarian Jewish Studies*, World Federation of Hungarian Jewry, New York

——1981 *The Politics of Genocide*, Columbia University Press, New York

——1985 'The uniqueness of the Holocaust in Hungary' *The Holocaust in Hungary: Forty Years Later* eds R. Braham and B. Vago, Columbia University Press, New York

——1988 'The rescue of Hungarian Jewry in historical perspective' *The Historiography of the Holocaust Period* eds Y. Gutman and G. Greif, Yad Vashem, Jerusalem

Braham, R. and Pok, A. eds 1997 *The Holocaust in Hungary: Fifty Years Later*, The Rosenthal Institute for Holocaust Studies of the City University of New York, New York, & The Institute of History of the Hungarian Academy of Sciences, Budapest

Browning, C. 1985 *Fateful Months: Essays on the Emergence of the Final Solution*, Holmes & Meier, New York

——1992 *Ordinary Men: Reserve Police Battalion 101 and the Final Solution in Poland*, HarperCollins, New York

Burleigh, M. and Wippermann, W. 1991 *The Racial State: Germany 1933–1945*, Cambridge University Press, Cambridge

Buzinkay, G. ed. 1988 *Mokány Berci és Spitzig Itzig, Göre Gábor mög a többiek . . . A magyar társadalom figurái az élclapokban 1860 és 1918 között* (Berci Mokany and Itzig Spitzig, Gabor Gore and the Others . . . The Figures of Hungarian Society in the Comic Magazines), Magvető, Budapest

Carsten, F.L. 1988 'Interpretations of fascism' *Fascism: A Readers Guide* ed. W. Laqueur, Wildwood House, Aldershot

Cesarani, D. ed. 1997 *Genocide and Rescue: The Holocaust in Hungary 1944*, Berg, Oxford

Cohen, G.B. 1989 'The social structure of Prague, Vienna and Budapest in the late nineteenth century' *Hungary and European Civilisation* ed. G. Ranki, Akadémiai Kiadó, Budapest

Csorba, L. 1990 'Zsidó szellemi élet a huszas-harmincas évek Magyarországán' ('Jewish intellectual life in the 1920s and 1930s in Hungary') *Hét Évtized a Hazai Zsidóság Életeben* (Seven Decades in the Life of Hungarian Jewry) eds L. Lendvai, A. Sohár and P. Horvath, MTA Filozofiai Intezet, Budapest

Darvas, J. 1945 'Vissza a néphez!' ('Back to the people!') *Szabad Szó*, 28 August, p. 2

Dawidowicz, L. 1990 *The War against the Jews, 1933–45*, Penguin, London

Deak, I. 1985 'The peculiarities of Hungarian fascism' *The Holocaust in Hungary: Forty Years Later* eds R. Braham and B. Vago, Columbia University Press, New York

——1992 'Historiography of the countries of Eastern Europe: Hungary' *American Historical Review*, October, pp. 1041–63

Diamond, L. and Plattner M. eds 1994 *Nationalism, Ethnic Conflict and Democracy*, The Johns Hopkins University Press, Baltimore

Dobos, I. 1990 'A csodarabbi alakja a néphagyományban' ('The figure of the wonder-rabbi in folklore') *A Hagyomány Kötelékében Tanulmányok a Magyarorszagi Zsidó Folklór Körebol* (Bound by Tradition: Essays in Hungarian Jewish Folklore) ed. I. Kriza, Akadémiai Kiadó, Budapest

Encyclopaedia Judaica 1973, corrected edn, Keter Publishing, Jerusalem

Engels, F. 1977 'The Magyar struggle' *Marx and Engels Collected Works* vol. 8, Lawrence & Wishart, London

Eötvös, K. 1968 *A nagy per mely ezer éve folyik, s még sincs vége* (The Grand Trial which has been on for the Last Thousand Years, and Still does not End), Szépirodalmi Kiadó, Budapest

Erdélyi, A. 1991 'Eltorzult kozmopolita alkat' ('Contorted cosmopolitan personality') *Bibó Emlékkönyv* (Bibó Memorial Volume), Századvég, Budapest

Erős, F., Kovacs A. and Lévai, K. 1985 '"Hogyan jottem ra hogy zsido vagyok?"—Interjuk' ('"How did I find out that I am Jewish?"—Interviews') *Medvetanc* no. 2–3, pp. 129–44

Eros, J. 1970 'Hungary' *European Fascism* 2nd edn, ed. S. Woolf, Weidenfeld & Nicolson, London

Ettinger, S. 1988 'Jew-hatred in its historical context' *Antisemitism through the Ages* ed. S. Almog, Pergamon, Oxford

Feher, F. 1980 'Istvan Bibó and the Jewish question in Hungary: Notes on the margin of a classical essay' *New German Critique* no. 21, pp. 3–46

Fein, H. 1987a 'Dimensions of antisemitism: Attitudes, collective accusations, and actions' *The Persisting Question: Sociological Perspectives and Social Contexts of Modern Antisemitism* ed. H. Fein, Walter de Gruyter, Berlin

——ed. 1987b *The Persisting Question: Sociological Perspectives and Social Contexts of Modern Antisemitism*, Walter de Gruyter, Berlin

Fejtő, F. 1959 'Conclusion' *1848—A Turning Point?* ed. M. Kranzberg, D.C. Heath & Co., Boston

——1990a *Budapesttől Párizsig: Emlékeim* (From Budapest to Paris: Memoirs) Magveto, Budapest

——1990b *Rekviem egy Hajdanvolt Birodalomért: Ausztria–Magyarország Szétrombolása* (Requiem for an Empire that Had Been: The Destruction of Austria–Hungary), Minerva, Atlantisz, Medvetanc, Budapest

Felkai, G. 1992 *A budapesti zsidó fiu- es a leánygimnázium története* (The

History of the Budapest Boys' and Girls' High School), Anna Frank Gimnázium, Budapest

Finkielkraut, A. 1992 *Remembering in Vain: The Klaus Barbie Trial and Crimes Against Humanity*, Columbia University Press, New York

Fountain, A.M. 1980 *Roman Dmowski: Party, Tactics, Ideology 1895–1907*, East European Monographs, Boulder & Columbia University Press, New York

Friedlander, H. and Milton, S. eds 1980 *The Holocaust: Ideology, Bureaucracy and Genocide*, Kraus International Publications, Millwood, New York

Frojimovics, K., Komoróczy, G., Pusztai, V. and Strbik A. 1995 *A zsidó Budapest: Emlékek, szertartások, történelem* (The Jewish Budapest: Memories, Rituals and History), Városhaza, Budapest

Fukuyama, F. 1994 'Comments on nationalism and democracy' *Nationalism, Ethnic Conflict and Democracy* ed. L. Diamond and M. Plattner, The Johns Hopkins University Press, Baltimore

Gellner, E. 1964 *Thought and Change*, Weidenfeld & Nicolson, London

——1983 *Nations and Nationalism*, Basil Blackwell, Oxford

Gerő, A. 1992 'Liberálisok, antiszemiták és zsidók a modern Magyarország születésekor' ('Liberals, antisemites and Jews at the birth of modern Hungary') *Zsidósag Identitás Történelem* (Jewishness, Identity, History) eds M. Kovacs, M. Kashti and F. Erős, T-Twins, Budapest

Gilbert, M. 1991 *Auschwitz and the Allies*, Mandarin, London

Glatz, F. 1989 'Előszó' ('Foreword') *Három Nemzedék és Ami Utána Következik* (Three Generations and What Happened After) G. Szekfü, Maecenas, Budapest

Gobineau, A. 1967 *Essai sur L'Inégalité des Races Humaines*, Belford, Paris

Goldhagen, D. 1996 *Hitler's Willing Executioners: Ordinary Germans and the Holocaust*, Alfred A. Knopf, New York

Gonda, L. 1992 *A zsidóság Magyarországon 1526–1945* (Jews in Hungary 1526–1945), Szazadveg, Budapest

Gutman, Y. and Greif, G. eds 1988 *The Historiography of the Holocaust Period*, Yad Vashem, Jerusalem

Gyani, G. 1993 'Az asszimilació fogalma a Magyar társadalomtörténetben' ('The concept of assimilation in Hungarian social historiography') *Valosag* no. 4, pp. 18–27

Habermas, J. 1986 'A kind of indemnification: The tendencies toward apologia in German research on current history' *Yad Vashem Studies* vol. XIX, pp. 75–92

——1992 'Citizenship and national identity: Some reflections on the future of Europe' *Praxis International* vol. 12, no. 1, pp. 1–20

Hanak, P. 1984a 'Problems of Jewish assimilation in Austria-Hungary in the nineteenth and twentieth centuries' *The Power of the Past: Essays for Eric Hobsbawm* eds P. Thane, G. Crossick and R. Floud, Cambridge University Press, Cambridge

——1984b *Zsidókérdés, Asszimilació, Antiszemitizmus* (The Jewish Question, Assimilation, Antisemitism), Gondolat, Budapest

——1985 *Jászi Oszkár dunai patriotizmusa* (Oscar Jászi's Danube Patriotism), Magvető, Budapest

——ed. 1988 *One Thousand Years: A Concise History of Hungary*, Corvina, Budapest

Handler, A. 1980 *Blood Libel at Tiszaeszlár*, East European Monographs, Boulder & Columbia University Press, New York

——ed. 1982 *The Holocaust in Hungary: An Anthology of Jewish Response*, University of Alabama Press, Tuscaloosa

Hertzberg, A. 1986 *The French Enlightenment and the Jews*, Columbia University Press, New York

Herzl, T. 1988 *The Jewish State*, Dover Publications Inc., New York

Hilberg, R. (1967 Quadrangle Books, Chicago) 1985 *The Destruction of the European Jews* 3 vols, rev. and definitive edn, Holmes & Meier, New York and London

——1980 'The significance of the Holocaust' *The Holocaust: Ideology, Bureaucracy and Genocide* eds H. Friedlander and S. Milton, Kraus International Publications, Millwood, New York

Hill, M. 1979 *Hannah Arendt: The Recovery of the Public World*, St. Martin's Press, New York

Hoffmann, R. 1980 *More Than a Trial: The Struggle over Captain Dreyfus*, Collier, Macmillan, New York

Ignatieff, M. 1993 *Blood and Belonging: Journeys into the New Nationalism* Farrar, Strauss & Giroux, New York

Ignotus, P. 1972 *Hungary*, Praeger, New York

Jaspers, K. and Augstein, R. 1966 'The criminal state and German responsibility: A dialogue' *Commentary* vol. 41, no. 2, pp. 33–9

Jászi, O. 1961 *Dissolution of the Habsburg Monarchy*, University of Chicago Press, Chicago

——1986 *A Nemzeti Államok Kialakulása és a Nemzetiségi Kérdés* (The Development of the Nation–State and the Nationalities' Question), Gondolat, Budapest

——1988 *A Monarchia Jövője* (The Future of the Monarchy), Maecenas, Budapest

Juhasz, F. 1985 'Hungarian intellectual life and the Jewish problem during World War II' *The Holocaust in Hungary: Forty Years Later* eds R. Braham and B. Vago, Columbia University Press, New York

Kállay, N. 1954 *Hungarian Premier: A Personal Account of a Nation's Struggle in the Second World War*, Columbia University Press, New York

Kamenka, E. ed., 1973a *Nationalism: The Nature and Evolution of an Idea*, Edward Arnold, London

——1973b 'Political nationalism: The evolution of the idea' *Nationalism: The Nature and Evolution of an Idea* ed. E. Kamenka, Edward Arnold, London

Kamenka, E. and Krygier, M. eds 1979 *Bureaucracy*, Edward Arnold, London

Kamenka, E. and Tay, A.E.S. 1979 'Freedom, law and the bureaucratic state' *Bureaucracy* eds E. Kamenka and M. Krygier, Edward Arnold, London

Karady V. 1984 'Szociológiai kísérlet a magyar zsidóság 1945 és 1956 közötti helyzetének elemzésére' ('Sociological attempt for the analysis of the situation of Hungarian Jewry between 1945 and 1956') *Zsidóság az 1945 utáni Magyarországon* (Jewry in Post–1945 Hungary), Magyar Füzetek, Paris

——1989 'Assimilation and schooling: National and denominational minorities in the universities of Budapest around 1900' *Hungary and European Civilisation* ed. G. Ranki, Akadémiai Kiadó, Budapest

——1993a 'Antisemitism in twentieth-century Hungary' *Patterns of Prejudice* vol. 27, no. 1, pp. 71–92

——1993b 'Asszimiláció és társadalmi krizis' ('Assimilation and social crisis') *Világosság* vol. XXXIV, no. 3, pp. 33–60

Karinthy, F. 1963 *Igy Irtok Ti* (This Is How You Write), Szepirodalmi Könyvkiadó, Budapest

Karsai, L. ed. 1992 *Kirekesztők: Antiszemita irások, 1881–1992* (Those Who Exclude: Antisemitic Writings, 1881–1992), Aura, Budapest

Katz, J. 1978 *Out of the Ghetto: The Social Background of Jewish Emancipation, 1770–1870*, Schocken Books, New York

——1980 *From Prejudice to Destruction: Antisemitism, 1700–1933*, Harvard University Press, Cambridge, Massachusetts

——1986 *Jewish Emancipation and Self-Emancipation*, The Jewish Publication Society, Philadelphia

Katzburg, N. 1966 'Hungarian Jewry in modern times: Political and social aspects' *Hungarian Jewish Studies* ed. R. Braham, World Federation of Hungarian Jewry, New York

——1985 'The tradition of antisemitism in Hungary' *The Holocaust in Hungary: Forty Years Later* eds R. Braham and B. Vago, Columbia University Press, New York

Klein, G. and Milan, J. eds 1981 *Politics of Ethnicity in Eastern Europe*, East European Monographs, Boulder & Columbia University Press, New York

Kohn, H. 1961a *The Habsburg Empire, 1804–1918*, Van Nostrand, Princeton

——1961b *The Idea of Nationalism: A Study in its Origins and Background* 2nd edn, Macmillan, New York

Kosary, D. 1989 'Enlightenment and liberalism in Hungary' *Hungary and European Civilisation* ed. G. Ranki, Akadémiai Kiadó, Budapest

Kovacs, A. 1985 'The Jewish question in contemporary Hungary' *The Holocaust in Hungary: Forty Years Later* eds R. Braham and B. Vago, Columbia University Press, New York

——1992 'Asszimiláció, antiszemitizmus, identitás' ('Assimilation, antisemitism, identity') *Hogyan Éljuk túl a Huszadik Századot?* (How to Survive the Twentieth Century?) ed. M. Vig, Narancs Alapitvány, Budapest

Kovacs, M., Kashti, M. and Erős, F. 1992 *Zsidóság Identitás Történelem*, (Jewishness Identity History), T-Twins, Budapest

Kranzberg, M. ed. 1959 *1848—A Turning Point?*, D.C. Heath & Co., Boston

Kren, G. and Rappoport, L. (1980) 1994 *The Holocaust and the Crisis of Human Behavior* rev. edn, Holmes & Meier, New York

Kriza, I. ed. 1990 *A Hagyomány Kötelékében: Tanulmányok a Magyarországi*

Zsidó Folklór Köréból (Bound by Tradition: Essays in Hungarian Jewish Folklore), Akadémiai Kiadó, Budapest

Kubinszky, J. 1976 *Politikai antiszemitizmus Magyarországon (1875–1890)* (Political Antisemitism in Hungary (1875–1890)), Kossuth, Budapest

Kupchan, C. 1995 'Introduction: Nationalism resurgent' *Nationalism and Nationalities in the New Europe* ed. C. Kupchan, Cornell University Press, Ithaca

Lacko, M. 1966 *Nyilasok: nemzetiszocialisták, 1935–1944* (Arrowcross Men: National Socialists, 1935–1944), Kossuth, Budapest

Langmuir, G. 1987 'Toward a definition of antisemitism' *The Persisting Question: Sociological Perspectives and Social Contexts of Modern Antisemitism* ed. H. Fein, Walter de Gruyter, Berlin

——1990 *Toward a Definition of Antisemitism*, University of California Press, Berkeley

Laqueur, W. ed. 1976 *Fascism: A Readers Guide*, Wildwood House, Aldershot

László, E. 1966 'Hungary's Jewry: A demographic overview, 1918–1945' *Hungarian Jewish Studies* ed. R. Braham, World Federation of Hungarian Jewry, New York

Lendvai, L., Sohár, A. and Horváth, P. eds 1990 *Hét Évtized a Hazai Zsidóság Életében* (Seven Decades in the Life of Hungarian Jewry), MTA Filozofiai Intezet, Budapest

Lévai, J. 1948 *Raoul Wallenberg: Regényes Élete, Hősi Küzdelmei es Rejtélyes Eltünesének Titkai* (Raoul Wallenberg: His Colourful Life, Heroic Struggles and the Secret of his Mysterious Disappearance), Magyar Teka, Budapest, reprinted 1988, Maecenas, Budapest

Lindemann, A.S. 1991 *The Jew Accused: Three Anti-Semitic Affairs, 1894–1915*, Cambridge University Press, Cambridge

Linz, J. 1988 'Some notes toward a comparative study of fascism in sociological historical perspective' *Fascism: A Readers Guide* ed. W. Laqueur, Wildwood House, Aldershot

Lipstadt, D. 1993 *Denying the Holocaust: The Growing Assault on Truth and Memory*, The Free Press, New York

Lloyd George, D. 1938 *The Truth about the Peace Treaties*, Gollancz, London

Lukacs, J. 1988 *Budapest 1900*, Weidenfeld & Nicolson, London

Macartney, C.A. 1961 *October Fifteenth: A History of Modern Hungary 1929–1945* 2nd edn, Edinburgh University Press, Edinburgh

——1971 *The Habsburg Empire 1790–1918*, Weidenfeld & Nicolson, London

McCagg, W.O. 1972a *Jewish Nobles and Geniuses in Modern Hungary*, Columbia University Press, New York

——1972b 'Jews in revolutions: The Hungarian experience' *Journal of Social History* vol. 6, no. 1, pp. 78–105

MacDonald, D. 1957a 'The responsibility of peoples' *The Responsibility of Peoples and Other Essays in Political Criticism* ed. D. MacDonald, Victor Gollancz, London

——ed. 1957b *The Responsibility of Peoples and Other Essays in Political Criticism*, Victor Gollancz, London

Magyar Zsidó Lexikon (Hungarian Jewish Encyclopaedia) 1929 Budapest
Marrus, M. 1987 *The Holocaust in History*, University Press of New England, Hanover
Márványi, J. 1991 'Köszönet helyett' ('Instead of thanks') *Bibó Emlékkönyv* (Bibó Memorial Volume), Századvég, Budapest
Marx and Engels Collected Works 1977 vol. 8, Lawrence & Wishart, London
Mason, T. 1981 'Intention and explanation: A current controversy about the interpretation of national socialism' *Der 'Führerstaat': Mythos und Realität* (The 'Führerstate': Myth and Reality) eds G. Hirschfeld and L. Ketteneckar, Keltt-Cotta, Stuttgart
Mate, I. ed. 1988 *Elméleti viták a nemzeti kérdésrol: A nemzeti kérdés lenini elméletének kialakulása* (Theoretical Debates on the National Question: The Development of the Leninist Theory on the National Question), Kossuth, Budapest
Meinecke, F. 1928 *Weltbürgertum und Nationalstaat* (World Bourgeoisie and Nation State), Oldenburg, Munich
Mendelsohn, E. 1974 'The dilemma of Jewish politics in Poland: Four responses' *Jews and Non-Jews in Eastern Europe, 1918–1945* eds B. Vago and G. Mosse, John Wiley & Sons, New York
——1983 *The Jews of East Central Europe: Between the World Wars*, Indiana University Press, Bloomington
Miháncsik, Zs. 1995 'Szóval azt mondja, aki zsidó, tartsa magát zsidónak?' ('So you say that a Jew should regard himself a Jew?') *Budapesti Negyed* vol. 8, pp. 227–60
Mikszáth, K. 1910 *A Gavallérok* (The Gentlemen), Pallas, Budapest
Milgram, S. 1973 *Obedience to Authority: An Experimental View*, Tavistock, London
Mosse, G. 1993 *Confronting the Nation: Jewish and Western Nationalism*, University Press of New England, Hanover, New Hampshire
Nagy-Talavera, N. 1970 *The Green Shirts and the Others*, Hoover Institution Press, Stanford
Nettl, P. 1969 *Rosa Luxemburg*, Oxford University Press, London
Nodia, G. 1994 'Nationalism and democracy' *Nationalism, Ethnic Conflict and Democracy* eds L. Diamond and M. Plattner, The Johns Hopkins University Press, Baltimore
Patai, J. 1918 'Az antiszemitizmus Magyarországon' ('Antisemitism in Hungary') *Múlt es Jövő* p. 283
Patai, R. 1989 'Szüleim' ('My Parents') *Múlt es Jövő* no. 2, pp. 23–30
Paxton, R. 1994 'Radicals' *New York Review of Books* 23 June, pp. 51–4
Pelle, J. 1991 '"Csaholyban nincs zsidó. '68-ban ölték meg az utolsót." A XX. századi paraszti antiszemitizmus kórképéhez' ('"In Csaholy there are no Jews left. The last one was murdered in 1968." To the pathography of 20th century peasant antisemitism') *Kritika* no. 4, pp. 22–4
——1992 'Vérvád Mátészalkán' ('Blood libel at Mateszalka') *Világosság* no. 1, pp. 68–80

Plamenatz, J. 1976 'Two types of nationalism' *Nationalism: The Nature and Evolution of an Idea* ed. E. Kamenka, Edward Arnold, London

Poliakov, L. *The History of Antisemitism* vol. 1, Vanguard Press, New York

——1973 *The History of Antisemitism* vol. 2, Vanguard Press, New York

——1975 *The History of Antisemitism* vol. 3, Routledge & Kegan Paul, London

——1985 *The History of Antisemitism* vol. 4, Oxford University Press, Oxford

Proctor, R. 1988 *Racial Hygiene: Medicine under the Nazis*, Harvard University Press, Cambridge, Massachusetts

Pryce-Jones, D. 1989 *The Closed Circle*, Paladin, London

Pynsent, R. ed. 1989 *Decadence and Innovation: Austro–Hungarian Life and Art at the Turn of the Century*, Weidenfeld & Nicolson, London

Ranki, G. 1968 *1944 Március 19* (19 March 1944), Budapest

——1985 'The Germans and the destruction of Hungarian Jewry' *The Holocaust in Hungary: Forty Years Later* eds R. Braham and B. Vago, Columbia University Press, New York

——1988 *A Harmadik Birodalom Árnyékában* (In the Shadow of the Third Reich), Magvető, Budapest

——1989 'The role of Budapest in Hungary's economic development' *Hungary and European Civilisation* ed. G. Ranki, Akademiai Kiadó, Budapest

Ranki, G., Tilkovszky, L. and Juhasz, G. eds 1968 *A Wilhelmstrasse és Magyarország: Német Diplomáciai Iratok Magyarországról, 1933–1944* (Wilhelmstrasse and Hungary: German Diplomatic Papers from Hungary, 1933–1944), Budapest

Ranki, V. 1971 'A jogi nyelv' ('The legal language') *Jogelméleti Tanulmányok* (Essays in Jurisprudence) ed. M. Samu, Budapest

——1990 'Goulash-fascism, a socio-legal analysis of Hungarian fascism in the 1930s' *Australian Journal of Law and Society* vol. 6, pp. 144–56

Royal Institute of International Affairs 1939 *South-Eastern Europe: A Political and Economic Survey*, Oxford University Press, Oxford

Rubinstein, W.D. 1997 *The Myth of Rescue: Why the Democracies Could Not Have Saved More Jews from the Nazis*, Routledge, New York

Sajo, A. 1990 'New legalism in East Central Europe: Law as an instrument of social transformation' *Journal of Law and Society* no. 17, pp. 329–44

Sartre, J-P. 1948 *Portrait of the Anti-Semite*, Secker & Warburg, Lindsay Drummond, London

Schmidt, M. 1987 'Provincial police reports: New insights into Hungarian Jewish history 1941–1944' *Yad Vashem Studies* vol. XIX, pp. 233–67

——1990 *Kollaboracio vagy Kooperació: A Budapesti Zsidó Tanács* (Collaboration or Cooperation: The Jewish Council of Budapest), Minerva, Budapest

Scholem, G. 1976 *On Jews and Judaism in Crisis: Selected Essays*, Schocken Books, New York

Senesh, H. 1973 *Hannah Senesh: Her Life and Diary*, Shocken Books, New York

Seton-Watson, H. 1977 *Nations and States: An Enquiry into the Origins of Nations and the Politics of Nationalism*, Westview Press, Boulder

Simpson, G. and Yinger, M. 1985 *Racial and Cultural Minorities: An Analysis of Prejudice and Discrimination* 5th edn, Plenum Press, New York

Smith, A. 1976 *Nationalist Movements*, Macmillan, London

Standeisky, E. 1995 'A kommunista polgarellenesseg' ('Communist ideology against the bourgeoisie') *Budapesti Negyed* vol. 8, pp. 209–23

Stark, T. 1989 *Magyarország Második Világháborús Embervesztesége* (The Human Losses of Hungary during the Second World War), MTA Történettudományi Intézet, Budapest

Stern, F. 1961 *The Politics of Cultural Despair,* University of California Press, Berkeley

Stern, S. 1990 'Versenyfutas az idovel' ('Race with time') *Kollaboráció vagy Kooperació: A Budapesti Zsidó Tanács* (Collaboration or Cooperation: The Jewish Council of Budapest) ed. M. Schmidt, Minerva, Budapest

Sternhell, Z. 1976 'Fascist ideology' *Fascism: A Readers Guide* ed. W. Laqueur, Wildwood House, Aldershot

——1994 *The Birth of Fascist Ideology: From Cultural Rebellion to Political Revolution*, Princeton University Press, Princeton

Strauss, H. 1988 'Antisemitism as a political tool' *Present-Day Antisemitism* ed. Y. Bauer, The Hebrew University of Jerusalem, Jerusalem

Sugar, P. 1971 'External and domestic roots of Eastern European nationalism' *Nationalism in Eastern Europe* eds P. Sugar and I. Lederer, University of Washington Press, Seattle

Szabó, R. 1995 'A zsidóság és a párt, a párt és zsidóság' ('Jewry and the party, the party and Jewry') *Mozgó Világ* no. 8, pp. 33–50

Száraz, G. 1984 'Egy előitélet nyomában' ('On the trail of a prejudice') *Zsidokerdes, Asszimilacio, Antiszemitizmus* (The Jewish Question, Assimilation, Antisemitism) ed. P. Hanak, Gondolat, Budapest

——1985 'The Jewish question in Hungary: A historical retrospective' *The Holocaust in Hungary: Forty Years Later* eds R. Braham and B. Vago, Columbia University Press, New York

Szegedy-Maszak, M. 1989 'Enlightenment and liberalism in the works of Széchenyi, Kemeny and Eötvös' *Hungary and European Civilisation* ed. G. Ranki, Akadémiai Kiadó, Budapest

Szekfü, G. 1989 *Három Nemzedék és Ami Utána Következik* (Three Generations and What Happened After), Maecenas, Budapest

Szelényi, I. 1990 *Városi Társadalmi Egyenlőtlensegek* (Urban Social Inequalities), Akadémiai Kiadó, Budapest

Szerb, A. 1972 *Magyar Irodalomtörténet* (History of Hungarian Literature), Magvető, Budapest (quotations from Szerb have been translated from the original text by the author)

Tatz, C. 1991 'Confronted by the Holocaust' *Australian Journal of Jewish Studies* vol. 5, no. 2, pp. 6–34

——1995 *Reflections on the Politics of Remembering and Forgetting*, Centre for Comparative Genocide Studies, Sydney

Thane, P., Crossick, G. and Floud, R. eds 1984 *The Power of the Past: Essays for Eric Hobsbawm*, Cambridge University Press, Cambridge

Toynbee, A. 1935 'Territorial arrangements' *The Treaty of Versailles and After* eds A. Toynbee et al., George Allen & Unwin, London

Vago, B. 1981 'Contrasting Jewish leadership in wartime Hungary and Romania' *The Holocaust as Historical Experience* eds Y. Bauer and N. Rotenstreich, Holmes & Meier, New York

——1988 'Fascism in Eastern Europe' *Fascism: A Readers Guide*, ed. W. Laqueur, Wildwood House, Aldershot

Vago, B. and Mosse, G. eds 1974 *Jews and non-Jews in Eastern Europe*, John Wiley & Sons, New York & Israel Universities Press, Jerusalem

Varga, L. 1992 'Zsidókerdes 1945–1956' ('The "Jewish question" 1945–1956'), *Világosság* no. 1, pp. 62–7

Venetianer, L. 1922 *A Magyar Zsidóság Története* (History of Hungarian Jewry), Fővárosi nyomda, Budapest

Vida, M. ed. 1939 *Itéljetek! Néhány Kiragadott Lap a Magyar Zsidó Életközösség Könyvéből* (You Judge! A Few Pages Torn from the Book of the Life of Hungarians and Jews Together), Budapest

Vig, M. ed. 1992 *Hogyan Éljük túl a Huszadik Századot?* (How to Survive the Twentieth Century?), Fidesz Akadémia, Narancs Alapitvány, Budapest

Volkov, S. 1978 *The Rise of Anti-modernism in Germany, 1873–1896*, Princeton University Press, Princeton

Vörös, E. 1994 'Újabb adatok egy pogrom történetéhez. Kunmadaras' ('Additional information on the history of a pogrom. Kunmadaras') *Múlt es Jövő* vol. 4, pp. 69–80

Walicki, A. 1982 *Philosophy and Romantic Nationalism: The Case of Poland*, Clarendon Press, Oxford

Weber, E. 1988 'Revolution? Counter-revolution? What revolution?' *Fascism: A Readers Guide* ed. W. Laqueur, Wildwood House, Aldershot

Weisberg, R. 1984 *The Failure of the Word: The Protagonist as Lawyer in Modern Fiction*, Yale University Press, New Haven

Wiesel, E. 1985 'Introduction' *The Holocaust in Hungary: Forty Years Later*, eds R. Braham and B. Vago, Columbia University Press, New York

——1981 *Night*, Penguin, Harmondsworth

Wistrich, R. 1982 *Socialism and the Jews: The Dilemmas of Assimilation in Germany and Austria–Hungary*, Rutherford, Madison, Associated University Presses, London, Toronto

——1990 *Between Redemption and Perdition: Modern Antisemitism and Jewish Identity*, Routledge, London

——1991 *Antisemitism: The Longest Hatred*, Pantheon Books, New York

Woolf, S. ed. 1970 *European Fascism* 2nd edn, Weidenfeld & Nicolson, London

Wyman, D. 1984 *The Abandonment of the Jews: America and the Holocaust, 1941–1945*, Pantheon Books, New York

Yahil, L. 1969 *The Rescue of Danish Jewry*, The Jewish Publication Society, Philadelphia

Zeke, G. 1990 'Statisztikai mellékletek' ('Statistical appendices') *Hét Évtized a Hazai Zsidóság Életében* (Seven Decades in the Life of Hungarian Jewry)

eds L. Lendvai, A. Sohár and P. Horváth, MTA Filozofiai Intezet, Budapest

Zsuppan, F. 1989 'The reception of the Hungarian feminist movement, 1910–14' *Decadence and Innovation: Austro–Hungarian Life and Art at the Turn of the Century* ed. R. Pynsent, Weidenfeld & Nicolson, London

Zweig, S. 1947 *The World of Yesterday: An Autobiography*, Cassell, London

Index